20TH CENTURY ROCK AND ROLL

GLAM

Dave Thompson

WATCH FOR THE REST OF THE SERIES

A GUIDE TO THE ARTISTS WHO MADE THE CENTURY'S GREATEST ROCK MUSIC

20th CENTURY ROCK AND ROLL

A COLLECTOR'S GUIDE PUBLISHING SERIES

Psychedelia	ISBN 1-896522-40-8
Alternative Music	ISBN 1-896522-19-X
Progressive Rock	ISBN 1-896522-20-3
Heavy Metal	ISBN 1-896522-47-5
Pop Music	ISBN 1-896522-25-4
Punk Rock	ISBN 1-896522-27-0
Glam Rock	ISBN 1-896522-26-2
Women In Rock	ISBN 1-896522-29-7

For ordering information see our web site at
www.cgpublishing.com

We acknowledge the financial support of the Government of Canada through
the Book Publishing Industry Development Program for our publishing activities.
Published by Collector's Guide Publishing Inc., Box 62034, Burlington, Ontario, Canada, L7R 4K2
Printed and bound in Canada
20th Century Rock and Roll - Glam
by Dave Thompson
ISBN 1-896522-26-2

20TH CENTURY ROCK AND ROLL

GLAM

Dave Thompson

Table Of Contents

Introduction

Glam was a British phenomenon, and a British pop phenomenon at that. It only makes sense, then, that it's Britain's pop charts which established this book's lay-out. The 40 bands included here are listed chronologically by the date of their first UK chart entry — except, of course, on those occasions when there was no UK chart entry to list them by, in which case their first attempt comes into play.

Of course, once past a handful of self-explanatory obvious inclusions, the divisions between glam, pop, and a host of other genres, blurs horribly. Steve Harley of Cockney Rebel insists his band had nothing at all to do with glam rock, and he may be correct — neither did ex-Jeff Beck Group drummer Cozy Powell, but his two 1973-74 hit singles ensure that he's a regular on sundry glam compilations anyway. So are Chicory Tip, the Wombles and the Rubettes, but chronology notwithstanding, it's difficult to establish a watertight case for the inclusion of any of them.

The decisions and inclusions made in this book, however, are my own — agree or disagree at your own discretion. But play the records carefully, before you open your mouth. Watch the old TV appearances, and dig out a few promo photographs. Appearances aren't always deceptive, you know.

Glam Is For Christmas, Not For Life

Between 1971 and 1975 a musical movement erupted which was to shatter the pop / rock continuum more thoroughly than it had ever been shattered before.

Brought on by rock's growing obsession with its own worth, socially, politically and historically, this new movement was to pay not the slightest attention to those pretensions. Rather, it represented nothing more than a return to the frivolous basics for which Rock And Roll had been condemned when it first appeared, with one profound difference — musically, culturally, sexually and anatomically, glam rock was to be the biggest, brightest, shiniest beast the music industry had ever known.

Sure it was manufactured, but it was manufactured by the people who needed it most — that amorphous mass of music fans too old for the nursery sing-alongs that crept out of the bubblegum factories of America and Britain, but not old enough to appreciate the mores of the progressive rock boom which blasted out of student common rooms the western world over.

And even when the kids had had enough of it, still glam exploded upward, and with such force that the fall-out is still being felt today.

The punks of the late 70's grew up on glam. The Damned got their first nationwide break on tour with Marc Bolan And T. Rex, Johnny Rotten joined the Pistols on the strength of his miming to *School's Out* on Malcolm MacLaren's jukebox. The Adverts' T.V. Smith was first sighted in a Steve Harley-esque glam band called Sleaze. Glen Matlock's Rich Kids were launched with a debut album produced by Mick Ronson, Joan Jett built her post-Runaways career around old Gary Glitter songs.

And so it goes on — the visual chicanery of Adam And The Ants; the debased sleazoid flash of Ratt, Mötley Crüe and Hanoi Rocks; the recherche camp of London Suede, Pulp and Placebo; the revived careers of Gary Glitter, Alvin Stardust, Suzi Quatro and Slade in the UK, KISS and Alice Cooper in the United States; the continuing cults of Jobriath and the New York Dolls; the art circuit smash movie VELVET GOLDMINE, reassessing the era's excesses in the guise of soft gay porn.

Acts which, in any other life, would have faded the moment their allotted chart-span was over, re-emerged through the 80's and 90's to ride their white swans once more around the hit parade, while a whole new generation of kids learned the dances from their parents and poured out to pay homage in full 70's drag without the slightest hint of revivalist self-consciousness. Despite all this, few people today give glam rock the attention it deserves. Perhaps they're afraid of appearing uncool, they're the people who spent their childhood hiding Gary Glitter records behind the Grand Funk collection every time their friends came round. Other people simply can't believe that something so superficial could ever have turned out to be so important.

In early 1974, after all, Lou Reed prophesied, "All this glamour scene will run its course. The only one who'll come out full intact is Bowie, and maybe he's gone too far. But the rest are all in his wake."

"I think all this posing stuff will be tolerated until — let's see — oh, the middle of 1974, and then it'll be dead," added Mick Jagger — no stranger to "all this posing stuff" himself. And even David Bowie was to look around at the mutant scene which had grown up around himself and Bolan and all the rest, and register not a little disapproval. Asked how he reacted to the increasing theatricality in rock and the ever increasing reliance on gimmickry he said, "More theater does not necessarily mean more props. We [Ziggy and the Spiders] were using no props. If we had a theatricality it came through us as people, not as a set environment or stage."

"Like playing an instrument, theater craftsmanship is something one learns. There are going to be a lot of clangers dropped and a lot of tragedies over the next few years, when a lot of bands try to become theatrical without knowing their craft. It's important to know about the things you do, and to have learned it. As a theatrical expression evolves a lot of it is going to be on a secondary modern school [vocational high school] amateur dramatics level. There will only be the odd few bands left who have the knowledge to master their theater."

Nearly three decades later the accuracy — or otherwise — of those comments are plain for all to see.

☆ 1 ☆
Marc Bolan And T. Rex

— Ride A White Swan —

Their first Glam hit, *Ride A White Swan*, entered the UK chart on October 24, 1970.

	Chart Hits	
	UK	**US**
Singles	33 (1988-88)	4 (1971-72)
Albums	30 (1968-91)	5 (1971-73)

In 1969, Marc Bolan was an itinerant drifter of no fixed musical abode, who wandered through the British underground with little more than raging self-belief and a string of minor hit singles to his name. By 1971, he was God, the founding father / figurehead of a musical genre which had been inconceivable a few short months before.

True, his first words to manager Simon Napier Bell, back in 1966, were "Hi, I'm a singer and I'm going to be the biggest British rock star ever." True, also, he was one of the most imaginative songwriters ever to put plectrum to pixiephone. But a short spell with psychedelic noise terrorists John's Children, and a few years operating under the unwieldy handle of Tyrannosaurus Rex, had done nothing more than endear him to the hippy crowd, and when the British press wrapped up the 60's by predicting its brightest hopes for the newborn decade, Marc Bolan And Tyrannosaurus Rex were nowhere in sight.

But even as Tyrannosaurus Rex sawed away at their bongo drums and one string fiddles, Bolan's destiny was always in sight. Three albums with original Rex partner Steve Peregrin Took saw Bolan's musical outlook growing increasingly more abrasive, while 1969's BEARD OF STARS album, his first with bongo player Mickey Finn, saw him really get down to shaking off the shackles. By the end of 1970, *Ride A White Swan* had catapulted Bolan — now operating under the abbreviated

Marc Bolan And T. Rex

title of T. Rex — to the top of the UK chart. By the spring of 1971, the monster was unstoppable.

Two consecutive No. 1 hits, *Hot Love* and *Get It On* (*Bang A Gong* in the innuendo-crazed US) followed in the new year, while a massive UK tour, with specially reduced ticket prices, attracted a vast army of adolescent girls, lured by T. Rex's captivating TOP OF THE POPS television appearances. Overnight, the group's older student hippy audience was all but obliterated and the rumbles of discontent from Bolan's old progressive stomping grounds were drowned out beneath a barrage of screaming which didn't let up for the next two years. The ELECTRIC WARRIOR album went on to spend the best part of the year on the chart. A new single, *Jeepster*, landed advance orders of 35,000 just in time for Christmas. T. Rextacy swept the land. Bolan had made it.

The first new pop idol of the new decade — the first since the Beatles, the epitome of the English 60's, had discorporated — Bolan's transition from underground anti-hero to superstar demi-god completely shattered all predictions and preoccupations for the new decade. At a time when Rock was Rock and Fun was just for the kiddies, Bolan cut through all the contradictions, flouncing on stage in sequins and satin, blasting out a joyous celebration of youth and potency. With just one flick of his corkscrew curls, he ushered in the era of glam rock, single-handedly dragging Rock And Roll out of the grave, and at the same time screwing down the coffin lid on pretension and reserve.

It has, over the years, been suggested that glam rock, or a close approximation thereof, would have happened anyway, that Bolan was simply the lucky first contestant. And it's true that at a grassroots level, the whole thing was little more than an hysterical reaction to the musical and cultural stagnation of the previous three years.

Just as the purity of the British Beat boom had mutated in the gutters of Haight-Asbury into a frenzied confection of acid and light shows, so the musical liberation which that supposedly brought, was swiftly to degenerate into a slough of intense introspection and forty minute solos.

That in itself is ironic, that within a genre which was to remain so English, the impetus for Bolan's success (and indeed of all those who followed him) was to come from the US and the LP revolution. Just as the new regime of American bands breaking through in the wake of the British Invasion concentrated almost exclusively on this exciting new format, so the groups who both pre- and post-dated that initial cross-fertilization (and who — in the first instance — were to survive the transition) also took to aiming their music not at the kids who put them where they were, but at a more "mature" audience who would be able to appreciate all the hours of work that went into creating every second of sound.

The Beatles, the Stones, the Who, the Kinks, all the leading lights of the 60's singles scene, suddenly gave up on custom-built 45's and opted instead simply to pull suitable songs off LP's as and when the marketing man demanded. In Britain, where only the offshore pirate stations entertained the same vices as American FM (Radio North Sea International, the on-again / off-again Radio Caroline), the backlash was even stronger, simply because there was no option to the pop charts.

There, the new high principles of the previous decade's most exciting bands weren't seen as progression by the average single buyer, they were seen as desertion. And with pasty studio outfits — Edison Lighthouse, the Cufflinks, Christie and Chicory Tip — having moved up to take advantage of the void, there had probably never been such a depressing time in which to be young.

There was no viable alternative left, there was nothing to sing to, dance to, make out to. The Cufflinks and Atomic Rooster were opposites in every way, but they were both non-starters in the teenage libido stakes. And that was the opening Marc Bolan had been waiting for.

In electrifying fashion, he relaunched the single as a work of art, shrugging aside the belief that it was impossible to have a revolution at 45 rpm, and letting rip in a surge of sequins and sex. Nobody that followed, not Gary Glitter, Slade, The Sweet, not even the recently revitalized David Bowie, could do anything more than stand on the outside, gazing enviously in on the universe Bolan had constructed around himself, a universe wherein the performer, the

Marc Bolan And T. Rex

performance and all the peripheral little things which Meant so much, were as one. Nothing else mattered — nothing else could matter. There was not one possible physical, emotional or critical response which could even dent the bubble.

1972 began precisely where 1971 left off. In January, *Telegram Sam* sold 97,000 copies before it was even released, debuting Bolan's own Hot Wax label with another fortnight in the pole position. In March, T. Rex sold out at the massive Wembley Empire Pool, then staged a barnstorming concert which would become the centerpiece of the timelessly ebullient BORN TO BOOGIE movie. *Metal Guru* followed, the album THE SLIDER, a host of chart busting reissues from his Tyrannosaurus days . . . And then came the crash.

With the frankly irrelevant exception of the playfully pseudonymous *Squint Eyed Mangle* single, released under the name Big Carrot, Bolan's early 1973 releases were little more than sad attempts to recapture the glory of the previous two years, with the TANX album a belated attempt to signpost his next, soul-fused, direction, at the same time as struggling to regain lost ground. By the time 1974 rolled around, T. Rex was pretty much spent as a commercial force. Bolan, who created the glam rock market, who saw it flourish and caused it to explode, had now been overtaken by it.

David Bowie, Gary Glitter, Alvin Stardust, The Sweet, Mud, were now all out-charting the bopping elf. And yet, chart positions can lie. Early in 1996, a British TV show highlighted what its makers called "the Glam Top Ten," showcasing the ten most successful artists of the era. Bolan romped home in second-place — only Slade, the pantomime Stones to his sepulchral Beatles, outsold him, but not even they out-performed him. Bowie, incidentally, didn't even rank.

Bolan reacted heroically to his sudden slide, riding out the February 1975, departure of Mickey Finn with no visible ill-effects, then returned to the chart with *New York City*, a sing-along knockabout which bore all the hallmarks of vintage T. Rex, while still managing to sound fresh. A year later, the sublime *I Love To Boogie* followed a similar pattern, and by early 1977, Bolan was once again poised on the edge of something special.

His latest album, DANDY IN THE UNDERWORLD, was his best in ages. He hosted a national TV series, MARC, and while *Celebrate Summer*, his summer 1977 single, is frequently cited as his absorption of the lessons of punk, it was also nothing less than a full-fledged return to his own early 70's basics, casually recrafted to show the new kids how it ought to be done. Creatively, his rehabilitation was complete. A month later, Bolan was dead, killed outright when the car in which he was a passenger slammed into a tree on Barnes Common, in London.

Marc Bolan never did become "the biggest British rock star ever" of his prophecies. In terms of vinyl units, a host of other talents were far more successful. But few people could argue that, even more so than David Bowie and the Sex Pistols (the only other possible claimants to that title) Bolan was the single most important artist to emerge from the post-Beatles era, a fact which at least places the 70's, 80's and the 90's in his thrall.

And even if only a handful of his records still stand up as the instant jukebox classics that they originally appeared to be, Bolan's influence on the course that rock has taken since his emergence, can never be over-estimated.

T. Rex Glam Years Discography:
UK Original Singles 1970-77
- *Ride A White Swan / Is It Love / Summertime Blues* (Fly BUG 1, 1970)
- *Hot Love / Woodland Rock / King Of The Mountain Cometh* (Fly BUG 6, 1971)
- *Get It On / Raw Ramp* (Fly BUG 10, 1971)
- *Jeepster / Life's A Gas* (Fly BUG 16, 1971)
- *Telegram Sam / Cadillac / Baby Strange* (T Rex 101, 1972)
- *Metal Guru / (Thunderwing) / Lady* (T Rex MARC 101, 1972)
- *Children Of The Revolution / Jitterbug Love / Sunken Rags* (T Rex MARC 2, 1972)
- *Solid Gold Easy Action / Born To Boogie* (T Rex MARC 3, 1973)
- *20th Century Boy / Free Angel* (T Rex MARC 4, 1973)
- *The Groover / Midnight* (T Rex MARC 5, 1973)
- *Truck On Tyke / Sitting Here* (T Rex MARC 6, 1973)
- *Teenage Dream / Satisfaction Pony* (T Rex MARC 7, 1974)
- *Light Of Love / Explosive Mouth* (T Rex MARC 8, 1974)
- *Zip Gun Boogie / Space Boss* (T Rex MARC 9, 1974)
- *New York City / Chrome Sitar* (T Rex MARC 10, 1975)
- *Dreamy Lady / Do You Wanna Dance / Dock Of The Bay* (T Rex MARC 11, 1975)
- *Christmas Bop / Telegram Sam / Metal Guru* (T Rex MARC 12, 1975)
- *London Boys / Soul Baby* (T Rex MARC 13, 1976)
- *I Love To Boogie / Baby Boomerang* (T Rex MARC 14, 1976)
- *Laser Love / Life's An Elevator* (T Rex MARC 15, 1976)
- *The Soul Of My Suit / All Alone* (T Rex MARC 16, 1977)
- *Dandy In The Underworld / Groove A Little / Tame My Tiger* (T Rex MARC 17, 1977)
- *Celebrate Summer / Ride My Wheels* (T Rex MARC 18, 1977)

UK Original Singles (pseudonymous) 1970-73
- *Oh Baby / Universal Love* (as Dib Cochran & The Earwigs) (Bell 1121, 1970)
- *Blackjack / Squint Eyed Mangle* (as Big Carrot) (EMI 2047, 1973)

UK Important Archive Singles
- DEMON QUEEN EP (Fly ANT 1, 1977)
- EXTENDED PLAY EP (NMC COPILOT 17, 1997)

US Original Singles 1970-77
- *Ride A White Swan / Summertime Blues* (Blue Thumb 121, 1970)
- *The Light Of The Magical Moon / Find A Little Wood* (Blue Thumb 212, 1972)
- *Hot Love / One Inch Rock / Seagull Woman* (Reprise 1006, 1971)
- *Bang A Gong (Get It On) / Raw Ramp* (Reprise 1032, 1971)
- *Jeepster / Rip Off* (Reprise 1056, 1971)
- *Telegram Sam / Cadillac* (Reprise 1078, 1972)
- *Metal Guru / Lady* (Reprise 1095, 1972)
- *The Slider / Rock On* (Reprise 1122, 1972)
- *The Groover / Born To Boogie* (Reprise 1161, 1973)
- *Light Of Love / Explosive Mouth* (Casablanca NB 808, 1974)
- *Precious Star / Space Boss* (Casablanca NB 810, 1974)

UK Original Flexidisc
- *Christmas Messages* (Fan Club [no catalog No.], 1972)

UK Original Albums 1970-77
- T REX (Fly HIFLY 2, 1970)
- ELECTRIC WARRIOR (Fly HIFLY 6, 1971)
- BOLAN BOOGIE (compilation) (Fly HIFLY 8, 1972)
- THE SLIDER (T Rex 5001, 1972)
- TANX (T Rex 5002, 1973)
- GREAT HITS (compilation) (T Rex 5003, 1973)
- ZINC ALLOY AND THE HIDDEN RIDERS (T Rex 7751, 1974)
- BOLAN'S ZIP GUN (T Rex 7752, 1975)
- FUTURISTIC DRAGON (T Rex 5004, 1976)
- DANDY IN THE UNDERWORLD (T Rex 5005, 1977)

US Original Albums 1970-77
- T REX (Reprise 6440, 1970)
- ELECTRIC WARRIOR (Reprise 6466, 1971)
- THE SLIDER (Reprise 2095, 1972)
- TANX (Reprise 2132, 1973)
- LIGHT OF LOVE (compilation) (Casablanca 7005, 1975)

UK Important Archive Albums
- GREAT HITS 1972-77: THE A-SIDES (Edsel EDCD 401, 1994)
- GREAT HITS 1972-77: THE B-SIDES (Edsel EDCD 402, 1994)
- RABBIT FIGHTER — THE ALTERNATE SLIDER (Edsel EDCD 403, 1994)
- LEFT HAND LUKE — THE ALTERNATE TANX (Edsel EDCD 410, 1995)
- UNCHAINED 1 — 1972 PT 1 (Edsel EDCD 411, 1995)
- UNCHAINED 2 — 1972 PT 2 (Edsel EDCD 412, 1995)

- CHANGE — THE ALTERNATE ZINC ALLOY (Edsel EDCD 440, 1995)
- UNCHAINED 3 — 1973 PT 1 (Edsel EDCD 441, 1995)
- UNCHAINED 4 — 1973 PT 2 (Edsel EDCD 442, 1995)
- PRECIOUS STAR — THE ALTERNATE ZIP GUN (Edsel EDCD 443, 1996)
- UNCHAINED 5 — 1974 (Edsel EDCD 444, 1996)
- UNCHAINED 6 — 1975 (Edsel EDCD 445, 1996)
- DAZZLING RAIMENT — THE ALTERNATE FUTURISTIC DRAGON (Edsel EDCD 522, 1997)
- ELECTRIC WARRIOR SESSIONS (NMC PILOT 4, 1997)
- ELECTRIC BOOGIE / LIVE 1971 (NMC PILOT 13, 1997)
- BBC RECORDINGS 1970-76 (NMC PILOT 17, 1997)
- SPACEBALL (US Radio 1971-72) (NMC PILOT 21, 1997)
- PRINCE OF PLAYERS — THE ALTERNATE DANDY IN THE UNDERWORLD (Edsel EDCD 523, 1998)
- UNCHAINED 7 — 1976-77 PT 1 (Edsel EDCD 524, 1997)
- UNCHAINED 8 — 1976-77 PT 2 (Edsel EDCD 525, 1997)
- LIVE 1977 (Edsel EDCD 530, 1997)
- MARC: SONGS FROM THE GRANADA TV SERIES (Edsel EDCD 545, 1998)

Notes: The Edsel releases represent the most complete archive project ever granted a major artist. After more than a decade of abuse at the hands of Bolan's so-called fan club, Edsel completely restructured Bolan's 1972-77 catalog, reissuing all original albums with bonus single sides; mirroring these with demo and out-take recreations of each individual album; and then rounding up all other available unissued material for the UNCHAINED series. These releases replace all previous versions of the same material.

☆ 2 ☆
Arnold Corns

— Hang Onto Yourself —

Their first Glam song, *Hang Onto Yourself*, was released in July, 1971.

By mid-1971, David Bowie was desperate. Almost two years had elapsed since his first, and only, hit single *Space Oddity*, two years during which the man that Music Now! magazine readers had once voted "the brightest new star of the year" had faded into the kind of obscurity which one hit wonders alone can appreciate.

Worse still, people he thought were his friends were deserting, marching off to fame and fortune while he was still stuck at the starter's post. School friend Peter Frampton, already a teenybop idol, was now a hard rock specialist as well. Tim Renwick, wizard guitarist on Bowie's 1969 album, was a critical God with his own band, Quiver. And Marc Bolan had stopped talking about becoming the biggest star in Britain ever, and gone and

become it instead. What was a poor boy to do?

Well, he could always talk to the American press. Captivated by Bowie's increasingly eccentric peacock appearance, and aware that he was still writing great songs, even if no-one was buying them, Rolling Stone despatched writer Mick Rock to Bowie's Haddon Hall home to talk about men who wear dresses and sing songs about spacemen. Instead, Rock got a world exclusive on the would-be Pop Chameleon's intended next move: Pop Svengali.

"I've got this friend who is just beautiful," Bowie simpered. "When you meet him, you don't even question whether he's a boy or a girl. He's just a person called Freddi, who's very nice to look at. That's what's important, to be a person, to be an individual." And Freddi was so individual, Bowie continued, that he would be the first man ever to appear on the cover of Vogue.

He outlined his plans. He had written a song for Freddi, a mogadon plod through a bass led freak out, *Moonage Daydream*. Working with another Dulwich student, guitarist Mark Carr Pritchard, he had pieced together a band for him: Arnold's Corn. He had even landed him a record deal, with the small but successful B&C label. Bowie himself would produce and sing on the record. All Freddi had to do was stand there and look ravishing.

"The Rolling Stones are finished," said Bowie. "Arnold's Corn will be the next Stones. This song is unique. There's certainly nothing to compare it with." And because he believed that "Freddi is right for now," the whole thing had been accomplished in just six days. "There's no point in waiting." Freddi was less immodest. "Actually, I can't just expect to bring Jagger back," he admitted. "Really, I'm just a dress designer."

Indeed he was. Freddi Buretti was an art student from south London's Dulwich College, who had wandered into the Bowie camp with his girlfriend Danielle, and swiftly been drawn into the flurry of sartorial reshaping which Bowie's wife, Angie, was in the process of executing.

"Every time David's band had an important gig," Angie recalls, "Freddi would design new clothes for them. I also made them realize that it was pointless going on stage in great clothes if they were going to be wearing jeans off stage, so Freddi made them clothes to wear offstage as well, from mohair, cashmere, silk … anything that would make them look out of the ordinary when they were on the street."

It was this look which Freddi himself would now be taking into the full public glare, as though Bowie wanted to check the reaction first, before relaunching himself in equally audacious style. If Freddi was simply laughed out of sight, then Bowie would return to the drawing board. But if people accepted him in all of his finery, then the door would be open for anything else: an alligator, a space invader, a mama / papa coming for tea.

Arnold Corns, as the project was slightly renamed, made a live debut of sorts on June 3, 1971. Bowie had been contracted to play BBC radio's IN CONCERT show, an excuse not only to air the best and the rest of his own repertoire, but also to give his friends some exposure as well.

Long time girlfriend Dana Gillespie dropped by to perform Bowie's *Andy Warhol*. Album sleeve designer, and the man whose playground punch-up fist was responsible for Bowie having odd colored eyes, George Underwood, performed *Song For Bob Dylan*. Another school friend, Geoffrey Alexander, handled Chuck Berry's *Almost Grown*, and Mark Carr Pritchard turned up to represent Arnold Corns on *Looking For A Friend*. Freddi, of course, designed all the costumes.

The BBC concert was broadcast on June 20, 1971. Three days previously, on June 17, Freddi, Carr Pritchard and Bowie commenced a week of sessions at Trident Studios in London. They were joined by the remainder of Arnold Corns, two more from Dulwich Art College who Freddi had apparently discovered playing alongside Pritchard in a band called Runk: bassist Polak de Somogyl and the magnificently named drummer Ralph St. Laurent Broadbent. The suggestion that the latter pair were, in fact, preposterous pseudonyms adopted by traditional Bowie cohorts Trevor Bolder and Mick Woodmansey, with Mick Ronson on uncredited lead guitar, has never been denied.

Indeed, Bob Grace, head of Bowie's Chrysalis Music publishers, suggests that the entire project was a hoax. The way he remembers it, Bowie and his own band were spending so much time making demos that they were getting "really slick, so finally we decided to lease three of the demos to B&C, simply to try and get some money back. I think we got 300 pounds for the masters. But because David was still contracted to Mercury, we couldn't use his name. So David came up with Arnold's Corn. He never told anyone what it meant."

In fact, Arnold was a tribute to Pink Floyd's debut hit *Arnold Layne*, while not three but four songs were recorded during the ensuing sessions: *Moonage Daydream* and *Hang Onto Yourself*, which were to be coupled on the band's first 45, *Man In The Middle* and *Looking For A Friend*. If they did well, Bowie enthused, a full album, LOOKING FOR RUDI, would follow.

Publicist Bill Harry was engaged to tout pictures of Freddi (who really was as lovely as Bowie reckoned) around the Fleet Street papers, while B&C's own PR machinery clanked into action, flooding the music press with copies of *Moonage Daydream*.

Their travails went unrewarded. Fleet Street was apathetic, the music press was appalled. Even the best review was a stinker. Commenting upon the single's B-side in the New Musical Express, journalist Charles Shaar Murray dismissed *Hang Onto Yourself* as "a thinly disguised rewrite of the Velvet Underground's *Sweet Jane*," and the only consolation was that Bowie would not dispute that charge. He'd been rewriting Velvets songs for years. The worst thing Murray's review imparted was that Bowie wasn't the only Velvets fan in town.

Of course he wasn't, but any others still remained thin on the ground, so thin that even Murray's words of wisdom could not induce them to sample Arnold's wares. *Moonage Daydream* flopped ignominiously. So did *Hang Onto Yourself* when it was released in its own right, backed by *Man In The Middle*.

And though Bowie himself still had high hopes for the projected third single, *Looking For A Friend* (it had already been played by the BBC, after all), B&C's interest in the whole affair was waning. The existing records were deleted, and Arnold Corns' dry run of two songs — which in later incarnations, would form the cornerstone of the most exciting live act Rock And Roll has ever seen — were left to founder in obscurity.

But of course the story doesn't end there. Bowie did, in fact, go on to make something of himself and in 1974 B&C's successor, Mooncrest, reissued *Hang Onto Yourself / Man In The Middle*. It didn't sell.

Eleven years later, in 1985, a 12 inch EP compiling all four Arnold Corns tracks was released. It didn't sell, either.

Rykodisc added Arnold's renditions of *Moonage Daydream* and *Hang Onto Yourself* to their bonus packed reissue of Bowie's own MAN WHO SOLD THE WORLD album in 1990. It did sell, but probably not on their account. Arnold Corns was never the next Rolling Stones, and Freddi was never on the cover of Vogue. But he did make the cover of Curious one month, seductively fondling a snake, and the subsequent immortality enjoyed by at least two of his songs does at least hammer home one truth. From little A. Corns, big Ziggys can grow.

Arnold Corns Discography:
UK Original Singles
  - *Moonage Daydream / Hang Onto Yourself* (B&C CB 149, 1971)
  - *Hang Onto Yourself / Man In The Middle* (B&C CB 189, 1971)
  - *Hang Onto Yourself / Man In The Middle* (Mooncrest, 1974)
  - *Moonage Daydream / Hang Onto Yourself / Man In The Middle / Looking For A Friend* (Krazy Kat PAST 2, 1985)

UK Original Album
  - MAN WHO SOLD THE WORLD (includes *Moonage Daydream / Hang Onto Yourself*) (Rykodisc RCD 10132, 1990)

☆ 3 ☆
Slade

— Coʒ I Luv You —

Their first Glam hit, *Coz I Luv You*, entered the UK chart on October 30, 1971.

Chart Hits		
	UK	US
Singles	40 (1971-91)	7 (1972-85)
Albums	16 (1972-91)	7 (1972-85)

The first band to break through in Marc Bolan's wake was Slade, a better than average Midlands club band whose last flirtation with marketability had been a singularly disastrous attempt at fobbing themselves off as skinheads. Cropping their hair and donning boots and suspenders, it took some time for them to realize that the look actually lost them more gigs than it won them. It was bad enough letting skinheads in to watch the bands. Putting the crop-topped little devils on stage as well was simply asking for trouble.

Under the aegis of Jimi Hendrix's old manager, Chas Chandler, Slade had nevertheless succeeded in making a lot of friends, and while public opinion was still totally oblivious to the band's true charms, their live reputation was at least good enough to stop their label, Polydor, from simply dropping them altogether. Instead, it simply gritted its teeth and allowed the band to get on with it.

Slade first showed signs of paying back this loyalty when *Get Down And Get With It*, a rousing revival of Little Richard's old-time chest-beater, rose to No. 16 in June 1971. But it wasn't the hit itself which impacted on Slade themselves. It was the realization that, Marc Bolan's T. Rex aside, there wasn't another band in the land to compete with them. "We did TOP OF THE POPS," Slade bassist Jim Lea recalled, "and there were acts like the Pipkins, Edison Lighthouse and Pan's People on ... I remember thinking to myself that we could rule this situation. None of those acts had anything like the experience we had. I knew then that we were going to make it, and with Chas at the helm, it was impossible for us not to."

Slade had already started dropping their most recent stage clothes, slowly replacing them with a brighter, more garish look which somehow put one in mind of a slightly deranged Max Wall. Blue jeans were replaced by checkered suits. Doc Martens were replaced by stack heels, shaven skulls by flowing manes. Vocalist Noddy Holder trained his sideburns down his face, and guitarist Dave Hill sprayed glitter across his ample forehead. Noddy found a mirrored top hat, Dave came up with a bottomless range of indoor overcoats and an equally perverse collection of thigh boots. By the time Slade was ready to return to the fray, with the self-penned *Coz I Luv You*, they were barely recognizable.

Quite how much this had to do with Bolan, we'll probably never know. Slade themselves maintained that theirs was a gradual change, that while Bolan literally emerged overnight, they had already been experimenting with dress for some time, and that even their most garish costumes were simply each a progression from the last.

Nevertheless, it was with the emergence of Slade at this time that it at last became apparent that Bolan was not an isolated phenomenon, that his success was not the be-all and end-all of the emotions that he had unleashed. Bolan's appeal always verged on the more cerebral side of life, in that his whole approach to music was a fey other-worldliness. Slade, on the other hand, were almost brutally common, out-of-town yobbos having a night on the tiles and intent on raising Hell everywhere they went.

Their songs weren't music, they were aural graffiti, slabs of working class consciousness spray painted across the wall of the Establishment, and each one more misspelled than the last.

The magnificent *Coz I Luv You*, all crazy stomp and spectral violin, set that particular ball rolling. Written by Holder and Lea, it had originally been titled *Because I Love You*. But, says Lea, "that sounded wimpy, so we changed it to *Cause I Love You*, because that's what we sang. And then Chas suggested the changes in spelling [and] that was the way it came out." The rest of the band's greatest hits simply followed in its wake . . . *Look Wot You Dun, Take Me Bak Ome, Mama Weer Orl Crazee Now, Gudbuy T'Jane* . . . Slade was a lexicographer's nightmare, and a dressmaking disaster as well.

"I think a lot of [our early success] was through the telly," Holder mused. "As soon as we'd got the colorful image sorted out, it just zoomed away for us. People just looked at us and thought, 'f***ing hell, these guys are mad,' and it just became an overnight thing."

But while Bolan concentrated on a narcissistic greatness, Slade went the opposite way entirely. You could visualize Bolan camping up simply to mow the lawn, but Slade were pantomime dames, dressing up for the show and changing back into flat caps and clogs when they came offstage. Bolan lived his image; Slade kept theirs' in the wardrobe with their parkas and wellington boots.

Yet their emergence a year after Bolan, but a good six months before the rest of the pack, was to set the scene for a sartorial struggle which couldn't help but translate itself into the music. Just as it had taken the emergence of the Rolling Stones to challenge the supremacy of the Beatles before the Beat Boom could truly be born, so now the movement created by Bolan needed its own anti-Christ. Slade's leering thugs were the total antithesis of Bolan's lisping, bopping elf, and with a suddenly burgeoning New Wave of British Bubblegum caught on the fence somewhere in the middle, so the Glitter pack began to divide into two very separate camps.

"Bolan said in a Melody Maker interview that Slade was no competition, and I had it in for him from that day on," Jim Lea told Slade biographer Chris Charlesworth. "Bolan was huge, and I respected him because the records he made were tremendous. But I still had it in for him." And he proved his point over the next two years. While Bolan's star waxed fast, then waned even faster, Slade remained inviolate through all the ensuing convolutions. *Coz I Luv You* went to No. 1 in November 1971. *Look Wot You Dun* dipped to No. 4, but from the moment *Take Me Bak Ome* topped the chart in September 1972, the juggernaut was unstoppable.

Mama Weer Orl Crazee Now entered the chart at No. 2. *Cum On Feel The Noize* went in at No. 1. Through 1973, every new single was a guaranteed No. 1 (or 2.) Throughout 1974, with the mania clearly drifting, and Slade themselves very obviously struggling out of the straitjacket of misspelled cosmic yobbishness, they still hit the Top 3 with monotonous regularity.

When the end came, however, it was swift. In October 1974, the yearning *Far Far Away* made No. 2 on the back of a box office smash movie, SLADE IN FLAME. In February 1975, *How Does It Feel* was fortunate to peak at No. 15. *Thanks For The Memory* recovered slightly, and reached No. 7, but that was it. Slade, in their 1970's guise at least, never made the British Top 10 again, and in spring 1976, the utterly unthinkable happened. A new single (the admittedly shoddy *Nobody's Fool*) failed to chart at all.

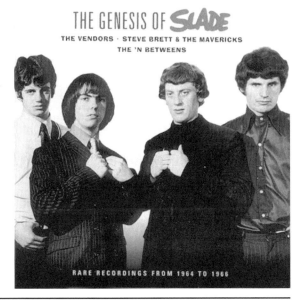

Slade

Part of the problem was of their own making — an ill-conceived attempt to break into the US, come what may round the rest of the world. And that, of course, was the kiss of death.

Slade succeeded in Britain because they were so straightforward, an irresistible blend of stomp, pomp and idiot yelling. America, however, had never gone for such crudities — through the first half of the 1970's, while the UK got down and got with it with abandon, America snoozed to the Eagles, James Taylor, Phoebe Snow ...And somewhere within the Slade song writing camp, that essential difference struck a chord. If Mohammed wouldn't go to the mountain, the mountain went to Mohammed. Then found he couldn't care less.

Slade relocated to New York in the spring of 1975, toured their legs off, and seemed to be making a dent. But Jim Lea recalled, "we worked a lot, but we weren't showing a profit. In fact we all lost a lot of money. I was getting an American influence into the music I was writing, and that wasn't good." But by the time they all realized what had happened, and fled back to the UK — "we'd blown it," Jim Lea sighed. In February 1976, *Let's Call It Quits* faltered at No. 11 on the British chart, and the bassist admitted, "No. 11 in the charts can seem like the end of the road when you've had six No. 1's."

The band kept going, returning to the small club circuit which had sustained them in the early days, but losing heart all the way. Finally, they told Chandler that they'd reached the end.

"Psychologically, they'd disbanded," manager Chas Chandler later said. "[But] after all the huge success they'd had, their last gig should be on a huge stage and not in an empty hall somewhere." Accordingly, he set up Slade's farewell show, halfway up the bill on the first night of Britain's annual Reading Festival in 1980, standing in for Ozzy Osbourne.

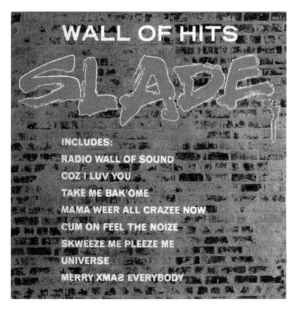

For an hour that evening, sandwiched between Girl and Def Leppard, Slade ran through a monstrous greatest hits set, omitting only *Merry Christmas Everybody* from their repertoire — and reeling with amazement when, as they left the stage, the audience performed it for them.

By Christmas, a live at Reading EP was in the chart, a hits compilation was racing to join it, and Slade were again selling out venues they hadn't seen in five years. *We'll Bring The House Down* returned them to the UK Top Ten in the new year, and at the Castle Donnington

Heavy Metal festival the following summer even the presence of AC/DC and Whitesnake couldn't dampen their ardor. After all, Slade could still remember when AC's new singer, Brian Johnson, had been impersonating Slade in mid-70's hopefuls Geordie!

The festive *Merry Christmas Everybody*, a No. 1 in 1973, rounded the year off by reaching the Top 20, and in 1983, Quiet Riot's cover of *Cum On Feel The Noize* sold more records in America than Slade themselves had ever done. In its wake, Slade signed their first US deal in six years, and were immediately rewarded. *Run Run Away* made the Top 20 singles, THE AMAZING KAMIKAZE SYNDROME hit the Top 40 albums.

But Slade in the 80's, raucous, rumbustious and ridiculous as ever, were a far cry from the Slade of the 70's. And not through any fault of their own. They were older, it's true, and they no longer had the roar of unanimous adulation to propel them along. But more importantly, their points of reference had changed. Once they were part of the glam scene, now they'd been adopted by the heavy metal lobby, and it was from within those confines that they needed to take their cue. The departure of vocalist Noddy Holder, to become a DJ in hometown Wolverhampton, and the group's subsequent reinvention as Slade 2, of course, only reduced their efficiency even further.

But the almost-annual success of *Merry Xmas Everybody* (reissued every Christmas for another round of festive bellowing), the speed with which a dance floor fills every time a Slade oldie hits the DJ turntable, Oasis' near-note perfect cover of *Cum On Feel The Noize* ... all these things prove just one thing — the spirit of Slade will never be slayed.

Slade Glam Years Discography:
UK Original Singles 1970-76
- *Know Who You Are / Dapple Rose* (Polydor 2058 054, 1970)
- *Get Down Get With It / Do You Want Me / Rasputin* (Polydor 2058 112, 1971)
- *Hear Me Calling / Get Down Get With It* (DJ only) (Polydor 2814 008, 1971)
- *Coz I Luv You / My Life Is Natural* (Polydor 2058 155, 1971)
- *Look Wot You Dun / Candidate* (Polydor 2058 195, 1972)
- *Tak Me Bak Ome / Wonderin'* (Polydor 2058 231, 1972)
- *Mama Weer Orl Crazee / Man Who Speaks Evil* (Polydor 2058 274, 1972)
- *Gudbuy To Jane / Won't Let It Appen Agen* (Polydor 2058 312, 1972)
- *Cum On Feel The Noize / I'm Mee, I'm Now* (Polydor 2058 339, 1973)
- *Skweeze Me Pleeze Me / Kill Em At The Hotclub* (Polydor 2058 377, 1973)
- *My Friend Stan / My Town* (Polydor 2058 407, 1973)
- *Merry Xmas Everybody / Don't Blame Me* (Polydor 2058 422, 1973)
- *Everyday / Good Time Gals* (Polydor 2058 454, 1974)
- *Bangin' Man / She Did It To Me* (Polydor 2058 492, 1974)
- *Far Far Away / OK Yesterday ...* (Polydor 2058 522, 1974)
- *How Does It Feel / So Far So Good* (Polydor 2058 547, 1975)
- *Thanks For The Memory / Raining* (Polydor 2058 585, 1975)
- *In For A Penny / Can You Just Imagine* (Polydor 2058 663, 1975)
- *Let's Call It Quits / The Chips Are Down* (Polydor 2058 690, 1976)
- *Nobody's Fool / LA Jinx* (Polydor 2058 716, 1976)

US Original Singles 1971-76
- *Get Down Get With It / Do You Want Me / Rasputin* (Cotillion 44128 (-), 1971)
- *Coz I Luv You / My Life Is Natural* (Cotillion 44139, 1971)
- *Look Wot You Dun / Candidate* (Cotillion 44150, 1972)
- *Tak Me Bak Ome / Wonderin'* (Polydor 15046, 1972)
- *Mama Weer Orl Crazee / Man Who Speaks Evil* (Polydor 15053, 1972)
- *Gudbuy To Jane / Won't Let It Appen Agen* (Polydor 15060, 1972)
- *Cum On Feel The Noize / I'm Mee, I'm Now* (Polydor 15069, 1973)
- *Feel So Fine . . . / Let The Good Times Roll* (Polydor 15080, 1973)
- *Skweeze Me Pleeze Me / Kill Em At The Hotclub* (Reprise 1182, 1973)
- *When The Lights Are Out / How Can It Be* (WB 7808, 1973)
- *How Does It Feel / So Far So Good* (WB 8134, 1975)
- *Nobody's Fool / When The Chips Are Down* (WB 8185, 1976)

UK Original Flexidiscs 1972-75
- *The Whole World's Going Crazee* (Polydor SF1122, 1972)
- *Slade Talk To Melanie readers* (Lyntone 2645, 1973)
- *Slade Talk To 19 readers* (Lyntone 2797, 1975)
- *Far Far Away / Thanks For The Memory* (Lyntone 3156, 1975)

UK Original Albums 1970-76
- PLAY IT LOUD (Polydor 2382 026, 1971)
- SLADE ALIVE (Polydor 2383 101, 1972)
- SLAYED? (Polydor 2383 163, 1972)
- OLD NEW BORROWED & BLUE (Polydor 2483 261, 1973)
- SLADE IN FLAME (Polydor 2442 126, 1974)
- NOBODY'S FOOLS (Polydor 2383 377, 1976)

UK Important Archive Albums
- SLADEST (compilation) (Polydor 2442 119, 1973)
- WALL OF HITS (compilation) (Polydor 5116 121, 1991)

US Original Albums 1970-76
- PLAY IT LOUD (Cotillion 9035, 1970)
- SLADE ALIVE (Polydor 5508, 1972)
- SLAYED? (Polydor 5524, 1972)
- STAMP YOUR HANDS, CLAP YOUR FEET (WB 2770, 1974)
- SLADE IN FLAME (WB 2865, 1974)
- NOBODY'S FOOLS (WB 2936, 1976)

US Important Archive Album
- SLADEST (Reprise 2173, 1973)

  Note: Incredibly the 1973 SLADEST collection of random hits, misses and B-sides, represents the only attempt to date to chronicle the origins of the biggest selling glam band of them all — 1998's GENESIS OF SLADE album (Music Corp TMC 9606) concentrated on the members' pre-Slade days; a string of greatest hits albums simply parrot back the 70's smashes; and CD reissues of the original albums have yet to unearth a single non-album B-side by way of bonus material. Yet if any band deserved a boxed-set . . .

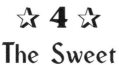

☆ 4 ☆
The Sweet

— *Poppa Joe* —

Their first Glam hit, *Poppa Joe*, entered the UK chart on February 5, 1972.

Chart Hits		
	UK	US
Singles	17 (1971-85)	9 (1971-78)
Albums	2 (1974-84)	6 (1973-79)

Few bands ever led so schizophrenic a life as The Sweet. In their British homeland, they were as unfashionable as last year's haircut, and that despite scoring 15 consecutive hit singles in under five years, and four best selling albums in three.

In America, on the other hand, they were the objects of a cult following which remained fanatical in its devotion, sticking with the band through the string of music and image changes which separated *Little Willy* (their first Stateside hit) from *Love Is Like Oxygen* (their last); applauding when Ritchie Blackmore conferred his own stamp of approval upon them by joining the band on stage; and giving The Sweet a higher, hipper, Stateside profile than anything else Britain flung at them — a barrage which includes T. Rex, Slade, David Bowie and Gary Glitter, none of whom even came close to eclipsing The Sweet's contemporary fame.

In Britain, The Sweet were stablemates of Mud and the Arrows, and were castigated accordingly. In America, they shared an audience with Deep Purple and Grand Funk.

Emerging out of a none too successful pedigree which included 60's non-starters Wainwright's Children (featuring vocalist Ian Gillan) and The Sweet Shop, The Sweet themselves were already onto a fast path to oblivion when their producer, former Quotations drummer Phil Wainman, introduced them to two aspiring young songwriters, Nicky Chinn and Michael Chapman. Although the pair had only been working together for a few months, since meeting in the club where Chapman then worked, they were also magnificently ambitious. All they needed was to find a band that was down on its luck, that needed some songs, and that would let the songwriters do the rest. The Sweet, with a string of flop singles behind them, were that band.

More confident musicians would have chafed at Chinnichap's demands, but The Sweet were in no position to argue. They would be the public face alone of the song writers' genius. Their actual records would be performed by session men, and that despite The Sweet's ranks having recently been bolstered by the arrival of a genuinely great guitarist, former Elastic Band maestro Andy Scott. For their first five singles, the full power of The Sweet could be heard on their B-sides only. Brian Connolly alone appeared on the hit songs.

In their own words, Chinnichap were still some way from finding their true musical selves, but that did not dull their ambition. *Funny Funny*, which was to give The Sweet their first hit, was in fact the first song the duo ever wrote together, and stemmed directly from Chapman's self-confessed "personal preferences," which were for Bubblegum music. "Basically, *Funny Funny* started off as a poor rip off of *Sugar Sugar* which is still, to this day, one of my favorite records of all time. Which is not to say *Funny Funny* is a bad song, but compared with what we went on to create, I think it was a little tedious."

Produced, of course, by Phil Wainman, the single was released by RCA (Bell in America) in February 1971. It rocketed to No. 13 in the British chart, to be followed with by the maddeningly infectious *Co-Co*. Simultaneously, New World's version of another Chinnichap composition, *Tom Tom Turnaround*, was released to similar success by Mickie Most's RAK label. In less than six months, Chinnichap had laid the foundations for what would become one of the most successful song writing partnerships in British pop history, and The Sweet were on their way to becoming one of the country's most popular bands — particularly once the song writers stopped to look around them.

In the months since they'd first hooked up with The Sweet, the British pop scene had undergone substantial change. Out went the faceless hard rockers who had dominated the listings around the turn of the decade. Out, too, went the identikit bubblegum merchants with names like Edison Lighthouse, Honeybus and the Mixtures. The emergence of Marc Bolan And T. Rex with an explosion of glitter, sequins and irresistible personality had seen to that. Suddenly, it was no longer enough to have a good song. You had to have a star to go with it.

With *Funny Funny* and *Co-Co* (their third single, *Alexander Graham Bell*, hadn't done quite so well), The Sweet had come close to attaining that status. Already Brian Connolly's blonde mane was a known commodity, and the band's infectious brand of glistening gum had given them a foothold which could easily be transformed into personal fame. Now *Poppa Joe* was to build the bridgehead. It hit No. 11, but more importantly, it finally cemented The Sweet into their hit making place.

Where *Poppa Joe* differed from its predecessors — indeed, where it differed from pretty much everything on the market at that time — was in its presentation. Hitherto, the band had been simply four good looking guys singing their song on stage. Now, they were four good looking guys in make-up, surrounded by belly dancing natives, and not simply singing, but living, their song. In that blissful age before MTV, a time when bands were still only just beginning to come to terms with the importance of visual image. The Sweet was suddenly streets ahead of virtually everyone but Bolan. Just one look and you knew this was no boring bunch of studio musos cobbled together to make a few cents — even though it was. The Sweet had given Bubblegum a public face which was as easy to swallow as the music. They looked great.

But were they happy? Not likely!

Nicky Chinn recalls, "Michael and I were definitely autocratic with our bands, and I became aware of that when we were told [by The Sweet] that *Little Willy* was a piece of rubbish and had no right to be released. It wasn't exactly a symphony, of course, but . . . it was a hit, and we told them it was going to be released whatever they thought of it."

And of course, he was right. *Little Willy*, the last of The Sweet's prefabricated hits, and their first American success, made No. 4 in Britain in June 1972. *Wig Wam Bam*, their first self-played A-side, hit the same peak in September. In January 1973, *Blockbuster* went all the way to the top. And of course, every new record brought with it a new image, American Indians for *Wig Wam Bam*, a camp Hitler Youth for *Ballroom Blitz*. Watching old clips of The Sweet on TOP OF THE POPS, one cannot help but marvel at the innocence (not to mention tolerance) of an age in which Andy Scott could appear on prime time television in full stormtrooper drag, Swastika armband included!

And though it was merely caricatured pop star role playing, it was role playing with a difference. Past bands had dressed up to make you fall in love. The Sweet wanted to make you laugh. Nobody believed The Sweet dressed like this all the time. Like the newly emergent Slade and Gary Glitter, the look was totally superficial. Indeed, Andy Scott goes even further, insisting that the band's growing penchant for elaborate cosmetics was due in no small way to the proximity of the TOP OF THE POPS make-up room to the dressing rooms used by the show's resident dance troupe, Pan's People. The longer you spent having your face painted, he laughs, the more chance you had "of getting a sniff of Pan's People."

That's as may be, but it was a startlingly original approach all the same, a living theater of bubblegum in which every last dash of face paint was integral to the music, and Scott's exaggeratedly camp lisping a trademark which was to endure over the next year or so's worth of hits.

Says Chapman, "In a way, at that time, we were the people responsible for telling the kids what they were going to buy. Not asking them what they wanted, but telling them. And it worked. We didn't copy anything that was there, we were front-runners along with Marc Bolan, and Mike Leander and Gary Glitter, Chas Chandler and Slade. We were like a little gang in those days, and we actually used to schedule our releases so that we wouldn't interfere with anybody else's No. 1's."

In actual fact, Chinnichap were some way ahead of the pack in that, unlike Leander and Chandler, they hadn't put all their eggs into the one basket. If Slade or Glitter hit a sticky patch, everyone would have to wait for them to extricate themselves. But if The Sweet ran into difficulties, there were always Mud . . . and Suzi Quatro . . . and Smokey . . . The empire was becoming a dynasty.

It was a sign of how rapidly The Sweet had grown that they were now blithely turning down new Chinnichap songs in hopes of the duo coming up with something better. They usually did, but their rejects weren't bad either. After *Crazy* and *Hypnosis* had given Mud a flying start in the charts (and attention turned towards building a cohesive image around what was already shaping up to be another startlingly successful career) it was *Dyna-mite*, one of The Sweet's cast-offs, that did the trick. There again, chart success wasn't the most important thing in The Sweet's world. They wanted the respect of their peers as well.

The gulf between The Sweet and the other chart busting glam rock stars of the age was already vast. T. Rex, Slade, even the absurd spectacle of Gary Glitter, "a Yogi Bear lido impersonating David Bowie," as the New Musical Express cruelly condemned him, were all guaranteed a certain respect. The Sweet, though, remained a laughing stock, a point which was made most apparent by their next single.

When Chinnichap bastardized the Yardbirds' *I'm A Man* riff, renamed it *Blockbuster* and threw it into the arena almost simultaneously with David Bowie's *Jean Genie*, we were treated to the rare spectacle of two varieties of the same theme fighting it out for supremacy not only at the top of the chart (The Sweet eventually won), but in the pages of the music press as well.

The Sweet were out-moded bubblebashers, Bowie the future of Rock And Roll. But where the twain met was a murky area in which one's reputation could not help but enhance the others'. But while Mick Ronson, later admitted, "I thought it was great; I always liked The Sweet, and *Blockbuster* was a great song," British critics were having a harder time of things.

Bowie was the press darling, the multi-faceted superstar spaceman who could do no wrong. The Sweet were a ridiculous travesty which should never have escaped the playground. But when they were both on the market with the self-same bastardization, what could a poor record reviewer do? The Sweet had received the best notices of their career to date, and now they wanted more.

In concert, their hits became an afterthought, as the band concentrated their attentions on their own compositions, B-sides mainly, and a few songs intended for their forthcoming fourth album. The gay innocence of their TV image, too, went by the board as The Sweet struggled to prove they were as hard and heavy as anyone. Early in 1973, the band was publicly banned from the prestigious Mecca ballroom circuit for what was described as "the overt sexual nature" of their stage act.

But if the worm was slowly turning, Chinnichap still controlled the hit-making strings. *Hell Raiser* reached No. 2 in the spring of 1973. The band's eponymous fourth (but first

American) album followed in July. And then came *Ballroom Blitz*, still one of Chinnichap's most insistent hits, and one which Chapman recalls as being most indicative of the way in which the duo worked. "We were trying to write songs that had no meaning, and *Ballroom Blitz* was one of them. I suggested the title and we sat down and wrote a song about a guy having a horrifyingly bad dream that his latest record hadn't made it — he was in this ballroom, in a discotheque, and maybe he was on drugs because he started hallucinating."

Aftre signing to Capitol in the United States, *Ballroom Blitz* returned The Sweet to the American charts, while providing them with a second successive No. 2 in Britain. *Teenage Rampage* echoed that UK success in the new year, while the May 1974 release of their SWEET FANNY ADAMS album proved that despite so much singles success, the band wasn't restricted solely to the three minute medium.

Indeed, in reaching No. 27, SWEET FANNY ADAMS (a popular euphemism for "nothing," or more commonly, "sweet f*** all") hinted that The Sweet might indeed be on the verge of transcending their pop image and joining that elite company which was just as comfortable on the albums and singles charts. But it wasn't to be. For all their earnest wishes to be taken seriously, for all their block busting Jean Genies, The Sweet were still regarded as a crass novelty band by the audience they wanted to woo. And their attempts to alter that perception only made things worse. Throughout 1974 The Sweet barely let an interviewer leave the room without complaining about their lot, and though pop fans might be gullible, they're very rarely stupid, and they certainly weren't going to sit tight while their idols slagged them off. The Sweet don't need the kids anymore?

Fine, the kids don't need The Sweet either — not when they had Queen, the one band who not only understood where The Sweet's burgeoning interest in harmonies and heaviness was heading, they were also able to hijack it before The Sweet themselves really figured it out.

And so, *The Six Teens*, a marginally convincing hard rock protest song barely scraped the Top 10. The DESOLATION BOULEVARD album didn't even sniff the chart, and matters just lurched from bad to worse. *Turn It Down*, their latest single, collapsed at No. 41. The Sweet's relationship with Chinnichap fell apart immediately after.

The duo were holidaying in the United States when their empire first showed signs of cracking. Anxious to break away from the manufactured stereotype which still haunted them, The Sweet waited until their mentors were safely out of the way, then went into the studio to record one of their own songs, *Fox On The Run*, for immediate release — and immediate success. The song reached No. 2 in Britain. Six months later it breached the American Top 5.

More importantly, however, the song proved — at least to The Sweet — that they no longer needed Chinnichap. Unfortunately, they made one major error in their calculations. The strength of their past reputation alone was enough to ensure a couple of hits, whatever the quality of the material. But no-one, apart from Sweet fans, was ever going to take the band as seriously as they thought they should be, especially the hardcore heavy metal fans that the band were now so desperate to court. And though

The Sweet themselves had long since acknowledged that they were quite prepared to sacrifice the high chart positions of old, if it meant they could progress as legitimate artistes, even they could not have been prepared for the speed with which their commercial stock dropped.

Action peaked at a lowly No. 15, *The Lies In Your Eyes* made it no further than No. 35, and after that . . . nothing. A comeback of sorts produced 1978's *Love Is Like Oxygen*, but while it proved that the band had finally come to terms with its own most immediate musical ambitions, it was to remain a flash in the pan. No follow-up materialized, and finally, singer Brian Connolly quit in mid-1979. Andy Scott took over on vocals, but three loser albums later The Sweet finally called it a day.

The Sweet would, of course, reform, not as one but as two separate groups, one led by Scott, the other by Connolly, whose own solo career amounted to just three singles in two years, and whose personal life had since been devastated by a series of heart attacks. Even before he left The Sweet, he was warned that cirrhosis of the liver left him with just months left to live. In fact, he would continue performing well into the 1990's, overcoming not only a string of mid-80's heart attacks (including 14 in one day), but also pneumonia, and a nervous disorder which in turn led to serious spinal problems. Interviewed on British TV in 1995, a pale reflection of the rock God he once had been, he simply shuddered, "I guess my metabolism just wasn't as hardy as I thought it was." He died from renal failure two years later.

Sweet Glam Years Discography:
UK Original Singles 1971-77
- *Funny Funny / You're Not Wrong* (RCA 2051, 1971)
- *Coco / Done Me Wrong Alright* (RCA 2087, 1971)
- *Alexander Graham Bell / Spotlight* (RCA 2121, 1971)
- *Poppa Joe / Jeanie* (RCA 2164, 1972)
- *Wig Wam Bam / New York Connection* (RCA 2260, 1972)
- *Blockbuster / Need A Lot Of Loving* (RCA 2305, 1972)
- *Hell Raiser / Burning* (RCA 2357, 1973)
- *Ballroom Blitz / Rock'n'Roll Disgrace* (RCA 2403, 1974)
- *Teenage Rampage / Own Up* (RCA 5004, 1974)
- *The Six Teens / Burn On The Flame* (RCA 5037, 1974)
- *Turn It Down / Someone Else Will* (RCA 2480, 1974)
- *Fox On The Run / Miss Demeanour* (RCA 2524, 1975)
- *Action / Sweet FA* (RCA 2578, 1975)
- *Lies In Your Eyes / Cockroach* (RCA 2641, 1976)
- *Lost Angels / Funk It Up* (RCA 2748, 1976)
- *Fever Of Love / A Distinct Lack Of Ancient* (RCA PB 5011, 1977)
- *Stairway To The Stars / Why Don't You Do It* (RCA PB 5046, 1977)

UK Important Archive Singles
- *It's The Sweetest Mix / Fox On The Run* (Anagram ANA 28, 1984)
- *Sweet 2th — The Wig Wam Willy Mix / Teen Action Mix* (Anagram ANA 29, 1985)

US Original Singles
- *Funny Funny / You're Not Wrong For Loving Me* (Bell 106, 1970)
- *Co-Co / You're Not Wrong For Loving Me* (Bell 126, 1971)
- *Poppa Joe / Jeannie* (Bell 184, 1972)
- *Little Willy / Man From Mecca* (Bell 251, 1973)
- *Blockbuster / Need A Lot Of Lovin'* (Bell 361, 1973)
- *New York Connection / Wig Wam Bam* (Bell 408, 1973)
- *Ballroom Blitz / Restless* (Capitol 4055, 1974)
- *Fox On The Run / Burn On The Flame* (Capitol 4157, 1975)
- *Action / Medusa* (Capitol 4220, 1976)
- *Fever Of Love / Heartbreak Today* (Capitol 4429, 1977)
- *Funk It Up (David's Song) / Disco Mix* (Capitol 4454, 1977)

UK Original Albums
- GIMME DAT DING (with the Pipkins) (MFP 5248, 1971)
- FUNNY HOW SWEET COCO CAN BE (RCA 8288, 1971)
- BIGGEST HITS (compilation) (RCA 8316, 1972)
- SWEET FANNY ADAMS (RCA 5039, 1974)
- DESOLATION BOULEVARD (RCA 5080, 1975)
- STRUNG UP (RCA SPC 0001, 1975)
- GIVE US A WINK (RCA 1036, 1976)
- GOLDEN GREATS (compilation) (RCA 25111, 1977)

UK Important Archive Albums
- SWEET SIXTEEN (compilation) (Anagram 16, 1984)
- ROCKIN' THE RAINBOW (Receiver RRCD 169, 1993)

US Original Albums
- THE SWEET (Bell 124, 1973)
- DESOLATION BOULEVARD (Capitol ST 11395, 1975)
- GIVE US A WINK (Capitol ST 11496, 1976)

US Important Archive Albums
- THE SWEET (compilation) (Razor & Tie 7930182189, 1999)
- BLOCKBUSTER! ALTERNATE TAKES (Cleopatra CLP 0474, 1999)

Notes: SWEET SIXTEEN is the most satisfying Sweet compilation, containing as it does all of the band's major hits (less *Funny Funny* and *Co-Co.*) The two earlier UK compilations feature a variety of B-sides and album cuts in addition to a side's worth of hits.

The 1999 THE SWEET album reissues the band's US debut in its entirety, plus bonus material completing a survey of all the band's pre-*Blockbuster* UK 45's / B-sides. The band's recent discography overflows with generally budget priced compilations and collections promising live and out-take material, generally without reference to which incarnation of the group is involved — needless to say, many feature latter-day (post RCA) and reunion projects. Cherry picked from a number of these titles, BLOCKBUSTER! ALTERNATE

TAKES compiles rare 1972-75 era television performances and out-takes, with material recorded by both The Sweet without Connolly, and Connolly without The Sweet.

☆ 5 ☆
Gary Glitter

– Rock'n'Roll –

His first Glam hit, *Rock And Roll (part 1)*, entered the UK chart on June 10, 1972.

Chart Hits	UK	US
Singles	23 (1972-95)	2 (1972)
Albums	6 (1972-97)	1 (1972)

Gary Glitter was absurd. Even at the time, there was nothing else like him, a slightly middle-aged, slightly over-weight, slightly daunting creation, a cross between the failed nightclub Rock And Roller he had once been and the space aged mutant he wanted to be. And as he aged, the absurdity grew. But through a career which comprised, equally, outrageous highs and mortifying lows, times when he could do no wrong, or moments when the entire world seemed to be ranged against him, he remained . . . The Leader. The fact that he also wrote the greatest record of all time is simply the icing on the cake.

Rock'n'Roll, parts one and two the first time around, parts three to six a decade later, remains the tribal war cry of the last quarter century. Forget its absorption into American sporting iconography. Forget, too, the fact that Gary himself built a five year career at the top of the British charts simply from recycling that same primeval formula. *Rock'n'Roll* is important because of its lyrics. And those lyrics, the most joyful, meaningful, and utterly, defiantly, triumphant lyrics in the entire history of modern music, go "rock'n'roll, rock'n'roll, rock'n'roll, rock'n'roll." That's part one, anyway. Part two is even better. That one goes "hey, hey, hey, hey, hey." Who needs "awopbopaloobop"? Who cares for "since my baby left me"? And who can even understand half of what Bob Dylan writes? Talk about Rock And Roll, and you only need to say one thing. *Rock'n'Roll*. Parts one, two, three, four, five and six. Hey!

"When I was a kid, my major influence was Elvis," says Glitter. "After that, I discovered people like Ray Charles; I liked his *What'd I Say* very much. Then I got into things like Gary US Bonds . . . Eddie Cochran . . . Gene Vincent's *Be Bop A Lula*. Those were my real influences," and those were the talismen he would carry through his greatest years.

When Gary Glitter first emerged, in the spring of 1972, the glam rock explosion which he necessarily joined was only one of the directions he was aiming in. The other was the Rock And Roll revival which was building slowly around the London underground, coalescing around increasingly regular visits by the likes of Jerry Lee Lewis, Chuck Berry and Little Richard.

It was the blending of the two into one seamless mass which made *Rock'n'Roll* so eternally divine. Instantly nostalgic, but like nothing else on earth, *Rock'n'Roll* sliced through everything else that was around that English summer, through the T. Rex sparkle and David Bowie sashay, through Slade's patent stomp and Sweet's candied pop, and though it didn't quite make No. 1, it hung around the chart so long that there's not another song on earth that recaptures the moment like that one. Even today, the pounding beat which opens the record, the chorusing guitars which carry the riff, and the opening calls of the Massed Vocals Of Hey convey a magic, a might, and most of all, an innocence which defies categorization. It might not be the most intellectual record ever made, but can anyone name a better one?

Gary did not always Glitter, of course. He was born Paul Gadd, in Banbury, Oxfordshire, on May 8 . . . 1944 was the official year, but estimates continue to vary. He got his first guitar at age 13, but he never really took to it. He wanted to be a singer, and recalls, "I was the typical boy posing in front of the bedroom mirror with my collar turned up, trying to sneer like Elvis."

Through the 1960's, Paul Gadd . . . Paul Russell . . . Paul Monday . . . Rubber Bucket . . . the name changes were as frequent as the 45's . . . rode every musical movement into oblivion. He tried his hand as a balladeer, and got nowhere. He moved into beat, and was beaten out. He sang protest and nobody listened, he went pop and nobody noticed. For a time, he was a warm-up performer on the now epochal READY STEADY GO television show. At another point, he pounded the same German club stages that the Beatles served their apprenticeship on.

In partnership with record producer Mike Leander, however, he kept on trying, and in 1969, operating out of the tiny Mayfair Studios in South Molton Street, London, Leander and Gadd launched into a long period of experimentation. It was there, they later agreed, that the pounding roar of the Glittersound was born, through the painstaking manipulation of tape loops and drum patterns. *Famous Instigator*, a track which eventually appeared on Gadd's first album, was demoed around this time. So was a boiling

Gary Glitter

rhythm which they called *Shag Rag, That's My Bag*, and which was tentatively scheduled as Paul Raven's first single of the new decade. At the last minute, however, Leander changed his mind. The hook was right, the beat was correct, but the song had something missing. It needed a bit more Rock And Roll.

Good, strong and energetic dance music was coming back into fashion — hits like Marc Bolan's *Bang A Gong* and Slade's *Get Down And Get With It* proved that. If *Shag Rag* could just be made a little more musically malleable, a touch more profound, and a shade less obscene (quaint though it sounds, "shag" remains an English colloquialism for sexual intercourse), it stood a good chance of following those classics up the chart.

Change! It was everywhere. The Beatles had changed, from a superhuman unit to four fallible individuals. The Stones had changed, the Who had changed. Without placing himself into those same exalted circles, Paul Gadd knew he, too, must change. So must Paul Monday, so must Paul Raven, so must Rubber Bucket. The man of a thousand aliases needed to come up with the thousandth-and-first, and even before he knew what he was going to record next, he was desperately trying to create a new name.

Glam rock was flowering everywhere. There was a clue in there, someplace. Vicki Vomit . . . Terry Tinsel . . . Stanley Sparkle . . . Late at night, the calm of Upper Montagu Street, where he was now living, would be shattered by Gadd leaping from his chair and announcing, "I want to be Horace Hydrogen!" Working backwards through the alphabet, Gary Glitter was simply the next alliteratively daft name he came up with. But this time, it stuck. And with it, there adhered a sound which summed up that name in perfect style.

Leander remembered, "Paul was very much into Rock And Roll, so I said to him, 'Let's go into the studio with a couple of friends, and you and I will write something as we go along . . . and see what we come up with." A tape of *Shag Rag, That's My Bag* was duly put on the deck, and they began playing along with it. "Friends dropped in during the evening, people came into the studio, played for a while and then drifted away, it was all very loose, and eventually this developed into an impromptu jam session as we started to get into a Rock And Roll rhythm, and then we built it up from there. And suddenly it all came together. We had produced something that was like all the records we had ever heard before, and yet was different to them all. We were writing and making the sort of record that we had both loved to listen to when we were 14 and 15 years old, yet it wasn't preconceived. We had not planned it that way. But when we played the tapes back the sound we heard was a revelation." What they came up with was a primeval mogadon stomp, 15 minutes long. They called it *Rock'n'Roll*. Edited down to a more manageable length, they renamed it *Rock'n'Roll (parts one and two)*.

Rock'n'Roll (either part) was to the most unique record of its era, and that despite the continued attempts on the part of Leander and Glitter to recreate it over the next three years' worth of follow-ups. Even at their finest — *I Didn't Know I Loved You (Til I Saw You Rock'n'Roll), I Love You Love Me Love* — the innocent chaos which underpinned the very rhythm of their first effort was to remain forever re-attainable.

Leander continued, "I took *Rock'n'Roll* to Dick Leahy at Bell Records and they were all astonished when they heard it — and more than a bit perplexed. There was nothing like it on the market at the time, and yet they, like me, had this instinctive feeling that the record had something." Bell pressed 1,500 copies of the single, and mailed them out to the usual BBC jocks. Everyone turned it down flat. But in the clubs, the song was making an impact. Leander relates a conversation he had with Dick Leahy, shortly after the single was released.

"He told me he'd been talking to the switchboard girl, and she'd mentioned that she was getting all these club DJ's phoning up asking for copies, that kids were going up to them night after night and asking to hear *Rock'n'Roll*. About a month after that, we started to get a change in the sales figures. Now record stores were starting to phone up and order copies because kids were coming in asking for that *Rock'n'Roll* record they'd heard at the disco."

It took *Rock'n'Roll* eleven weeks to get on the radio, twelve to get into the chart. But despite that, its success took Gary and Leander by surprise. Gary Glitter, to them, was still just a name, they needed an image — and it wasn't to come cheaply. Within weeks, Gary had spent nearly $10,000 on clothes, $15,000 on stage and lighting equipment, and more on hiring staff for Leander's management offices. "I wanted us to be a totally self-contained unit," Leander explained simply. "And I never had any doubts about our eventual success."

Gary's earliest television appearances were restrained compared with what he later accomplished. In a tight-fitting black jumpsuit which only accentuated the folds of blubber collecting around his mid-riff, and open to the waist to reveal his chest (or was it a chest wig? The gossipmongers could never decided) in all its matted glory, he was no-one's idea of a teen idol. Which was, no doubt, the idea behind it in the first place. While he was by no means ugly, Glitter could never hope to be teen meat per se. So he exaggerated his faults, put on too much make-up, showed too much flesh, and developed into the perfect caricature of a Rock And Roll superstar.

Like an obscene vaudeville stripper, he used his body as a weapon, to shock, to titillate the audience. Said the New Musical Express, "Gary Glitter . . . is the ultimate test of a liberated mind. If you can't live with the sight of Gary Glitter, the Michelin man of Glam Rock, quivering like Fosdyke's tripe factory, you're just another bigoted straight."

Rock'n'Roll was barely out of the chart before Leander and Glitter unleashed the follow-up. Aside from the fact that it had more lyrics, *I Didn't Know I Loved You (Till I Saw You Rock'n'Roll)* was very similar to its predecessor, and lost no time in racing into the Top 5. *Do You Wanna Touch Me (Oh Yeah)* and *Hello Hello, I'm Back Again* followed suit in the new year.

In March 1973, Gary played his first ever London concert. Although he had toured heavily in the wake of *Rock'n'Roll*, including a handful of shows which have ascended into legend for their inappropriate surroundings — village halls booked before the record took off, with Gary hugely incongruous in full costume on those little stages — he had purposely avoided playing the capital. Now, a full year after his breakthrough hit, there was no excuse. He would take the city by storm.

With untouchable class, he booked into the London Palladium, a venerable old pile better known for hosting pantomimes and plays. It was one of the first rock shows ever staged there, and it was one of the last for a long time. Afterwards, the theater management swore they'd seen the balcony visibly swaying. That never happened during PUSS IN BOOTS.

I'm The Leader of The Gang (I Am) became Gary Glitter's first British chart topper in the summer of 1973. It wasn't one of his greatest records, but Glitter fever was at its peak, and Gary could do no wrong — as he proved that fall, when *I Love You Love Me Love* shattered the classic Glittersound bubble by slowing everything down to half the speed. Another No. 1, without even breaking sweat.

The team turned its attention to America. *Rock'n'Roll* was a major hit, reaching No. 7, and giving the country's sporting fraternity a brand new national anthem. But they soon turned away again. *I Didn't Know I Loved You* scraped in at No. 35, then scraped its way out again, and GLITTER spent a couple of months at the foot of the chart, but never climbed above No. 186. When a handful more singles failed to match even that, Glitter pretty much left America to its own devices. America retaliated by sending Brownsville Station's cover of *Leader* to No. 48.

In November 1973, Gary played his biggest shows yet, a season at the London Rainbow. Filmed for a planned documentary on the Glitter phenomenon, the shows eventually became simply the backdrop and climax of REMEMBER ME THIS WAY, a full-blown feature film in which an ever-so-ludicrous plot allowed our hero to indulge in his wildest rock star fantasies. The Kung Fu sequence alone is worth the price of admission.

REMEMBER ME THIS WAY also spawned Gary's finest album, a non-stop live recording from those same Rainbow shows. Loaded down with hits — eight of the album's eleven tracks were Top 5 smashes — REMEMBER ME THIS WAY remains the perfect document of Gary Glitter's peak period, vividly capturing the full-on glittering excitement and frenzy of both his live show and his audience.

"The glam thing was always great fun," Gary reflected years later. "We — Marc Bolan, David Bowie, myself, Slade, Sweet — were working in pre-video times, but we'd be thinking visually. When we did TOP OF THE POPS, which was our major outlet, we devised some outrageous props. I used to come out on motorbikes, or moons to stand on." And his visual extravagance was only half the story. Tales of Gary's spending were manifold, and tended to be true. Importing sequins from Switzerland, he thought nothing of dropping between two and three thousand pounds on one suit. At one point he owned 30 glitter suits, maybe 50 pairs of monstrous silver platforms, and when questioned about his expenditure now, he happily admits, "I needed that many because there were always people around. It's what they wanted from me, just like anybody today would be disappointed if they dropped in on Prince and found him slopping about in an old cardigan."

But the bubble was perilously close to bursting.

Always Yours, a return to the high energy thump of old, gave Gary his eighth successive hit, and third No. 1, in June 1974, yet he was to enjoy just three more Top Tenners. Another ballad, *Oh Yes! You're Beautiful*, reached No. 2, the insistent *Love Like You And Me* made No. 10, and finally, *Doing Alright With The Boys* hit No. 6. But his next single, *Papa Ooh Mow Mow* was lousy. And while *You Belong To Me* was certainly a solidly contagious rocker, its signal lack of old-time stomp served only to alienate his once so-loyal audience even further. They didn't want Gary Glitter to mature as an artist, they wanted him to be physical, vulgar, crude and raw.

Gary bowed out of the concert arena in early 1976, saying good-bye via a massive, televised, farewell show. But of course it wasn't really good-bye — Glitter's 1991 autobiography, THE LEADER, speaks openly of the financial and psychological pressures which first forced him into retirement, then dragged him out again. Hounded into bankruptcy by the voracious sharks at the Inland Revenue, bruised and battered by his sudden decline, drinking heavily, "the self-destruct button was firmly pushed." Finally, in early 1980, he attempted suicide.

He failed. So slowly he began piecing his life back together, throwing himself headlong into the only thing he really understood — entertaining. His hits had served him in good stead in the past, and they were still selling healthily now. Without stooping so low as the cabaret party, Gary realized what his mistake had been — "progressing" as an artist, trying to move with the times. The kids wanted the hits, and it was his job, his duty, to give them those hits, returning to the public glare as a grotesque parody even of the parody he'd once set out to be. For a new generation raised on the scratchy old singles they found in big sister's closet, it was suddenly possible to see just what all the fuss had been about in the first place.

By 1984, Glitter was back in the chart with the adorable *Dance Me Up*. By 1986, he was hamming it with Doctor & The Medics, and their Glitter-esque reworking of *Spirit In The Sky*. It was only a matter of time, and a very short time at that, before Gary Glitter was right back where he belonged, sitting at No. 1 with *Rock'n'Roll*, when the Timelords took the sound-alike'n'sampled *Doctoring The Tardis* to the top of the pile. His Gangshow concerts were filling every venue in the country, and when the Who reworked their Quadrophenia concept in 1996, Gary was in on that as well.

Gary Glitter was always the unlikeliest of pop stars, and at his peak, his strongest point was always his knowledge of why he was where he was. It wasn't ego, it wasn't artistic fulfillment. Even in the beginning, his live show was a battering ram at the twin gates of Taste and Decency, his imminent descent into grotesque buffoonery prevented only by the sheer absurdity of the whole occasion.

No gesture was too hammy. Whether he was thrusting his pelvis forward and demanding, "Do you wanna touch me there," or shedding real tears, overcome at the intensity of his reception, turning on the house lights to see how beautiful the audience really was, or throwing roses to the crowd at the end of the show, he was Super-Pop personified. He could have died after that first record but he would have always have been a Star.

And why is that? Because he's the man who wrote *Rock'n'Roll*" How could he be anything else?

Gary Glitter Glam Years Discography:
UK Original Singles
- *Rock'n'Roll Parts 1/2* (Bell 1216, 1972)
- *I Didn't Know I Loved You / Hard On Me* (Bell 1259, 1972)
- *Do You Wanna Touch Me / I Would If I Could* (Bell 1280, 1973)
- *Hello Hello I'm Back Again / IOU* (Bell 1299, 1973)
- *Leader Of The Gang / Just Fancy That* (Bell 1321, 1973)
- *I Love You Love Me Love / Hands Up It's A Stick Up* (Bell 1337, 1973)
- *Remember Me This Way / It's Not A Lot* (Bell 1349, 1974)
- *Always Yours / I'm Right* (Bell 1359, 1974)
- *Oh Yes! You're Beautiful / Thank You Baby* (Bell 1391, 1974)
- *Love Like You And Me / I'll Carry Your Picture Everywhere* (Bell 1423, 1975)
- *Alright With The Boys / Good For No Good* (Bell 1429, 1975)
- *Papa Oom Mow Mow / She Cat* (Bell 1451, 1975)
- *You Belong To Me / Rock'n'Roll Part 1* (Bell 1473, 1976)
- *It Takes All Night Long pts 1/2* (Arista 85, 1977)
- *A Little Boogie Woogie / Lay It On Me* (Arista 112, 1977)
- *Oh What A Fool I've Been / 365 Days* (Arista 137, 1977)
- *I Dare You To Lay One On Me / Hooked On Hollywood* (Arista 154, 1977)
- *Superhero / Sleeping Beauty* (GTO GT 247, 1979)
- *Whatcha Momma Don't See / Another Pretty Face* (Eagle ERS 004, 1980)
- *Eagle When I'm On I'm On / Wild Horses* (ERS 009, 1981)
- *Then She Kissed Me / I Love How You Love Me* (Bell 1497, 1981)
- *All That Glitters / Reach For The Sky* (Bell 1498, 1981)
- *Be My Baby / Is This What Dreams Are Made Of* (Bell 1503, 1982)
- *Dance Me Up / Too Young To Dance* (Arista 570, 1984)
- *Shout Shout Shout / Hour Of The Day* (Arista 586, 1984)
- *Another Rock'n'Roll Christmas / instrumental* (Arista 592, 1984)
- *Love Comes / Boys Will Be Boys* (Arista 615, 1985)
- *Rock'n'Roll Parts 3/4* (Priority GLIT 1, 1987)
- *Rock'n'Roll Parts 3,5,6* (Priority 12GLIT 1, 1987)
- *House Of The Rising Sun / Rock Hard Men / Rock'n'Roll pt 2* (Attitude OYCD 002, 1996)

US Original Singles
- *Rock'n'Roll Parts 1/2* (Bell 237, 1972)
- *I Didn't Know I Loved You / Shaky Sue* (Bell 276, 1972)
- *Do You Wanna Touch Me / I Would If I Could* (Bell 326, 1973)
- *Baby Please Don't Go / ?* (Bell 345, 1973)
- *Happy Birthday / ?* (Bell 375, 1973)
- *Leader Of The Gang / Just Fancy That* (Bell 398, 1973)
- *I Love You Love Me Love / Hands Up It's A Stick Up* (Bell 438, 1973)
- *Rock'n'Roll* (live version) / ? (Bell 6012, 1974)

UK Original Albums
- GLITTER (Bell 216, 1972)
- TOUCH ME (Bell 222, 1973)
- REMEMBER ME THIS WAY (live) (Bell 237, 1974)
- GG (Bell 257, 1975)
- SILVER STAR (Arista SPARTY 1020, 1978)
- BOYS WILL BE BOYS (Arista 206 687, 1984)
- GARY GLITTER'S GANGSHOW (live) (Castle CCSCD 234, 1989)

UK Important Archive Albums
- GREATEST HITS (compilation) (Bell 262, 1976)
- THE ULTIMATE GARY GLITTER (compilation) (Snapper GGCD 001, 1997)

US Original Album
- GLITTER (Bell 1108, 1972)

US Important Archive Album
- ROCK AND ROLL (compilation) (Rhino 70729, 1991)

  Note: Gary never stopped making Glitter records. The above discography is therefore incomplete.

Gary Glitter

☆ **6** ☆
David Bowie

– *Starman* –

His first Glam hit, *Starman*, entered the UK chart on June 24, 1972.

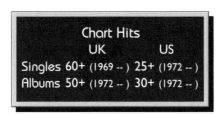

It was no coincidence that David Bowie's rise to glory coincided almost exactly with Marc Bolan's fall from grace. Bolan's success had relied on his almost unaccompanied breakthrough — when he first hit the scene he was unique. The people who followed couldn't help but take his lead, and with it a facet of his own personality. Gary Glitter took the primeval stomp, Slade took the terrace chant simplicity, The Sweet took the prepubescent awareness, and David Bowie took the sex.

Bolan's own sexuality had never been dwelt upon. He could drag up and act the "prima donna fag" as much as he wanted, rumors of his impending sex change and marriage to bongo player Mickey Finn could circulate freely, but not once did Bolan step forward to end the speculation. That responsibility was left to Bowie, and with it, the rewards.

After the fact, Bolan was furious that David had beaten him to the punch — but by then, of course, it was too late. With as much pride in his powers of invention as Bolan had, there was no way he was going to say — or do — something someone else had already done. There was no point. Indeed, for some time, the two superstars were scarcely even on speaking terms, a sad turnabout from the days when they'd been virtually inseparable.

Bowie, however, couldn't see what all the fuss was about. "The only thing saying I was gay ever did was sell records," he said several months after his original "confession." "As soon as [the] article come out in Melody Maker (in January 1972), people rang me up and said 'Don't buy the paper. You know what you've gone and done? You've just ruined yourself!' They said, 'You told him you were bisexual'; I said, 'I know, he asked me. Nobody is gonna be offended by that, everybody knows most people are bisexual.' And I got the paper and it looked alright. But from then on, the way the other papers picked up on it and just tore at it like dogs . . . they made this enormous thing out of it."

Although Bowie continued to express amazement at just how quickly the news spread, and the impact it created — even Cliff Richard denounced him for furthering the disintegration of society — he certainly had some awareness of the effect it would have.

Homosexuality had only been legal in the United Kingdom since 1967. To many people it was still one of society's greatest taboos, to be discussed — and practiced — secretly in darkened doorways and quiet corners.

Now here it was being quite literally shoved down everybody's throat — not least of all those of David and wife Angie. One day they were plain old Mr. and Mrs. Jones, living in a cheap flat in Beckenham, the next they were sexual deviants, abhorred and adored throughout every corner of the country, their private life a meal ticket for everybody who has ever made a living from scandal mags and gossip sheets.

Yet they reflected a very real need, present in a very real audience. It was not only homosexuals who had the obligation to feel grateful to the Bowies — for simple pop fans they were the culmination of Bolan's year long tease.

Bolan might have taken adolescent sex out of the back seat of the car and served it up on TOP OF THE POPS, but it was David and Angie who showed everybody how it worked. And however unwillingly (or otherwise) they did so, they made a bigger impact on a pubescent audience only just beginning to come to terms with its own body's needs and functions than anybody since the Beatles first made little girls wet their cinema seats.

In an age when sex was served up to a nation's teenyboppers in the form of vacuous teenage / teenaged idols, neatly sanitized by cellophane shrink-wrap and unfamiliar religious persuasions, Bowie cut across all the barriers with two simple words — I'm gay" — and the ability (or at least the promise of the ability) to back them to the hilt.

To an audience almost actively encouraged to be ashamed of its feelings, the Bowies touched upon the raw nerve, the hungry energy and the inability to channel any of it. It didn't matter that they would ultimately become as untouchable as any idol past or present. They were the figureheads, and their promise was of broken taboos, not broken hearts.

David Bowie

Like Bolan, Bowie spent the 1960's drifting aimlessly through a succession of image changes. Unlike Bolan, however, he never once stumbled upon the means of releasing, or disciplining, his dilettante meandering. While Bolan freaked out with John's Children, Bowie sang of Laughing Gnomes and Rubber Bands. While Bolan won underground support with Tyrannosaurus Rex, Bowie sold out with a song about a spaceman. Three years later, having become a space invader in his own right, he admitted that he wished he could erase *Space Oddity* from the memory banks of pop altogether.

That, perhaps, was the great difference between Bolan and Bowie, and in the long run the reason why Bowie was to sustain his success while Bolan was not. If Bowie made a mistake, sooner or later he would admit it, then place the blame on whichever mask he was wearing at the time. In 1976 he swept into Britain saying that what the country really needed was a fascist dictator, and rounding such remarks off with a Nazi salute at Victoria Station. But brought to book, it wasn't him that did it, not little David Jones. It was the Thin White Duke, whose latest album, STATION TO STATION, was hot in the shops.

Bolan never admitted his mistakes. He made some bad records, he even made some awful records. But ask him about them and he'd shrug, toss his curls, smile and say, "But man, they're what I was feeling at the time." And after a while, you just got sick of him feeling like that.

Ziggy Stardust, the character through whom Bowie projected himself upon the world, was born of any number of outside factors. Ziggy was a corruption either of Iggy (as in Pop) or Twiggy (as in the fashion face of the 1960's), Stardust was a tribute to the Legendary Stardust Cowboy, a mismatched country and western singer whose band included a one-legged drummer, and whose sole public appearance of any note was on ROWAN AND MARTIN'S LAUGH IN. "They all laughed at him and he walked off and cried," Bowie sighed. "It was so sad, he really believed in what he was doing."

So did Vince Taylor, an American Rock And Roller who was committed after going on stage one night clad only in a white sheet, and announcing he was really Jesus Christ. Ziggy, said Bowie, learned a lot from him as well. However, if any one event was to bring life to the seeds of thought which Bowie claimed to have been harboring for some time past, it was PORK, the latest play to escape the fervent imagination of New York playwright Andy Warhol.

Created from what assistant director Lee Black Childers describes as "Boxes and boxes and hours and hours of cassette tapes of every single conversation Andy had had in the past three years," PORK hit London in August 1971, booking in to a six week run at the London Roundhouse.

Childers and PORK star Cherry Vanilla were the first to discover David Bowie. Back in the States, Childers had read an interview with the singer in Rolling Stone, in which Bowie's penchant for wearing dresses was dwelt on at length. "When we got to London I was always looking out for David's name — hey, let's go see a man who wears a dress on stage. One day we saw he was playing at a place called the Country Club, so Cherry and I went down there."

A friendship, and mutual respect, swiftly blossomed. When Bowie introduced his song, *Andy Warhol*, Vanilla leaped up "and popped her tit out." Later the party — Childers and Vanilla, David and Angie, guitarist Mick Ronson and singer Dana Gillespie — went out to a nightclub, the following night they met up again at the Roundhouse for a performance of PORK. Actor Wayne County remembers, "We were all dressed up; glitter, ripped stockings, make-up. You couldn't get Crazy Color in those days so Lee had done his hair with Magic Marker. And David was just fascinated with us. We were freaks, and that was where he started thinking, 'Oh, I'll be a freak as well.'

"We were doing things in 1971 which he was still doing four years later, like painting our fingernails different colors, we all had blue and multi-colored hair, we were wearing big blonde wigs and huge platform boots and purple stockings. And he was wearing those floppy hats and the long, stringy hair, and he took one look at us and you could see that this was what he wanted to do. Lee and Cherry looked at him and said 'You can't keep on like you are. You've got to put on lots of make-up and freak yourself out a little.' Then Angie chimed in."

In January 1972, Bowie said he was gay. Six months later the whole world knew about it. When *Starman* became Ziggy Stardust's first hit single, it was not the song which started the stampede, it was the image. *Starman* was a pleasant enough vehicle, all about a little spaceman who wanted to come to Earth to play, but it was Bowie performing the song on TOP OF THE POPS, flame red hair and jumpsuit, odd eyes gleaming and one arm draped so languorously across Mick Ronson's shoulder, that did the trick.

Daniel Ash, later to record Bowie's own *Ziggy Stardust* as one-quarter of Bauhaus, remembers, "I went into town the next day and I was shaking when I went to buy that record. Because I knew it was going to change my life, and I didn't know if I really wanted my life changed."

By the time Bowie's on-going tour had reached its conclusion it was impossible even to breathe in the tiny clubs where Bowie and his band, the Spiders From Mars, touched down. And over the next twelve months, prior to his kicking it all in the head on a Hammersmith stage in July 1973, Bowie was to lift the best moves from everyone and put on the best show in town.

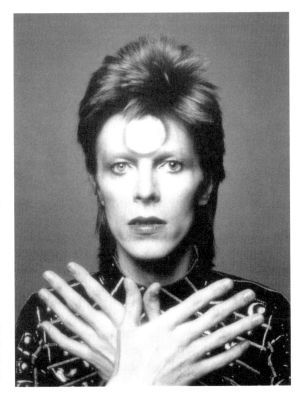

David Bowie

Shamelessly he plundered his own heroes' cabinets. *Hang Onto Yourself*, rewritten to become one of Ziggy's best licks, had already been revealed as a rewrite of the Velvets' *Sweet Jane*. *Rock'n'Roll Suicide* lifted its hook from Mort Shuman's translation of Jacques Brel's *Jef* (Brel's *Amsterdam* and *My Death* were also in-concert regulars.) Scratch the surface of almost any Bowie song, and its prototype was lying there as plain as day.

Even in conversation, the jackdaw rejoiced in cultural piracy. Somebody compared Bowie's vision to author Christopher Isherwood's I AM A CAMERA. A short time later, Bowie was announcing, "I am a photostat machine," and happily confessing, "I haven't got a new concept, I simply juggle with everybody else's. What I'm saying has been said a million times before." He described himself as a reflective surface. If he was degenerate, then the world around him must be degenerate too. Conversely, if he was wonderful, then the world must be pretty damn good as well. To praise Bowie was to praise yourself, to knock him was to knock yourself. It was, quite simply, brilliant.

And it was true, Bowie wasn't really offering anything new. The Rolling Stones and the Kinks, to name but two, had been experimenting with make-up and androgyny a good half decade before the rest of the world caught up with them, yet neither bothered exploiting the head start they had.

The Stones' greatest contribution to the ongoing madness was probably the promo film they made to accompany 1974's *It's Only Rock'n'Roll* single, sailor suits drowning in a sea of bubbles. Nobody took it seriously of course — having already plumbed the depths of sexual decadence (the black heart of even the most innocuous of glam bands) in his role as the reclusive Turner in the movie PERFORMANCE, Jagger had already said all that he needed to on the subject. Now he was simply taking the piss.

The same could be said for Ray Davies and the Kinks. *Lola*, a 1970 chart topper, was sufficiently explicit in its treatment of Lola's battered gender for many American journalists to blame it almost single-handedly for David Bowie's excesses of two years later. For some reason, such things were important to them. But while Davies could have gone for the jugular, he started backtracking furiously.

The mock Bolan-isms he employed on the 1969 B-side, *King Kong*, proved he was aware of what was going on — indeed, they proved he was somewhat ahead of his time. But for the most part, Davies spent the early 1970's wallowing in his desire to out-Tommy TOMMY and create the ultimate rock opera — a dash of pancake make-up, a wistful pout, a crooked smile and a suggestive wriggle were his sole concessions to the monster he had co-created, then it was back to village greens and midday suns.

Thus the way was open for Bowie, by fusing together two of rock's greatest talents, to painstakingly create a third — himself. Faced with an audience whose idea of a rock star was a great glittering beast of unspeakable debauchery and perversion, Bowie could have built one. Faced with an audience who wanted a down-home country boy with pointy shoes and baggy trousers, Bowie could have built one of them as well.

Bowie's impact was astonishing, but his ambition — if anything — was even wider. He saw Bolan telling his audience what sex was, but not showing them how to do it. He saw Slade coming the cosmic yobs without actually knowing what a cosmic yob was. He saw so much and suddenly everything fell into place.

The kids needed Rock And Roll. He picked up a down-at-heel suburban blues band called Mott The Hoople, gave them a face lift and a great single, *All The Young Dudes*, and Mott was off and running.

The kids needed squalor. He wrangled an introduction to Lou Reed, former guiding light of the Velvet Underground, and the pair hatched TRANSFORMER.

And they needed excitement, and he had that in abundance. *John I'm Only Dancing* followed *Starman* into the UK charts, *Jean Genie* followed that. A new album ALADDIN SANE, proved that ZIGGY STARDUST's breakthrough brilliance was no freak. And then, on July 3, 1973, David "retired." On stage at Hammersmith Odeon, facing an audience almost as breathless as he was, he announced that was it. "Not only is this the last show of the tour, it's the last show we'll ever do." Then he flew to France to record his next album, a tribute to the 60's called PIN UPS.

Though he has remained tarred with the Glam brush ever since, Bowie's active involvement in the scene had lasted 18 months, ending with one final slab of teenaged rock rebellion, the effervescent *Rebel Rebel* in early 1974. But like Bolan, what he helped to create would take him over. Even today, the Ziggy clones still turn out at his concerts; even today, lazy journalists still call him a glam idol; and even today, he can still breathe new life into a quarter century old repertoire.

He has indeed built his career on a succession of masks, shedding old identities the moment a new one suggests itself. And some of them have been good as well — the apocalyptic doom warrior of DIAMOND DOGS, the plastic soul boy of YOUNG AMERICANS, the concrete outcast of LOW and HEROES, the Italian waiter of LET'S DANCE and TONIGHT.

But few of these faces stick in the memory, and none of them changed peoples' lives. Ziggy Stardust did all that and then some.

David Bowie Glam Years Discography:

UK Original Singles 1972-76
- *Prettiest Star / Conversation Piece* (Mercury 1135, 1970)
- *Memory Of A Free Festival 1/2* (Mercury 6052 026, 1970)
- *Holy Holy / Black Country Rock* (Mercury 6052 049, 1971)
- *Changes / Andy Warhol* (RCA 2160, 1972)
- *Starman / Suffragette City* (RCA 2199, 1972)
- *John I'm Only Dancing / Hang Onto Yourself* (RCA 2263, 1972)
- *Jean Genie / Ziggy Stardust* (RCA 2302, 1972)
- *Drive In Saturday / Round And Round* (RCA 2352, 1973)
- *Life On Mars? / Man Who Sold The World* (RCA 2316, 1973)
- *John I'm Only Dancing / Hang Onto Yourself* (RCA 2263, 1973)
- *Sorrow / Amsterdam* (RCA 2424, 1973)
- *Rebel Rebel / Queen Bitch* (RCA 5009, 1974)
- *Rock'n'Roll Suicide / Quicksand* (RCA 5021, 1974)
- *Diamond Dogs / Holy Holy* (RCA 0293, 1974)

UK Important Archive Singles
- *Space Oddity / Changes / Velvet Goldmine* (RCA 2523, 1975)
- *Suffragette City / Stay* (RCA 2726, 1976)
- *John I'm Only Dancing 1972 / 75* (RCA BOW 4, 1979)
- *White Light White Heat / Cracked Actor* (RCA 372, 1983)

US Original Singles 1970-74
- *Memory Of A Free Festival 1/2* (Mercury 73075, 1970)
- *All The Madmen* (mono / stereo) (Mercury 73173, 1971)
- *Changes / Andy Warhol* (RCA 74065, 1972)
- *Starman / Suffragette City* (RCA 740719, 1972)
- *Jean Genie / Hang Onto Yourself* (RCA 0838, 1972)
- *Space Oddity / Man Who Sold The World* (RCA 0876, 1973)
- *Time / Prettiest Star* (RCA 0007, 1973)
- *Let's Spend The Night Together / Lady Grinning Soul* (RCA 0028, 1973)
- *Rebel Rebel / Lady Grinning Soul* (RCA 0287, 1974)
- *1984 / Queen Bitch* (RCA 10026, 1974)

Notes: Mercury recordings of *Prettiest Star* and *Holy Holy* are different versions to those released on the 1973 ALADDIN SANE album and the 1974 B-sides (*Prettiest Star* features Marc Bolan of T. Rex on guitar.)

Memory Of A Free Festival parts one and two is an electric version of the track on the 1969 MAN OF WORDS, MAN OF MUSIC album, and is the first Bowie recording to feature Mick Ronson.

The 1973 *John I'm Only Dancing* single is an alternate take of the 1972 single, recorded during the ALADDIN SANE sessions and released as a single after RCA pulled the wrong master while repressing the original single. The 1979 release takes two further mixes, one from 1972, one from the YOUNG AMERICANS album sessions of 1975.

The US release of *Rebel Rebel* is wholly different from that released in the UK and included on the DIAMOND DOGS album. *Velvet Goldmine* is a HUNKY DORY era out-take.

The *White Light / Cracked Actor* single is taken from the live ZIGGY STARDUST — MOTION PICTURE soundtrack

US Original EP
- *Space Oddity / Moonage Daydream / Life On Mars? / It Ain't Easy* (RCA 45103, 1972)

UK Original Flexidisc
- Excerpts from past singles (Lyntone 2929, 1974)

UK Original Albums 1971-74
- THE MAN WHO SOLD THE WORLD (Mercury 633804, 1971)
- HUNKY DORY (RCA 8244, 1971)
- THE RISE & FALL OF ZIGGY STARDUST & THE SPIDERS FROM MARS (RCA 8287, 1972)
- ALADDIN SANE (RCA 1001, 1973)
- PIN UPS (RCA 1003, 1973)
- DIAMOND DOGS (RCA 0576, 1974)

Archive Important Albums
- ZIGGY STARDUST: MOTION PICTURE (RCA 84862, 1983)
- SANTA MONICA 72 (Golden Years GY 002, 1994)
- RARESTONEBOWIE (Golden Years GY 014, 1995)

US Original Albums 1971-74
- THE MAN WHO SOLD THE WORLD (Mercury 61325, 1971)
- HUNKY DORY (RCA 4623, 1971)
- RISE & FALL OF ZIGGY STARDUST & THE SPIDERS FROM MARS (RCA 4702, 1972)
- ALADDIN SANE (RCA 4852, 1973)
- PIN UPS (RCA 0291, 1973)
- DIAMOND DOGS (RCA 0576, 1974)

Archive Important Albums
- ZIGGY STARDUST — MOTION PICTURE (RCA 84862, 1983)
- SOUND AND VISION (3CD boxed-set) (Rykodisc 90120-2, 1989)
- SANTA MONICA 72 (Golden Years GY 002, 1994)
- ESSENTIAL 1969-74 (EMI 21320, 1998)
  Notes: THE MAN WHO SOLD THE WORLD was reissued by RCA in 1972 (UK RCA 4816 / US RCA 4816), upon which occasion it charted. Bowie's entire Mercury / RCA catalog, briefly available on CD in the mid-1980's, returned to the racks during 1989-98 (Rykodisc US / EMI UK), the original albums appended with selected rare / unreleased material.

ZIGGY STARDUST — MOTION PICTURE was the abridged soundtrack to DA Pennebaker's 1973 film of Bowie's July 4, 1973 retirement concert.

SANTA MONICA 72 was the first in a series of releases from the Mainman archives. Other US titles included the unreleased Astronettes album (produced by Bowie, 1973) and a projected 3CD BBC collection. RARESTONEBOWIE included a number of live and out-take recordings previously widely circulated on bootleg.

EMI's ESSENTIAL 1969-74 included Bowie's ALADDIN SANE era studio out-take version of *All The Young Dudes*, eight years after Rykodisc publicly denied its existence. An alternate take was included on RARESTONEBOWIE.

☆ 7 ☆
Alice Cooper

– School's Out –

Their first Glam hit, *School's Out*, entered the UK chart on July 15, 1972.

Chart Hits		
	UK	US
Singles	19 (1972-94)	21 (1971-91)
Albums	16 (1972-91)	18 (1969-91)

Legend has it that Alice Cooper's big TV break came when they were asked to appear in an advertisement for an indigestion powder. They played and your stomach went sour until you took the cure. But legend says a lot of things about Alice Cooper — how, at the Toronto Peace Festival, they beat each other up on stage. How, when they flew to London for the first time, the old lady in the seat beside Alice dropped dead. And how a 20 foot cardboard Alice, naked except for a strategically-placed snake, brought London traffic to a halt when the lorry it was on broke down. "We act as a mirror," was the group's only explanation. "People see themselves through us."

What is certain is that they made two albums for Frank Zappa's Straight label, and that after they quit, Zappa kept an Alice Cooper put-down routine in his act for years. And it's also true that they were on a hot rail to nowhere until they released *I'm Eighteen* (they were all closer to 28 at the time, but no matter), the ultimate teen anthem of the 70's . . . and that's when everything fell into place.

Alice Cooper himself was actually Vince Furnier, the son of a Michigan preacher man. Moving to Phoenix, he changed his name and, after experimenting with such titles as the Nazz, the Earwigs and the Spiders, he built a band around it. With school friends Glen Buxton (guitar), Michael Bruce (guitar), Dennis Dunaway (bass) and Neal Smith (drums),

Alice swiftly built a reputation as the worst band in Arizona. They moved to Los Angeles and became the worst band in California as well.

One night Alice threw a chicken into the audience. He thought it would fly away ("I mean, they have wings, don't they?") Instead the audience ripped it to pieces, and the next day the press swore blind Alice had bitten off the bird's head and sucked out its blood. "After that we had to check in with the Humane Society every town we played."

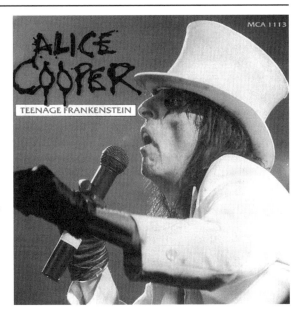

But *I'm Eighteen* turned everything around. The KILLER album became the shock hit of the year ... by June 1972, Alice's reputation in the US was hotter than hell. In Britain it took a little longer, but only a little, because all summer long, the entire country shook to *School's Out*, teenage perversity of the first degree, and an emphatic celebration of . . . what? The end of term? The end of the year? The end of institutionalized education as we know it? Nobody knew, but the sight of Cooper and his cronies whipping it up on TOP OF THE POPS was enough to outrage even the most liberal sensibilities.

But worse was yet to come. The daily tabloid press started filing pictures of rock's latest sensation as seen on their most recent American tour. They sang of Dead Babies and Killers, they re-enacted street fights and executions. Their latest LP had

Alice Cooper

been held up because they wanted it wrapped in a pair of frilly knickers, in violation of the fire code. They took snakes on stage with them, and inflatable sex dolls. If something was sacred they would spit on it, if it was Holy they'd hack it to pieces. The kids, needless to say, loved every minute of it.

Said Life magazine, "Confessing fantasies most people'd rather die than reveal, Alice Cooper became the scapegoat for everybody's guilts and repressions. People project on him, revile him, ridicule him. Some would doubtless like to kill him."

"People put their own values on what we do," said Alice, "and sometimes those values are warped. They react the way they do because they are insecure. They consider it shocking, vulgar … people who are really pure enjoy it. If Edgar Allan Poe were alive today, he'd do the same things as we do." And to justify his on-stage antics, "Of course we're in bad taste. There isn't anything in America which isn't in bad taste. That's wonderful, isn't it?"

The Coopers reached their peak with their sixth album, BILLION DOLLAR BABIES. They talked of giving away real money with it, then back-pedaled when they realized how much it would cost if the album sold even a fraction of its predecessors. Instead they gave away a dummy bill, a pack of custom made bubblegum cards and a collection of songs which paid homage to sick things, mad dogs and the dentist's drill. The last thing you heard was Alice screaming how much he loved the dead. Loved the dead.

And just in case you got to thinking maybe it was all a con, that maybe Alice really was a beer-drinking, golf-playing vicar's son, well there was always *Elected* (rewritten from a track on the band's very first album, *Reflected*.) The US elections were just around the corner, Richard Nixon was running for re-election to the most powerful gig in the world, and there was Alice, saying he wanted to run too, for the new party, the third party, the WILD party. He spoke of people's problems, because he knew everybody had them … "and personally, I don't care." Nobody dared ask him what his platform would be, but maybe it's just as well they never gave the vote to snakes.

Alice retired, halfheartedly, just before his bubble burst, and has been making sporadic comebacks in a variety of guises ever since — Alice Cooper from 1975 on referred to the man, not the now sundered band, and after a few years of confused drifting, he finally grasped his destiny when he was adopted by the heavy metal brigade, hosted MTV's Halloween Night special, and celebrated the end of the 80's with his first real hits in years, *Poison* and *House Of Fire*.

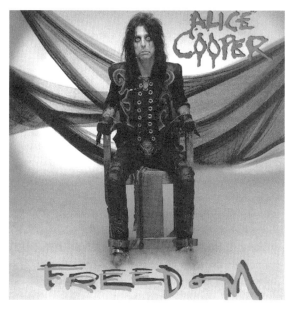

In between times, though, the old devil just kept churning it out, sometimes good, sometimes bad, and sometimes so damn ugly you couldn't help but admire the nerve of the man. 1975's WELCOME TO MY NIGHTMARE, the album and the tour, spawned some of the best reviews of his life, and even gave Alice a shot at MOR credibility when actress Julie Covington covered his *Only Women Bleed*. Another track, *Department Of Youth*, two or three years previous, might even have given him the biggest hit of his life, it was that good . . . especially the bit where Alice asks the kiddie chorus who gave them their freedom. He expects them to say he did. They tell him it was Donny. Alice's roar of surprise gives the record player palpitations.

But his greatest triumph came a couple of years later, in 1977, when he delivered WHISKEY AND LACE, a Philip Marlowe crime novel set to music. Overall, it allegedly was one of the most forgettable things he'd ever done. But one song alone proved there was schlock left in the old rocker after all.

The King Of The Silver Screen was the tale of a construction site worker who wanted to be a Hollywood starlet. "I could have been Greta Garbo if I'd been born in another time," he mourns, before the band strikes up *The Battle Hymn Of The Republic* and the singer fades out telling the world how much he loves wearing dresses, make-up, long hair. "I don't care anymore! Just don't hit me!"

Alice Cooper Glam Years Discography:
UK Original Singles
  ○ *Eighteen* / *Is It My Body* (Straight S 7209, 1971)
  ○ *Under My Wheels* / *Desperado* (WB K16127, 1972)
  ○ *Be My Lover* / *Yeah Yeah Yeah* (WB K16154, 1972)
  ○ *School's Out* / *Gutter Cat* (WB K16188, 1972)
  ○ *Elected* / *Luney Tune* (WB K16214, 1972)

○ *Hello Hooray / Generation Landslide* (WB K16248, 1973)
○ *No More Mr. Nice Guy / Raped & Freezing* (WB K16262, 1973)
○ *Teenage Lament '74 / Hard Hearted Alice* (WB K16345, 1974)

UK Original Flexidisc

○ *Slick Black Limousine /* excerpts from BILLION DOLLAR BABIES (Lyntone 2582, 1973)
    Note: *Billion Dollar Bits*, as the B-side of the above became known, was also released in the US as a promotional mini-LP (WB 208) and is most notable for the otherwise unavailable snippet from *Unfinished Suite*, in which Alice dons a dental coat to ask, "Have you ever had GAS before . . . ?"

US Original Singles

○ *Caught In A Dream / Eighteen* (Straight 7141, 1971)
○ *Eighteen / Is It My Body?* (WB 7449, 1971)
○ *Caught In A Dream / Hallowed Be Thy Name* (WB 7490, 1971)
○ *Under My Wheels / Desperado* (WB 7259, 1972)
○ *Be My Lover / Yeah Yeah Yeah* (WB 7568, 1972)
○ *School's Out / Gutter Cat* (WB 7596, 1972)
○ *Elected / Luney Tune* (WB 7631, 1972)
○ *Hello Hooray / Generation Landslide* (WB 7673, 1973)
○ *No More Mr. Nice Guy / Raped & Freezing* (WB 7691, 1973)
○ *Billion Dollar Babies / Mary Ann* (WB 7724, 1973)
○ *Teenage Lament '74 / Hard Hearted Alice* (WB 7762, 1974)
○ *Muscle Of Love / Crazy Little Child* (WB 7783, 1974)

US Original EP

○ excerpts from BILLION DOLLAR BABIES (WB 208, 1973)

UK Original Albums

○ LOVE IT TO DEATH (Straight STS 1065, 1971)
○ KILLER (WB K56005, 1971)
○ SCHOOL'S OUT (WB K56007, 1972)
○ BILLION DOLLAR BABIES (WB K56013, 1973)
○ MUSCLE OF LOVE (WB K56018, 1973)

UK Important Archive Album

○ GREATEST HITS (WB K56043, 1974)

US Original Albums

○ LOVE IT TO DEATH (Straight 1883, 1971)
○ KILLER (WB 2567, 1971)
○ SCHOOL'S OUT (WB 2623, 1972)
○ BILLION DOLLAR BABIES (WB 2685, 1973)
○ MUSCLE OF LOVE (WB 2748, 1973)

US Important Archive Albums
  ○ GREATEST HITS (WB 2803, 1974)
  ○ LIFE AND CRIMES (boxed-set) (Rhino R2 75680, 1999)

☆ **8** ☆
Mott The Hoople

– *All The Young Dudes* –

Their first Glam hit, *All The Young Dudes*, entered the UK chart on August 12, 1972.

	Chart Hits	
	UK	US
Singles	7 (1972-74)	3 (1972-74)
Albums	8 (1970-75)	7 (1970-75)

All The Young Dudes. It's the greatest 3 minutes and 33 seconds worth of pop ever consigned to seven inches of vinyl. A rallying cry, a requiem, a love song, a death march, *All The Young Dudes* has been covered more often, and more successfully, than any song outside of *Louie Louie.* In fact, if Richard Berry's little chest beater is the heartbeat of the American 60's, then *All The Young Dudes* is the soul of Britain, ten years later, conceived at the height of the Glam rock explosion, but so rapidly transcending that genre's limitations that today any one of a dozen different versions can be held up as somehow definitive.

There's the punk swagger of the Skids, gathering up the disparate tribes of late 70's rebellion; and the rhinestone swagger of Angel, recasting suicide Billy and shoplifting Lucy in the malls of middle America. There's the sultry harmonizing of the Chanter Sisters, realizing the song's inherent musicality; and the rebellious folk vibe of World Party, redressing the injustices of a decade under Thatcher and Reagan.

Bruce Dickinson injected the song with weary nostalgia. Mick Ronson, at his last recorded live performance, imbibed it with soaring sadness. Michael Aston's Gene Loves Jezebel have added a gritty gothic glamour; Jill Sobule, a sad, sweet dreaminess. And, of course, there are the multitudinous renditions which the song's own composer, David Bowie, has unveiled over the years, as he himself struggled to match the peerless perfection of Mott The Hoople's original version, recorded back in 1972, and still as relevant today as it ever was back then.

"To be honest, I much prefer our version," Mott The Hoople's Ian Hunter wrote of Bowie's first attempt at the song, later in 1972. "This seems too slow, and he's done it in a lower key." And Bowie would appear to have agreed with him. Plans to include the song on 1973's ALADDIN SANE album were abandoned, and it was another 20 years before that particular performance finally saw the light of day. In the meantime, though, Bowie bashed the song till it bled; rearranged it for soul and barber's shop quartet; jangled it up and jungled it down — he even gave it away to his fans.

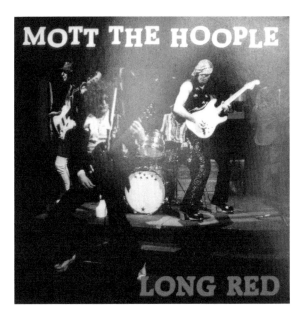

"This song was written 25 years ago," he announced from the stage on his 1997 American tour. "Do with it what you will." Then Reeves Gabrels would launch into the riff that once powered a generation's naive dreams, and a quarter of a century rolled back like candy wrappers, until 25 years were 25 minutes, and the kids still had hope and youth on their side, the old really were back at home with their Beatles and their Stones, and T. Rex and TV truly were all that mattered. *All The Young Dudes* did more than zap the zeitgeist of early 70's pop. Up there with *Rock'n'Roll*, it created it.

And it recreated Mott The Hoople, although the story began years earlier with a string of nowhere 60's R&B stalwarts — the Buddies, the Shakedown Sound, the Silence, the Doc Thomas Group, a slowly fermenting pool of musicians who became Mott The Hoople following encounters with producer Guy Stevens — who gave them a record deal, and vocalist Ian Hunter — who gave them a voice.

But four albums for Island Records went nowhere, and though Mott was among the biggest draws on the British live circuit, they were stone broke and sinking. "The strange thing was," says Hunter, "we were making money on the records, we weren't doing as badly as people thought. They didn't chart, but they kept selling. We were losing money on the live gigs, because we had all these ideas of what we wanted to do, and it cost so much, so we were losing money there. And because Island had us for publishing, agency, management, we couldn't get any money, because the money we were losing live, they were rolling over to the records. I got a check one morning for ten grand for the records, and it was canceled about two hours later by the gig section of Island, to go against that debt. So the records were doing well, it was the gigs — which were selling out — which were costing the money."

The end of Mott The Hoople came in Switzerland, slogging around a hastily arranged circuit while back home, Island Records despatched terse reminders of the group's failure — cut back on the lighting, cut back on the PA; oh, and we've got you a gig tomorrow night in a converted gas holder in Zurich. It was there, on March 26, 1972, that Mott The Hoople broke up.

According to drummer Buffin, "somebody played a wrong note, there was a push and a shove, nothing very much, but a bit of snarling, followed by 'there's better things to do in life than play f***ing gigs in places like this.' So it was decided, 'that's it. We'll flounce off and not be a group anymore'." The following day, the five band members went to the movies, to see a John Wayne film. They were — a month's worth of outstanding commitments around the UK notwithstanding — finally free.

"We got home," bassist Overend Watts recalled, "and I thought, 'well, it's all over now, what do I do?' So I rang David Bowie." This was not such a momentous event as it sounds; in the spring of 1972, in terms of bottoms-on-seats, or even sales-in-stores, Bowie was barely even as well-known as Mott The Hoople themselves were, a one hit wonder from three years before who'd had a few nice reviews for his last album, HUNKY DORY. Maybe Ziggy Stardom would be hitting him hard and fast within the next few weeks, but when he picked up the phone to Watts, he was no-one.

But he'd sent the band a demo a year or so before, and though Mott The Hoople just couldn't imagine themselves ever wanting to actually record *Suffragette City*, Watts wanted to thank him for the thought, tell him the news about the band's sad demise, "and ask him if he knew of any jobs going anywhere. We got talking for an hour, an hour and a half, and I was telling him about the group. He said, 'look, I've got a song I've half-written, let me ring you back in an hour or two, I have to speak to my manager.'"

"He rang back and asked if I'd like to go and listen to the song. I said I didn't know how the rest of the group would feel, but I'd come over. In fact, he came and picked me up in a battered old Jag. He was nervous to meet me, and I was nervous to meet him. We went round to [manager] Tony DeFries' place in Chelsea, and David played part of *All The Young Dudes* on acoustic guitar. He'd got all the chorus words, but he hadn't got some of the verse words, but you could tell it was a great song." Watts alerted his bandmates, and Mott regrouped on the spot.

"When I first saw them," Bowie reflected, "I couldn't believe a band so full of integrity and a really naive exuberance could command such enormous followings, and not be talked about." He admitted that he was fully expecting to have to nursemaid the band through the entire album, "contribute a lot of material. Now they're in a wave of optimism, and they've written [almost] everything on the LP."

All The Young Dudes, Mott The Hoople's first single for their new label, CBS, was released on July 28, 1972, and it was apparent from the moment Mick Ralphs' guitar chimed in the opening refrain, while Verden Allen's stately Hammond rode almost unheard, but certainly not unfelt, beneath the melody, that this was the perfect song for the summer. The phenomenon of glam rock was in full swing, and from Gary Glitter baring his chest and eulogizing *Rock'n'Roll*, to Alice Cooper predicting the downfall of education, the British rock scene was blazing with an intensity it hadn't known in five years.

That was the fire which *All The Young Dudes* tapped, as it so utterly transcended its running time, to capture the mood of the times like no other song ever did. Indeed, bookend *All The Young Dudes* with Mott The Hoople's final single, 1974's *Saturday Gigs*, and the entire schism of British rock and pop through this one golden era is preserved in all its living, breathing purity.

All The Young Dudes crashed to No. 3 on the British chart, but while there was little doubt that its success was in no small way attributable to Mott's association with Bowie — who himself had broken through in a very big way that same summer — Bowie did not reinvent, or even revamp, Mott The Hoople. He simply gave them the focus they had been searching for all along. That, and the nudge which shattered the band's original democracy, and established vocalist Hunter as the leader of the gang. "The first afternoon we met," Watts concludes, "Bowie said to me . . . 'in the 70's, you are going to be enormous.' And it made me feel great, because I thought we were buggered."

It was with great reluctance, of course, that Mott The Hoople felt themselves being squeezed into the glam bag. With the exception of Overend Watts, who had always boasted a sartorial flair to match his flamboyant name, the rest of the group were (as Buffin once delightfully put it) "hoary old bastards" who really did not fit in with the air of studied androgyny and camp which was the new movement's favorite party trick.

But they succumbed anyway, and while their old underground following burned its denim jackets in protest, furious that good ol' Mott The 'Oople had sold out to the painted Lucifer of Bowie and bubblegum, the band started plotting its follow-up single, another Bowie composition called *Drive In Saturday*.

What a record that could have been. No matter how many great records Bowie has made, he's written no more than a handful of truly great songs — *All The Young Dudes* was one, *Life On Mars?* is another, and *Drive In Saturday* is an unimpeachable third. Of course he would have been mad to give it away, but if he had, Mott The Hoople's next masterpiece would have been assured.

Sanity prevailed. "I tried to get *Drive In Saturday* because I didn't think he was doing it as well as we could," Hunter explained later. "I had this real different kind of arrangement for it. Listening to the song now, God knows what was in my mind, because I can't see what we could have done with it. But anyway, he wouldn't give it to me." Instead, Bowie suggested Hunter cast around to see if he could come up with a suitable single of his own. Hunter obliged, and turned up *Honaloochie Boogie*. Bowie listened, suggested a tentative lyric change, and Mott was on course for their second successive hit.

Overcoming the successive departures of organist Verden Allen and guitarist Mick Ralphs — who quit to form Bad Company, even as Mott The Hoople's latest album, MOTT, raced towards its UK chart peak of No. 7 — Mott entered their next golden age with former Spooky Tooth guitarist Luther Grovesnor on board, under the immortal name of Ariel Bender. They celebrated with another new single, the rousing *All The Way From Memphis*.

Bender joined the band in September 1973, on the eve of their next American tour. "When I joined," Bender reflected, "I believe that I gave them a shot in the arm. I said 'f*** it' — they were very down when I joined Mott The Hoople, so it was great for them, but it was also great for me, and the fact is, we spent the most commercial time together."

Mott The Hoople rang out 1973 with a new single, a tight and delightful piece of 50's-flavoured fluff called *Roll Away The Stone*. Originally recorded while Ralphs was still in the band, but reworked once Bender came aboard, *Stone* rolled all the way to No. 8 in Britain, Mott The Hoople's highest chart position since *All The Young Dudes*. And they launched the new year by going back to the studio, to begin work on their next album.

THE HOOPLE is not Mott The Hoople's greatest album. In fact, it could lay serious claim to being their worst, alternately gimmicky (*Marionette*), corny (*Alice*), overblown (*Through The Looking Glass*) and clichéd (*Crash Street Kidds*.) But it possesses a personality, and a sense of inner purpose, which no Mott The Hoople album since 1971's BRAIN CAPERS had managed to capture, a grotty grandeur and a weary wisdom which took its cue from the opening line of its finest cut, *Pearl'n'Roy (England)*, and never let up from there — "it's 'clean the chimneys, kids,' and it's 1974." THE HOOPLE was the sound of Mott The Hoople taking the studio by storm. Which is one of the reasons why the end of the band — the real end, this time, not another of those are-they / aren't-they pastiches of the past — came as such a total surprise.

First, a new single, a Spector pastiche called *Foxy Foxy*, died a death, scraping to a lowly No. 33 in June 1974. Then Bender quit, halfway through the sessions for a follow-up which Hunter himself had already decided was barely worth bothering with. He was already looking towards a solo career; he just needed to find a way to tell his bandmates. He couldn't, so he recruited Mick Ronson into the group.

"Mick Rock, the photographer, suggested I talk to Mick Ronson," Hunter recollected. "So I did. It started endless complications, but we didn't care because the two of us got on great, and Mick was right at the top of his game. We thought all the creativity would return, the band were over the moon about it."

From a fan's point of view, too, Ronson's arrival into Mott The Hoople was regarded as a marriage made in Heaven. The guitarist had already confessed to some bewilderment over what was expected of him in the solo shoes which he'd been struggling to fill since he and David Bowie parted ways earlier in the year. Admittedly, his best work came as an interpreter of other people's ideas, rather than as a vehicle for his own. When Angie Bowie sent a telegram proclaiming his union with Mott The Hoople "The Wedding Of The Year", few people argued with her.

David Bowie, of course, had already burned his bridges by this point. *Rebel Rebel*, a teenage strut of the first order, was his farewell to the magic that made him, an exultant roar of defiance which was the very heart of his last truly great album, DIAMOND DOGS. Now everybody looked to Mott The Hoople for the glories that Ziggy had promised, and which the band itself had already come at least halfway to delivering across their last three albums, and even closer if you only counted a string of delirious singles.

But the marriage was not to be a happy one. Hunter was hospitalized following a nervous breakdown which scuppered all of the band's live plans, bar a short tour of Scandinavia. Mott The Hoople's long-promised live album, taped in London and New York the previous spring, was released to widespread apathy, and a meager chart peak of No. 32 — it featured Ariel Bender, of course, but it was Ronson who the fans wanted to hear now. And Ronson himself was miserable as sin, stuck on the road with a group who, Hunter aside, apparently viewed his recruitment, his stature and his expense account with vitriolic distrust.

"Two limos were turning up, one from Columbia for Mott, one from RCA for Mick. And the others in the band got upset," Hunter sighed. "And so, a split developed." Ronson's wife, Susie, agreed, adding, "Mick couldn't buy a drink without four pairs of eyes watching him." And the bitterness didn't fade, either — years later, when Overend Watts came to compile the first Mott The Hoople greatest hits album, Ronno was relegated to a sleeve credit no larger than that afforded the session men who'd helped out on everything else.

To the public at large, of course, the whole world was rosy . . . and about to get even rosier. Despite its sordid aftermath, Hunter insisted the Scandinavian outing was "one of our best tours ever," while the first fruits of the new line-up's studio debut were also sounding great. Hunter had resuscitated the desultory sessions for the band's next single, rewritten *Saturday Kids* as *Saturday Gigs*, and reworked it around Ronson's explosive guitar solo. It would be out in early fall 1974.

An elegiac recounting of Mott The Hoople's entire history, *Saturday Gigs* came close to justifying every hope Mott The Hoople had ever inspired. With Ronson's soaring guitar as perfect as any he had played with Bowie, with Hunter's voice as scathing and saddening as ever, these ingredients alone made all the recent troubles seem worthwhile. But then you got to the fade-out.

Two years before, wrapping up *All The Young Dudes* in the studio, Hunter started to ad-lib over the fade, a few lines of exhortation, calling the audience to his side. Now he started to do it again, only this time it wasn't a call to arms. It was the last rites.

On the single, all you really hear is a distant chorus singing good-bye. The *All The Young Dudes* boxed-set, however, creates a collage from a handful of the band's working mixes and alternate takes, and there, Hunter's intentions are revealed as plain as day. "We're just going to sleep for a little while," he cries. "See you again, sometime." And, "don't you ever forget us — we'll never forget you."

A month later, on December 12, 1974, with *Saturday Gigs* having already stalled in the low 40's, Ian Hunter and Mick Ronson left Mott The Hoople.

Mott The Hoople Discography:

UK Original Singles 1972-74
- *All The Young Dudes / One Of The Boys* (CBS 8271, 1972)
- *Honaloochie Boogie / Rose* (CBS 1530, 1973)
- *All The Way From Memphis / Ballad Of Mott* (CBS 1734, 1973)
- *Roll Away The Stone / Where Do You All Come From* (CBS 1895, 1973)
- *Golden Age Of Rock And Roll / Rest In Peace* (CBS 2177, 1974)
- *Foxy Foxy / Trudi's Song* (CBS 2439, 1974)
- *Saturday Gigs /* live medley (CBS 2754, 1974)

US Original Singles 1972-74
- *All The Young Dudes / One Of The Boys* (Columbia 4-45673, 1972)
- *One Of The Boys / Sucker* (Columbia 4-45754, 1972)
- *Sweet Jane / Jerkin' Crocus* (Columbia 4-45784, 1972)
- *Honaloochie Boogie / Rose* (Columbia 4 45882, 1973)
- *All The Way From Memphis / Ballad Of Mott* (Columbia 4 45920, 1973)
- *Roll Away The Stone / Through The Looking Glass* (Columbia 4 46076, 1974)
- *Golden Age Of Rock And Roll / Rest In Peace* (Columbia 4 46035, 1974)
- *All The Young Dudes / Rose* (live) (Columbia 3-10091, 1974)

UK Original Albums
- ALL THE YOUNG DUDES (CBS 65184, 1972)
- MOTT (CBS 69038, 1973)
- THE HOOPLE (CBS 69062, 1974)
- LIVE (CBS 69093, 1974)

UK Important Archive Albums
- GREATEST HITS (CBS 81225, 1976)
- SHADES OF IAN HUNTER & MOTT THE HOOPLE (CBS 88476, 1980)
- ALL THE YOUNG DUDES — THE ANTHOLOGY (Columbia 491400 2, 1998)
- ALL THE WAY FROM STOCKHOLM TO PHILADELPHIA (live)
  (Angel Air SJPCD 029, 1998)
  Notes: SHADES OF IAN HUNTER & MOTT THE HOOPLE includes previously unreleased live material.

  ALL THE YOUNG DUDES is a 3CD boxed-set featuring one disc of pre-1972 rarities, one disc of remastered post-1972 hits and classics, and a third disc of material spanning the band member's entire careers. A cleverly reworked version of David Bowie's original *Dudes* demo is included.

  The live ALL THE WAY FROM STOCKHOLM TO PHILADELPHIA double CD includes gigs from 1971 and 1972, the latter featuring a guest appearance from David Bowie.

US Original Albums
- ALL THE YOUNG DUDES (Columbia KC 31750, 1972)
- MOTT (Columbia KC 32425, 1973)
- THE HOOPLE (Columbia PC 32871, 1974)
- THE HOOPLE (quadrophonic) (Columbia PCQ 32871, 1974)
- LIVE (Columbia PC 33282, 1974)

US Important Archive Albums
- GREATEST HITS (Columbia PC 34368, 1976)
- SHADES OF IAN HUNTER & MOTT THE HOOPLE (Columbia C2 36251, 1979)
- THE BALLAD OF MOTT: A RETROSPECTIVE (Columbia C2K 46973, 1993)
  Note: The 2CD collection THE BALLAD OF MOTT includes previously unreleased live and studio out-take material.

☆ 9 ☆
Roxy Music

— *Virginia Plain* —

Their first Glam hit, *Virginia Plain*, entered the UK chart on August 19, 1972.

Chart Hits		
	UK	US
Singles	18 (1972-96)	3 (1975-80)
Albums	15 (1972-96)	11 (1973-89)

No other artist ever repeated David Bowie's impact, but several were able to refine his original vision and create something immeasurably more sophisticated from the components he left lying about. And none more so than Roxy Music, a band who was quite the most explicit example of how the media could be put to one's own uses without degenerating into the no-holds-barred hyperbole which was to be employed elsewhere. At a time when art-as-artifice was becoming common currency, Roxy Music reversed the roles completely, creating artifice-as-art. And not even Bowie, whose own British breakthrough pre-dated Roxy Music's by a matter of weeks, had pulled that off yet.

Essentially the vision of a northern English school teacher, Bryan Ferry, Roxy Music had been around since the end of 1970 and, by late 71, had evolved into a line-up comprising Ferry, saxophonist Andy Mackay, drummer Paul Thompson, bassist Graham Simpson, and sound engineer Brian Eno, with a succession of guitarists coming and going as Ferry again and again made his bid for attention.

Nothing succeeded and what would now be a priceless treasure-trove of early demos circulated the music business to no avail. It wasn't until Ferry was able to add former Nice guitarist Davy O'List's name — and more importantly, fame — to the group's résumé that people began taking notice. "By the time I joined," O'List says, "Roxy Music had been rejected at least once by every record company in the land." And no wonder. One of the unsuccessful applicants for O'List's job, Quiet Sun guitarist Phil Manzanera, remembers, "their tape was done with a very abstract, sort of classical drummer and all that sort of thing. It was very different."

Whether recruited as an astute exercise in self-promotion or, as O'List himself claims, as a role model for Manzanera, who would of course become the band's eventual guitarist, O'List's arrival did change Roxy Music's future. The first notice came when the band's latest demo was reviewed in Melody Maker, in December 1971. Writer Richard Williams described it as "one of the most exciting tapes ever to come my way," and that despite it having been recorded "on a small tape recorder in what sounds like a Dutch barn." More succinctly, he later said, "It was a mess. It sounded like people mucking around — and there was this bloke in the middle who wanted to be a pop singer."

Nevertheless his enthusiasm was contagious. Within days of the review appearing, Roxy Music was booked for a session on John Peel's SOUNDS OF THE SEVENTIES radio show. Aired in late January 1972, the session featured just two songs, the fragmentary *The Bob (Medley)*, and a lengthy, eleven minute, version of *If There Is Something*, a recording which remains among the most exciting in the entire Roxy Music canon.

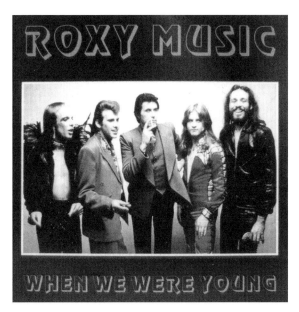

Live bookings followed. O'List remembers shows at Reading University's Fine Arts department and Battersea Art College, together with a handful of more mundane outings, opening for Quintessence in Bristol and Cambridge. The most incongruous of them all, though, was with the Pretty Things in Aylesbury. "We were sitting in this freezing cold dressing room, while outside the place was filling up with greasers (the British equivalent to Hell's Angels.) We just wanted to get the gig over with, we were expecting it to be really bad. In fact, we went down great. Bryan had made a quick quiff with a pot of Brylcreem, and there were all these greasers out there, actually jiving to the music! It was an amazing sight!"

Interest in the unsigned Roxy Music was growing, and in February 1972, Ferry decided to make overtures towards EG Management, a company to whom he had been introduced by one of the band's few "big name" admirers, Robert Fripp (Ferry actually auditioned for Fripp's King Crimson during 1971. He didn't get the job. According to legend Fripp advised him that with a voice, and an approach like his, Ferry would be better off persevering with his own group.)

EG was interested, but only in Ferry. They offered him a contract as a solo artist, but Ferry, to his ever-lasting credit, had not come through a year of intensive rehearsals simply to have his own master plan discarded at the drop of a checkbook. Instead, he persuaded EG head David Enthoven to accompany him to a disused cinema in Wandsworth, where an apprehensive Roxy Music was preparing to go through its paces.

Bemused, but impressed, Enthoven agreed to take the entire package, and within a week had signed the band to Island records, one of the companies that had rejected the group in the past. A few days later, O'List was dismissed, in favor of Phil Manzanera. "They asked me to audition again, and by that time I'd secretly learned all their material, sussed out what they wanted to do. I didn't tell them this, of course, didn't tell them for a long time, but I played and they thought 'Christ, he must be a genius!'"

The handful of live performances thus far undertaken had gifted the band with a very Art-School crowd, cool, sophisticated and stylish. It was exactly the audience Ferry had dreamed of courting, but to observers still desperately coming to terms with the pantomime androgyny of Bolan, the ice-cold fatales who followed Roxy formed an elite which immediately set outsiders on the defensive.

The band's music, too, permeated an other worldly reserve. Roxy Music looked like Glam rockers: Eno in feathers, furs and ladies' shoes; Ferry a mutant James Dean; Manzanera in human fly spectacles; but they sounded like computers locked into genetic overdrive. Everything about the band, from the canned lyrics that Ferry would warble with complete disregard for the conventions of melody, through to the presence of musicians not as an integral part of the band but as "featured soloists," seemed harsh and calculating.

When the band appeared on the BBC's weekly progressive rock show, OLD GREY WHISTLE TEST, performing *Ladytron* and *Remake Remodel*, host Bob Harris admitted on camera that they were there entirely against his personal judgment, that in his opinion they were nothing more than a talentless hype.

Yet at the Lincoln Festival that summer, Roxy Music was the star of the show. And when the band released its debut album, the Pete Sinfield-produced ROXY MUSIC, the reviews might have been written by their record company staff members. "The finest album I've heard this year and the best debut I can ever remember," championed the New Musical Express, "the answer to a maiden's prayer."

Even Bob Harris seemed to have changed his tune. Introducing Roxy Music on the BBC radio IN CONCERT program, he told listeners, "I don't usually say this . . . but I've been looking forward to this evening very much, particularly to see Roxy Music." Maybe he was simply being ironic. The next time Roxy Music graced the WHISTLE TEST studios, he was slagging them off as much as before.

If Bob Harris blew hot and cold, however, he was the only person who did. Released in July 1972, *Virginia Plain*, the band's first single, shot straight into the UK Top 5, its success so sudden that by the time Roxy Music came to support first, Alice Cooper at Wembley, and then David Bowie at the Rainbow Theater, they might well have been even bigger than either of the headliners. And *Virginia Plain* itself remains one of the most memorable singles of an already overly-memorable year, three minutes of word play and riffing that starts out with an orgasm and keeps getting better.

Still regarded by many as Roxy Music's finest hour, the band's second album, FOR YOUR PLEASURE, followed in the new year. Containing any number of future classics, *Do The Strand*, *The Bogus Man*, and the blow-up-dolly delirium of *In Every Dream Home A Heartache* included. Indeed, as recently as the late 1980's, Bryan Ferry's solo shows still featured these three tracks, proof that he, too, appreciated just how much they meant to his old audience — in 1996, Goth mainstays Rozz Williams and Gitane Demone titled their own album after a cover of that song.

Throughout its long history, Roxy Music was to be troubled by vacancies in the bassist department. Graham Simpson, who recorded the first album, had already quit before its release. John Porter, a friend from Ferry's pre-Roxy band the Gas Board, stepped in briefly, before producer Pete Sinfield introduced Rik Kenton.

He lasted eight months, before Porter returned for FOR YOUR PLEASURE. The strength of the remainder of the band, of course, was such that these comings and goings meant little to the general public. During the summer of 1973, however, a far more tumultuous departure hit the headlines when Eno quit. For a year now, he'd been regarded as the group's second leader. But Bryan Ferry wasn't into sharing any longer.

Eno was replaced by Eddie Jobson, Curved Air's young violinist and another of Ferry's pre-Roxy friends. Johnny Gustafson was drafted to plug the now-habitually vacant bass stool, and in this form, work began on the band's third album. Heralded with the *Street Life* single, STRANDED appeared considerably closer to the Rock And Roll mainstream than its predecessors. But was it really? Played alongside so much else that came out that fall, it wasn't Roxy Music who had moved backwards, but the mainstream itself which had stepped forwards.

Both Cockney Rebel and Sparks, two bands over whom Roxy Music's influence loomed large, were poised to break through, while Queen, then a far cry from the semi-metal monster they would eventually become, was nevertheless already allying tongue-in-cheek bombast with equally self-deprecating preposterousness in a manner which could not help but acknowledge Roxy Music's influence. Behind them, the rest of the UK scene was deliriously following suit.

America, however, remained firmly impervious to Roxy Music's appeal. All three of their albums to date had won US releases, spread across three different labels, with FOR YOUR PLEASURE and STRANDED even making the lowest end of the Top 200. That hardly translated into a healthy career, however, and in June 1974, eighteen months after their first US visit, the group kicked off what they described as their second American tour, but which, in reality, was little more than a fact-finding mission. It was, after all, just six shows long.

America's refusal to embrace Roxy Music at their sonic peak is not hard to understand. In a land where, well ahead of the modern preoccupation with generic pigeon-holing, music could be sold only if there was an audience for the pluggers to target it towards, Roxy Music filled too many pigeon-holes, and satisfied none. They were art rock, they were glam rock, and with a solo Bryan Ferry now sporting tuxedos and singing *Smoke*

Gets In Your Eyes in his concurrent guise as a solo smarm, they were even pre-rock. No wonder that many people opted to simply close their eyes to the whole thing, and write them off as just another obscure European thing.

All that changed with the band's fourth album, COUNTRY LIFE. Already trailing a British hit single, the thunderous *All I Want Is You*, and wrapped in a sleeve depicting two near naked young ladies, COUNTRY LIFE broke the American Top 40 (in a tastefully modified sleeve, naturally), and a full American tour was scheduled for 1975. Visits to Australia and Japan followed. There was a break to record the next album, and then in the fall, the whole routine began again, this time in Europe. It's no wonder that when that album, SIREN, did appear, for the first time in Roxy Music's recorded career, the sound appeared to be getting tired. It probably was.

Yet contradictory as always, Roxy Music still had one brilliant trick up their sleeve. Disco music had been making increasingly heavy inroads into the rock consciousness over the past year or so, with Robert Palmer and David Bowie having already proven its cross-over potential. *Love Is the Drug*, Roxy Music's contribution to the genre, left their competition in the dust. The consummate rock-disco record, in pure musical terms it would remain the most successful song of its type for another three years, until the Rolling Stones imbibed its own appeal into *Miss You*. In Britain, *Love Is The Drug* soared to No. 2 on the chart, Roxy Music's biggest hit yet. Even more rewardingly, it made No. 30 in America, and though SIREN itself crept no higher than No. 50, the breakthrough had been achieved.

Love Is the Drug was followed into the British chart by *Both Ends Burning*, while the band toured incessantly. In the space of less than six months, two American tours were crammed in, together with a British outing which culminated with two sold-out nights at the gigantic Wembley Empire Pool.

Such solidarity, however, did not disguise the fact that Roxy Music was falling apart — that it had, in fact, already done so by the time Island released one final, magnificent album. VIVA! ROXY MUSIC was recorded live over the past three years' worth of touring, a sensational collection which highlighted every stage of the band's development, every facet of their personality. The version of *If There Is Something* alone is worth the price of admission, while the similarly lengthy *In Every Dream Home A Heartache* has never sounded so dramatic.

If this was to be the end of Roxy Music (and of course, it wasn't; they resurfaced three years later, tighter, smoother and better dressed than ever), what an ending it was.

Roxy Music Glam Years Discography:
UK Original Singles 1972-76
- *Virginia Plain / The Numberer* (Island WIP 6144, 1972)
- *Pyjamarama / Pride & The Pain* (Island WIP 6159, 1973)
- *Street Life / Hula Kula* (Island WIP 6173, 1973)
- *All I Want Is You / Your Application's Failed* (Island WIP 6208, 1974)
- *Love Is The Drug / Sultanesque* (Island WIP 6248, 1975)

- *Both Ends Burning / For Your Pleasure* (Island WIP 6262, 1975)
  Note: A single from the live VIVA album, *Do The Strand* / the unreleased Andy Mackay composition *War Brides* was scheduled for UK release in late 1976 but failed to materialize.

UK Important Archive Singles

- *Virginia Plain / Pyjamarama* (Polydor 2001 739, 1977)
- *Do The Strand / Editions Of You* (Polydor 2001 756, 1978)

US Original Singles 1972-76

- *Virginia Plain / The Numberer* (Reprise 1124, 1972)
- *Do The Strand / Editions Of You* (WB 7719, 1973)
- *Thrill Of It All / Your Application's Failed* (Atco 7018, 1974)
- *Do The Strand / Virginia Plain* (WB, 1974)
- *Love Is The Drug / Both Ends Burning* (Atco 7042, 1975)

UK Original Albums 1972-76

- ROXY MUSIC (Island 9200, 1972)
- FOR YOUR PLEASURE (Island 9232, 1973)
- STRANDED (Island 9252, 1973)
- COUNTRY LIFE (Island 9303, 1974)
- SIREN (Island 9344, 1975)
- VIVA! ROXY MUSIC (live) (Island 9400, 1976)

UK Important Archive Albums

- GREATEST HITS (Polydor 2302 073, 1977)
- THE ATLANTIC YEARS (EG EGLP 54, 1983)
- STREET LIFE: THE BEST OF BRYAN FERRY / ROXY (EG EGT.V. 1, 1986)
- THE ULTIMATE COLLECTION (EG EGT.V. 2, 1988)
- THE THRILL OF IT ALL (boxed-set) (Virgin CDBOX 5, 1995)
  Notes: Both STREET LIFE and ULTIMATE COLLECTION also feature Bryan Ferry solo material.

  The boxed-set features no unreleased material, but does round up one disc's worth of non-LP B-sides.

US Original Albums 1972-76

- ROXY MUSIC (Reprise 2114, 1972)
- FOR YOUR PLEASURE (WB 2629, 1973)
- STRANDED (Atco 7045, 1973)
- COUNTRY LIFE (Atco 36106, 1974)
- SIREN (Atco 36127, 1975)
- VIVA! ROXY MUSIC (live) (Atco 36139, 1976)
  Note: The US version of ROXY MUSIC differs from the UK in that it contains *Virginia Plain*, a discrepancy evened up by the track's eventual inclusion on British CD's of the album.

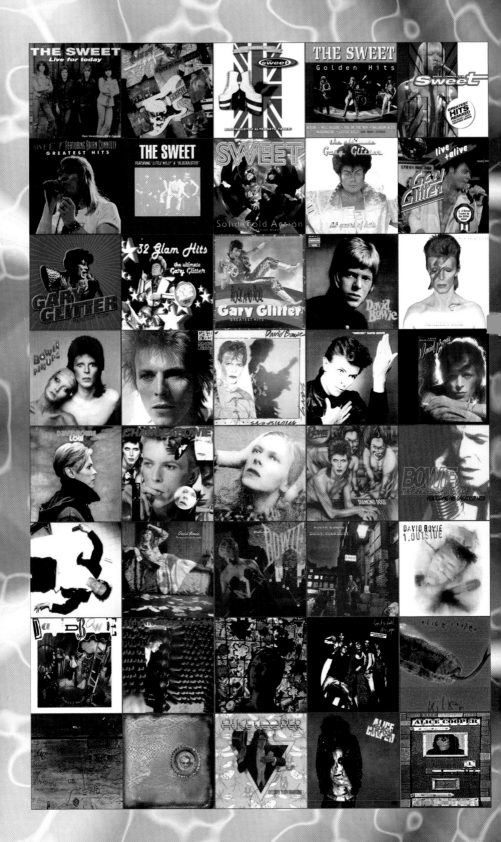

☆ 10 ☆
The Jook

– *It's Alright With Me* –

Their first Glam song, *It's Alright With Me* was released in August 1972.

Stomping, stamping, crass and crazy, The Jook was the brainchild of Marc Bolan's old John's Children bandmate, bassist John Hewlett. He was about to move into management (Sparks would become his first clients), and it was he who introduced guitarist Trevor White to singer-songwriter Ian Kimmet, in the summer of 1971.

"We hit it off straight away," remembers White. "So we packed up our families and went to live in the wilds of Scotland." They leased neighboring cottages near Jedburgh, and spent the next nine months earnestly getting their heads together in the country, "working every day and getting virtually nothing done. In the end, we decided to come back to London."

Accompanied by an Inverness bass player, Ian Hampton, and with another John's Children refugee, drummer Chris Townson, completing the line-up, the band launched into two months of intensive rehearsal, while Hewlett cast around for a deal and a name. He settled on RCA for one, and The Jook for the other, with the latter being derived from what was then his favorite oldie, Gene Chandler's immortal *Jook Of Earl*. Or so Chris Townson once said.

The Jook was launched in the summer of 1972, amidst cries of "there's nothing special about us at all, we just hope someone likes our music." So did RCA. For an unknown band, The Jook had been signed for an almost record fee, and the company was anxious to exploit every possible selling point — namely, Townson's illustrious past. Marc Bolan was at his peak, interest in his past was no less fervent, and Townson at least shared a few months of that heritage. RCA promptly dubbed The Jook "the 70's John's Children," and even today, Townson shrugs. "The only real comparisons were the anti-social attitude, and the fact that I didn't like the records we made."

What, none of them? — "No."

Over the next two years, The Jook produced five singles and one unreleased album, DIFFERENT CLASS, each displaying more and more recklessness as the band bid for that elusive first hit. According to Trevor White, "our music was getting so contrived that at one point, we were listening to whatever was the No. 1 single that week, to see what it had got, apart from success, that we hadn't. Then we'd borrow it. Integrity just went out of the window. We'd hear something and say, 'that's it, that's what we should be sounding like.'"

"We were great in rehearsal, or at gigs," Townson continues. "Everything sounded great, really relaxed. But when we got down to recording a single, it was like someone had said, 'okay, that's the fun over, now let's get down to some work.' And it was dreadful, really horrible. There were only a couple of things we put out that sounded like we might be enjoying ourselves." One of these was *Rumble*, the instrumental B-side to the band's fourth single, *King Kapp* ("Krapp" corrects Townson), which the band simply made up on the spot, from a riff White had been messing with in rehearsal one day. "There was us and Pete Wingfield, sitting in on piano, and okay, it was a bit self-indulgent, but at least it was fun."

Then there were *City And Suburban Blues* — which songwriters Gallagher and Lyle described as "a complete abortion", and the Jimmy Reed's *Shame Shame Shame*, recorded live in the studio and never, ever intended for public consumption. Unfortunately, no-one told RCA that, and the two songs appeared in the stores in March 1973, there to meet the fate which usually awaits rehearsal tapes . . . which was a shame, because that single was possibly the nearest The Jook ever came to their live sound.

Away from their uncontrollable urge to see their name emblazoned on the back of period RCA singles bags, up there with The Sweet, Jim Reeves and Jefferson Airplane ("if you enjoyed this record, you're sure to enjoy . . ."), the band really came into their own, and *Shame Shame Shame* had already earned its spurs highlighting The Jook's once a month residency at the Edmonton Sundown in north London. There, the predominantly Skinhead audience that the band had attracted turned out in the sort of numbers that even Slade, at the height of their flirtation with the crop-cut masses could only dream of. "Oh, if only they'd known what sort of people we really were," Townson smiles. "They'd have slaughtered us."

"We're not Skinheads," Kimmet used to reprimand passing journalists. "We're Rudies. Skinhead is the totally wrong word. We want to be masculine, but not violent. We just want to have a good time." And in answer to the accusation that they were indeed out to "slay Slade" — the band which Music Star magazine solemnly declared were "the latest Teeny and Weeny craze" — they would look down at their boots and braces and say, "we weren't really planning any image. It just happened."

It wasn't only Music Star and the skins who dug The Jook's image either. No less a personage than Mickie Most signed them to a publishing deal without ever having heard them play, while a visit to Edinburgh in early 1974 introduced The Jook to what Townson recalls as "the very hairy, very scruffy" local band who dropped by the dressing room to rave about yon bonnie image. A few weeks later, The Jook stared in horror as those same scruffy hairies, scruffy and hairy no more, cavorted around TOP OF THE POPS clad in almost precisely the same clothes as The Jook had been wearing for years. The Bay City Rollers had arrived, "and that was the end of The Jook."

Ironically, it was right at the end of their career that The Jook finally took to making the sort of music they wanted to, rather than what they thought everyone else did. Four songs produced at their final recording session (and which posthumously appeared on a 1978 EP) were, according to White, "the best things we'd ever done. Everything was just as we wanted, and if we'd stayed together, we might just have made the breakthrough."

But there's a big difference between "might just have made the breakthrough" and having already done so. When John Hewlett called to tell White and Hampton of disarray in the ranks of the country's most popular band of the moment, Sparks, it took them no time at all to put The Jook, and all its seeming potential, behind them, and launch into a life where fame and fortune were well within reach.

White got to make a solo single, re-recording The Jook B-side *Crazy Kids*. He and Hampton were screamed at in the streets and mobbed in the dressing room . . . they even came to fulfill a remark which White made to one of the teenybop magazines two years before. "If we ever make any big money, we're going to buy the most ridiculous cars."

The Jook Discography:
UK Original Singles
 ○ *It's Alright With Me / Do What You Can* (RCA 2279, 1972)
 ○ *City & Suburban Blues / Shame Shame Shame* (RCA 2344, 1973)
 ○ *Oo—oo Rudi / Jook's On You* (RCA 2368, 1973)
 ○ *King Kapp / Rumble* (RCA 2431, 1973)
 ○ *Bish Bash Bosh / Crazy Kids* (RCA 5024, 1974)
 ○ *Watch Your Step / La La Girl / Aggravation Place / Everything I Do*
   (Chiswick SW 30, 1978)

☆ **11** ☆
10cc

— *Donna* —

Their first Glam hit, *Donna*, entered the UK chart on September 23, 1972.

Chart Hits		
	UK	US
Singles	14 (1972-95)	9 (1973-79)
Albums	12 (1973-87)	9 (1974-80)

10cc's roots lie in the northern English town of Manchester, a city which has constantly been at the forefront of British pop. Today, it's Oasis who carries the city's banner. A decade earlier, it was the Happy Mondays. Before them, New Order, who in turn sprang out of Joy Division. And then there was the Smiths, whose vocalist, Morrissey, subsequently paid his own tribute to 10cc when he recorded Graham Gouldman's *East West*.

The group's members were similarly disparate. Gouldman was the best known, one of the classiest British songwriters of the 1960's, author of hits for the Yardbirds, Herman's Hermits (who recorded the original *East West*), the Hollies, Cher and more.

Eric Stewart was guitarist with Wayne Fontana and the Mindbenders, and lead vocalist following Fontana's departure — he sang lead on their hit *A Groovy Kind Of Love* and led them through one of the most underrated albums of the entire psychedelic age, WITH WOMAN IN MIND.

Lol Creme and Kevin Godley were film students who flirted with bands on their way through the 60's — Godley's first was alongside Gouldman in the Whirlwinds. Creme wrote that band's debut B-side. The pair also formed a psychedelic Simon and Garfunkel outfit in 1968, Frabjoy and the Runcible Spoon. All four knew one another, but it wasn't until the quartet came together as musicians in 1970 that things began happening. Gouldman was working as a contract writer for American bubblegum maestros Kasenatz-Katz, Stewart owned the studio where his demos would be recorded, and Creme and Godley were the session men who'd help bring the songs to life.

Three of the four had also formed a band together — that same year, Stewart, Creme and Godley landed a monster hit with the percussive *Neanderthal Man*, released under the odd name of Hotlegs. No further releases succeeded, however, and by mid-1972, their fortunes were at an all time low. Or so it seemed.

"We were doing sessions and it was terrible", said Godley. "We did a lot of tracks in a very short time, it was really like a machine. Twenty tracks in about two weeks, a lot of crap really, real shit. We used to do the voices, everything. It saved them money. We even did the female backing vocals!"

Early in 1972, Gouldman got together with producer Eric Woolfson (later a member of the Alan Parsons Project, and later still an aspiring solo artist, whose 1990 album would feature contributions from Eric Stewart), to record a new solo single, *Growing Older*. It was followed by a group decision that while session work was all well and good, it wasn't making any of them feel particularly fulfilled. There and then, Gouldman remembers, they made a pact. They wanted to create "something good and lasting".

Donna was initially intended as a possible B-side to a Stewart-Gouldman composition, *Waterfall*. A falsetto-voiced Rock And Roll spoof, it was considered a joke by the band. "But we knew it had something," Stewart remembered, and with *Waterfall* having been written off, *Donna* was immediately promoted to the top of the band's pile of potential singles. The trouble was, according to Eric, "we only knew of one person who was mad enough to release it, and that was Jonathan King."

The arch entrepreneur of British pop, King had known Eric Stewart since the early 60's when the Mindbenders were being followed around the country by a university student who claimed he could make them even bigger than the Beatles. The band laughed him off, "and the next thing we knew he'd had a hit with *Everyone's Gone To The Moon*. We never saw him again."

Stewart called King that same day, and by evening, King was on his way to Stewart's Strawberry Studios. Stewart remembers, "he listened to *Donna* and fell about laughing, saying 'it's fabulous, it's a hit'. So we agreed to let him release it on his UK label, and he was right. It was a hit."

It was King who also supplied the band's name, 10cc. Apparently it came to him in a dream. However, a feature on BBC Radio Two unearthed several other accounts of how the name was conceived, from Peter Tattershall and Graham Gouldman. "It was either a very small motorbike," Tattershall explained, "or it was the overdose of a heroin addict." Gouldman countered, "mythology has it that the name 10cc came from the average male ejaculation being 9cc, and, of course, being big, butch, Mancunian guys, we're gonna be, y'know, 1cc more than that."

It took Eric Stewart to end the speculation. "No, the name actually did came from Jonathan King. He said he'd had a dream the night before he came up to Manchester to listen to *Donna*. And, he saw a hoarding over Wembley Stadium or Hammersmith Odeon or something like that and said, "10cc: The Best Group in the World". So we . . . well, that sounds great to us, we'll call ourselves 10cc. And that's how it came about."

Initial worries that the band would simply be dismissed as another of King's little jokes were dispelled when they appeared on TOP OF THE POPS in September 1972.

King had given them two alternatives: either appear wearing their normal everyday denims, or "go the whole hog, be outrageous and appear in polythene hot pants". They opted for everyday wear and, as they walked into the studio, the program's host, DJ Tony Blackburn (whose choice of *Donna* as a Pick Of The Week had been instrumental in the record's success) greeted them with the words "Good God, you're normal! What a great gimmick!" *Donna*, backed by the instrumental *Hot Sun Rock* (based around a track Gouldman had had lying around for several years), reached No. 2 on the British chart. Immediately, work began on a follow-up.

In retrospect, the band admit that their choice was a mistake. *Johnny Don't Do It* was another 50's-type song, this time with the theme of a motorcycle accident. Unfortunately, the Shangri-Las' *Leader Of The Pack* was reissued at the same time, and while that epic tale of teenaged dismemberment reached No. 3, *Johnny Don't Do It* sank without trace. You can have too much of a good thing.

10cc's third single, *Rubber Bullets* (backed with *Waterfall*), also ran into problems, but of a very different kind. The British army had recently started using rubber bullets in their bid to bring peace to embattled Northern Ireland, and many BBC radio producers thought that with a title like that, the record had to have something to do with protest, and banned it accordingly. In fact, the song dealt with a riot in an American prison, a fact which BBC TV (who must have actually played the record) were quick to recognize. In April 1973, 10cc appeared on TOP OF THE POPS with barely a radio play to their credit. A month later, *Rubber Bullets* was No. 1, and well on its way into the American Top 75.

The success of *Rubber Bullets* more than paved the way for the band's eponymously-titled debut album. It included all three of their A-sides to date (although both *Donna* and *Johnny Don't Do It* were remixed, while *Rubber Bullets* appeared in an extended form), plus *The Dean And I*, which further established the band in the singles chart when it was culled from the album in August. The six other tracks further compounded the belief that 10cc was fast developing into a force to be reckoned with.

SHEET MUSIC

The Dean And I reached No. 8, and the similar success of the album prompted them to make their first foray onto the live circuit. On August 26, 1973, with Paul Burgess operating as second drummer to allow Godley to take his own vocal parts, 10cc debuted at Douglas Palace Lido on the Isle of Man. The show was a success, and they followed it with intermittent gigs around the country until the start of November, when they returned to Strawberry to begin work on their next album, sharing the studio with Mike McGear, who was recording the MCGEAR album under the auspices of his brother Paul McCartney.

10cc's own second album was the next phase in what Stewart calls, the band's "master plan to control the universe. The Sweet, Slade and Gary Glitter are all very valuable pop," he proclaimed, "but it's fragile because it's so dependent on a vogue. We don't try to appeal to one audience, or aspire to instant stardom, we're satisfied to move ahead a little at a time as long as we're always moving forward." SHEET MUSIC, perhaps the most widely adventurous album of what would become a wildly adventurous year, more than justified that claim.

First, however, there was another hiccup to surmount; the band's first single of 1974 was *The Worst Band In The World*, once again released at Jonathan King's insistence. And, for once, he was wrong. As was so often the case with 10cc singles, initial airplay was minimal, but when TOP OF THE POPS also proved hesitant, the release was doomed.

The problem this time was the use of the phrase "up yours" in the chorus, and a couplet in the first verse (the first line!) which rhymed "admit" with "we don't give a …" An edited version was hurriedly produced, but it was too late. *The Worst Band In The World* flopped, and that despite boasting a B-side, *18 Carat Man Of Means*, which might well have been an A-side in its own right.

Still, the offending song did make it onto the BBC at least once, when 10cc recorded a live session for SOUNDS ON SUNDAY on January 20. They performed six songs, *Worst*

Band, *Somewhere In Hollywood* and *Oh Effendi* from the new album, plus *Sand In My Face*, *Rubber Bullets* and *Headline Hustler* from their debut. More new material, *Hotel*, *Old Wild Men*, *Clockwork Creep*, *Silly Love* and a reprise of *Oh Effendi* appeared in May, in a studio session for DJ Bob Harris.

In February 1975, meanwhile, 10cc made their first visit to America. It was a storming success, even if Gouldman does recollect some very peculiar billings. "We used to have some interesting combinations that the promoters used to put us together with. Slade. Slade and 10cc, that is pretty bizarre, but you know what? It didn't work. It was strange. Slade were topping the bill and most people came to see them. We just went on, played, then went off again. Interesting."

Rory Gallagher was another regular star of 10cc's American shows, but the band were spared any further, even more incomprehensible, couplings when Kevin Godley fell victim to an unscheduled illness. The band took the change in plans as an excuse for a holiday, returning home in time to see their latest single, *Wall Street Shuffle* (backed by the self explanatory instrumental *Gismo My Way*) restore them to the Top 10.

SHEET MUSIC swiftly followed. The album was eventually to become one of the most successful of 1974, remaining on the British charts for over six months, and qualifying for a gold disc (it made No. 81 in America.) It was also the album that cemented 10cc's reputation as one of the most inventive and exciting British bands of the decade.

"It grips the heart of rock'n'roll like nothing I've heard before", raved Melody Maker, before describing 10cc as "the Beach Boys of *Good Vibrations*, the Beatles of *Penny Lane*, they're the mischievous kid next door, they're the Marx Brothers, they're Jack and Jill, they're comic cuts characters, and they're sheer brilliance." Eric Stewart certainly agreed — he told that same paper, 10cc's music is "better than 90% of the sheer unadulterated crap that's in the charts."

Gouldman agrees. "SHEET MUSIC is probably the definitive 10cc album. What it was, our second album wasn't our difficult second album, it was our best second album. It was the best second album we ever did."

In August, *Silly Love* became the third single to be lifted from SHEET MUSIC (and the first ever to have an album track as a flip side.) It wasn't a wise choice. Despite appearances on TOP OF THE POPS, and such lesser bastions of British rock TV as LIFT OFF WITH AYSHEA, the band was rewarded with a mere two weeks in the lower reaches of the Top 30, at the same time as they were selling out theaters all across the country on their latest tour and headlining the legendary Reading Festival.

Silly Love was 10cc's last official single for UK. On February 22, 1975 it was announced that they had signed to Phonogram for around the then unprecedented sum of $1 million. According to Ric Dixon, 10cc's co-manager (with Harvey Lisburg), "we decided that if 10cc were to reach their full potential we must change to a truly international record company", and a spokesman for UK, while expressing disappointment at losing the band, added that "a million dollars buys a lot of loyalty."

"There were certain regrets socially," Lol Creme acknowledged. "We like Jonathan, even though he's a bum and a punk and tight, but we love him because he's one of those very likable people. But regrets as far as our career went, there were none."

The band's third album, THE ORIGINAL SOUNDTRACK, had already been recorded, and it appeared two weeks later with a single, the brilliant *Life Is A Minestrone*, trailing in its wake. Once again, the album was a remarkable achievement, but as so often happens, last year's critical darlings were in line for a good kicking. Few reviews were immediately complimentary, while the handful that could praise the album were also swift to damn it. Too clever, too perfect, too smug, 10cc had effectively reduced Rock And Roll to a science, and no matter how much one marveled at their brilliance, still a part of one's body cried out for some good old fashioned boogie.

That's what the critics reckoned, anyway, and 10cc themselves would eventually confess that the album was not as good as it could have been, that a couple of tracks had not been intended for inclusion, but were thrown on at the last minute because they'd run out of time to record anything else.

Elsewhere, however, THE ORIGINAL SOUNDTRACK proved the band's most successful album, reaching No. 3 in Britain, and No. 15 in the US, before spawning a single which remains a perennial in those "All Time greats" popularity polls, the breathless *I'm Not In Love*.

Famously, *I'm Not In Love* required in the region of 256 vocal overdubs to complete. Less famously, it also required a guest appearance from Kathy Warren, the receptionist at Strawberry.

"They were trying to work out what to put in the middle eight, and a telephone call came through for Eric. So I went to the studio door and just opened it quietly and whispered, 'Eric, there's a phone call for you.' And they all said, 'That's it!' The line they asked me to say was, '[whispered] Be quiet, big boys don't cry'."

The band themselves believed *I'm Not In Love* was a risky release. "We decided to put it out, thinking it would either be a hit, or a resounding flop," Lol Creme admitted, with Gouldman adding, "Phonogram said that as well." 10cc's second British No. 1, and a No. 2 smash in America, *I'm Not In Love* was included on the soundtrack to the movie THE STUD ("I'm dying to see Joan Collins' bum working away to it," Eric Stewart sniggered), and has also spawned a wealth of cover versions, something which Graham Gouldman (one of the song's co-authors) remains uneasy about. "Petula Clarke's *I'm Not In Love*, disco style, is probably the worst cover I've ever heard of any song. Chrissie Hynde's was a bit plain. Her voice is brilliant, so you can't knock her for that, but it sounded a bit like we've got three hours to do this, so let's knock it out."

October 1975, saw Justin Hayward and John Lodge take a break from the Moody Blues and chart with *Blue Guitar*, a song which featured 10cc as both producers and accompanying musicians. Then, the following month, 10cc reemerged in their own right with *Art For Art's Sake*, their seventh British Top 10 entry (but a lowly No. 83 in America.)

An uncharacteristically unmemorable song, *Art For Art's Sake* had not been 10cc's own choice for a single. Indeed, Lol Creme acknowledged, "[Phonogram] wanted a single out in America to coincide with the tour, and to follow up *I'm Not In Love* as quickly as possible, because there'd been too long a delay already. They thought *Art For Art's Sake* was a good idea, so they released it there, then Phonogram in England released it here. We just went along with it, thinking we'd give them the opportunity to make that sort of decision, and in fact they were wrong in America . . . it didn't happen there, but it did happen here. [But] if it had been up to us, I doubt we'd have put it out."

It was not the band's greatest ever record. Many fans actually preferred the B-side, a non album ballad called *Get It While You Can*, which itself would later reappear as *Anonymous Alcoholics* on 1978's BLOODY TOURISTS album.) Unfortunately, however, it proved an all too accurate introduction to the new album, HOW DARE YOU. The four writers in the band had always naturally gravitated into two distinct schools of thought (Godley / Creme and Gouldman / Stewart), with the most entertaining results usually occurring when they swapped partners.

Throughout HOW DARE YOU, however, the once healthy friction between the pairs was becoming uncomfortable. The band was evidently struggling for ideas, and while a handful of tracks (notably *I Wanna Rule The World* and *I'm Mandy, Fly Me*, another hit single) did bear repeated listening, the collection as a whole showed 10cc to be suffering from an acute dearth of inspiration. Creme admitted that the title track itself was "three or four" years old, "it was an experiment that we tried, which somehow worked its way into that song." There again, *Lazy Days* sneaked into the soundtrack of the soft porn epic EMMANUELLE 2, so obviously 10cc was doing something right!

Their live credentials, too, came under sustained assault when it was revealed that not only were they incapable of reproducing several of the greatest hits (*The Dean And I* and *I'm Not In Love*) live, without resorting to a ton of tapes, the new album, too, was utterly unsuited to the concert environment.

Neither were the band members impervious to this abuse. Indeed, further damage was done when Eric Stewart, enraged by a scathing review in the New Musical Express, wrote an indignant letter to the editor, which of course was duly published in all its apparent soiled brat glory. As another magazine, Street Life remarked, "it was predictable that [NME] would allow the reviewer equal space to reply, and so make Stewart's impassioned outburst look rather silly. The NME always has the last word."

Band interviews from the time appeared as strained as their music. Gouldman recalls, "I remember a conversation with Lol in the front office of the studio. We'd just recorded I'm Mandy, Fly Me, and we'd almost finished recording it. Eric and I were really pleased with it. We thought it was just really good. But Lol was, sort of, mewing about it, y'know, like, 'is this the direction we should be going in? Was it interesting enough? And, was it music? And was it this?' And, I thought, 'What're you talking about?' For me, the seeds of doubt were planted then, that this was leading to some inevitability, that the end was nigh."

It was. In October, under the banner headline, "We're Not In Love," the now defunct British rock weekly National Rock Star reported that Godley and Creme had left the band to work on "a revolutionary new instrument they have invented and developed." This, of course, was the Gismo, and while the duo's initial intention was to simply record a single that would showcase the Gismo's many talents, by Christmas the project had become a triple album telling the story of "man's last defense against an irate nature", CONSEQUENCES.

The pair had already begun work on this ambitious project before announcing their departure, and Eric Stewart remarked at the time, "I heard the first side of [it] as they were doing it, just before the split, and that was the last thing I really wanted to know about what they were doing." Later, he would admit, "if you must know, I thought CONSEQUENCES was absolute rubbish. I think Graham and I held them in check when they were in the band, and when they left . . . I don't know, they just lost control."

Gouldman and Stewart, meanwhile, decided to carry on as 10cc (rumors that Moody Blue Justin Hayward was set to join them proved unfounded), having moved their base of operations down to the recently completed Strawberry South studio in Dorking, leaving the Strawberry studio with drummer Paul Burgess. "We read everywhere that the creative side [of the band] had gone," Stewart complained to Melody Maker, "and everyone brought us down. We were the commercial ones, we were looked down on because we weren't stuck in a garret in Stockport anymore, so we felt we had more to prove."

Well, they certainly proved they were still commercial. The Things We Do For Love, the truncated line-up's first single, appeared in time for Christmas 1976 — a pleasant pop romp which reached No. 2 in Britain, No. 5 in America, and joyously previewed the early 1977 release of their new album, DECEPTIVE BENDS, a set which itself duplicated the single in proving totally innocuous to all but the most cynical palate.

Gouldman willingly concedes this point. "I'm very proud of the early period, and I understand why the earlier period is the definitive 10cc," Gouldman admits today. "In a way there were always two main writing teams, so there were already two separate teams, but of course it was the combination of the four of us. Kevin and I wrote a song called *The Sacro-Iliac*, which I think is a charming little piece, Lol and I wrote *Worst Band In The World*. There was that chemical thing, you can't get it back."

"I listen to the records, and I understand why it was so great and why it was different. When Kevin and Lol left, it was a blow, an artistic blow and although we carried on and we had hits, and some tracks show all the humor and imagination and style of the early 10cc, we lost Kevin and Lol's abstract, bizarre attitude, and there was nothing we could do about it."

Over the next two years, the hit machine cranked on as though nothing had happened — the band even scored another No. 1 with the reggae pastiche *Dreadlock Holiday*. But their fall thereafter was fast. With just one more Top 50 entry, 1982's *Run Away*, and ever-declining sales for subsequent albums, when 10cc finally broke up in 1982, very few people even noticed.

There were reunions. In 1991 the original quartet worked together on at least a handful of songs for a new 10cc album, MEANWHILE. Stewart and Gouldman alone reconvened for some live recordings and a new album, 1995's MIRROR MIRROR. But the magic was gone and so was the thrill.

10cc Glam Years Discography:

UK Original Singles
- *Donna* / *Hot Sun Rock* (UK6, 1972)
- *Johnny Don't Do It* (45 edit) / *4% Of Something* (UK22, 1972)
- *Rubber Bullets* (UK45 edit) / *Waterfall* (UK36, 1973)
- *The Dean and I* (45 edit) / *Bee In My Bonnet* (UK48, 1973)
- *The Worst Band In The World* / *18 Carat Man Of Means* (UK57, 1974)
- *Wall Street Shuffle* / *Gismo My Way* (UK69, 1974)
- *Silly Love* / *The Sacro-Iliac* (UK77, 1974)
- *Life Is A Minestrone* / *Channel Swimmer* (Mercury 6008 010, 1975)
- *Waterfall* / *4% Of Something* (UK100, 1975)
- *I'm Not In Love* (45 edit) / *Good News* (Mercury 6008 104, 1975)
- *Art For Art's Sake* (45 edit) / *Get It While You Can* (Mercury 6008017, 1975)
- *I'm Mandy, Fly Me* / *How Dare You* (Mercury 6008 019, 1976)

US Original Singles
- *Donna* / *Hot Sun Rock* (UK49005, 1972)
- *What's So Great About UK Records* (various artists promo) (UK101, 1972)
- *Rubber Bullets* (US 45 edit) / *Waterfall* (UK49015, 1973)
- *Headline Hustler* / *Speed Kills* (UK49019, 1973)
- *Wall Street Shuffle* / *Gismo My Way* (UK49023, 1974)
- *I'm Not In Love* (45 edit) / *Channel Swimmer* (Mercury 73678, 1975)
- *Art For Art's Sake* (45 edit) / *Get It While You Can* (Mercury 73725, 1975)
- *I'm Mandy, Fly Me* / *How Dare You* (Mercury 73779, 1976)
- *Life Is a Minestrone* / *Lazy Ways* (Mercury 73805, 1976)

UK Original Albums
- 10cc (UK UKAL 1005, 1973)
- SHEET MUSIC (UK UKAL 1007, 1974)
- THE ORIGINAL SOUNDTRACK (Mercury 9102500, 1975)
- 100cc (UK UKAL, 1975)
- HOW DARE YOU (Mercury 9102 501, 1976)
- GREATEST HITS 1972-78 (Mercury 9102 504, 1979)

US Original Albums
- 10cc (UK UKS 53105, 1973)
- SHEET MUSIC (UK UKS 53107, 1974)
- THE ORIGINAL SOUNDTRACK (Mercury 1029, 1975)
- 100cc (UK UKS 53110, 1975)
- HOW DARE YOU (Mercury 1061, 1976)
- KING BISCUIT FLOUR HOUR LIVE IN CONCERT 11/11/75 (KBFH 88003, 1995)
  Note: All 10cc Mercury albums have since been reissued with relevant bonus tracks drawn from B-sides. Earlier UK era non-album material has appeared on a variety of compilations.

☆ 12 ☆
Sensational Alex Harvey Band

– FRAMED –

Their first Glam album, FRAMED, was released in October 1972.

	Chart Hits	
	UK	US
Singles	3 (1975-76)	—
Albums	6 (1974-76)	—

It wasn't an especially promising union. Tear Gas was a Scottish hard rock band whose two album career had been met with nothing but disappointment and poor sales. Alex Harvey was a 30+ year old veteran of 15 years of banging his head against the walls of the music business, recording a string of blues and rock records, none of which had stuck for a second.

Yet together, the pair were to forge one of the most dynamic partnerships of the early 1970's, a band which wasn't really glam by a long shot, but which wore the clothes, walked the walk, grinned the grin and — what the hell, carried the whole shtick off a lot better than acts half their age, and with twice the tinsel. They called themselves the Sensational Alex Harvey Band, and that is what they were. Sensational.

Not that many people thought so when the band first started playing in London throughout late 1971. Guitarist Zal Cleminson was wearing make-up, the thick white mask of a Pierrot. Harvey was introducing props and theatrics to his own act . . . early audiences hated S.A.H.B., unable to comprehend why such a seemingly traditional rock group should so readily have embraced glam-flavoured gimmickry. Yet, by the end of the summer of 1972, that so pivotal time when everyone from Gary Glitter to Alice Cooper, and David Bowie to Roxy Music, had nailed their colors to the glam rock mast, S.A.H.B. was ranked amongst the biggest draws on the London club circuit.

That fall, the group signed to Vertigo Records, who despatched them straight into the studio. Five days later, S.A.H.B. emerged with their debut album, FRAMED, and a special Yuletide single, the decidedly unseasonal *There's No Lights On The Christmas Tree, Mother, They're Burning Big Louie Tonight.* Released, in Britain only, in December 1972, FRAMED took its title from the Lieber-Stoller song which was already established as the centerpiece of S.A.H.B.'s live show, and now became a highlight of their recorded repertoire.

S.A.H.B. toured Britain constantly through the first half of 1973 in support of both FRAMED, and a brace of new singles, the non-album *Jungle Jenny*, and *Giddy Up A Ding Dong*, a preview of S.A.H.B.'s imminent second album, the barnstorming NEXT — the record which proved, after so long in the shadows, that Harvey was now out for blood. Throughout S.A.H.B.'s early career, the most constant criticism was that their vinyl never reflected their live performance. NEXT, dynamically produced by Phil Wainman (a man who would become considerably better known for his work with the Bay City Rollers), would change that forever.

Sensational Alex Harvey Band

Once again, the title song was a cover; a dramatic version of Jacques Brel's *Au Suivant*, transformed into the apocalyptic tango. At a time when Brel was simply a name dropped by David Bowie, Harvey's recitation of this homo-erotic tale of army whorehouses, gonorrhea and having his ass slapped by "the queer lieutenant," while a masked string section sawed away behind him, was absolutely captivating, and leagues away from Bowie's effete renditions of the same writer's *Amsterdam* and *My Death*.

In July 1974, S.A.H.B. appeared at the first Knebworth Festival, down the bill from the Allman Brothers, John McLaughlin, Van Morrison and the Doobie Brothers — a soporific line-up which simply didn't stand a chance. Harvey pulled out all the stops, building both his show and the stage set around S.A.H.B.'s forthcoming third album, THE IMPOSSIBLE DREAM, and the inner-city psychosis of his alter-ego, Vambo — "a cross between Father Christmas and Captain Marvel," as Harvey himself explained.

A month later in August, S.A.H.B. headlined the first night of the Reading Festival above 10cc and Camel, and by October S.A.H.B. was celebrating its first Top 20 British hit with a show at that most hallowed of venues, the London Palladium. And watching the audience file in, one knew immediately just what an impact Alex Harvey had made. It was as though every kid in the crowd was wearing the same trademark striped T-shirt that Harvey had sported for years. The impossible dream had been fulfilled.

Hardly surprisingly, TOMORROW BELONGS TO ME dominated the band's live set. But with considerably sounder commercial sense than many other, more successful, artists seemed capable of. When the inevitable S.A.H.B. LIVE set appeared in September 1975, only one cut, *Give My Compliments To The Chef*, was taken from the album. Across the remaining cuts, each preceding album was represented by arguably its finest moment: *Framed*, *Faith Healer* and *Tomahawk Kid*, with *Vambo* making an appearance in a wildly extended, improvised form, and the Tom Jones chest beater *Delilah*" rounding it off to remind listeners of Harvey's abilities as an interpretative singer.

And *Delilah* it was that finally catapulted S.A.H.B. into the British Top 30. Six months past his 40th birthday, Harvey rolled out on TOP OF THE POPS for the first time, performing the song which would take him all the way to No. 7. At the same time, LIVE made it to No. 14, and in December, S.A.H.B. played a triumphant Christmas party-like show at the New Victoria Theatre.

April 1976, saw LIVE followed to its chart peak by THE PENTHOUSE TAPES, an eccentric album that brought together a career's worth of live favorites which hadn't made it onto any previous S.A.H.B. album. Many of them were covers: *Gambling Bar Room Blues*, *School's Out*, *Crazy Horses*, Del Shannon's *Runaway* (which became the group's next single), a remarkable version of Jethro Tull's *Love Story*, dedicated to a band who had offered S.A.H.B. so much encouragement during their earliest days, and a couple of pre-rock standards, Leadbelly's *Irene Goodnight*, and Irving Berlin's *Cheek To Cheek*, recorded at S.A.H.B.'s triumphant Christmas show at London's New Victoria Theatre. But the best gauge of the album's strength arrived 12 years later, when K-Tel put together a S.A.H.B. "Greatest Hits" package. THE PENTHOUSE TAPES dominated the proceedings. After all, most of its contents had been hits at one time or another!

S.A.H.B. STORIES, S.A.H.B.'s seventh album, arrived in July 1976, two months after *Boston Tea Party* restored the group to the Top 20. Success, however, appears to have taken its toll on S.A.H.B., or at least on Harvey. In November 1976, he announced he was quitting the music industry. "I don't wanna be a rock'n'roll star," he told National Rock Star magazine. "I'm not saying I haven't had a good time. I'm not knocking it. I can still get a terrific buzz out of performing with guys who really know how to play. But I don't wanna crash through walls on stage anymore."

Vambo was gone, then, and the poor mug who was "Framed." So was Adolf Hitler, a parody routine which Harvey first developed during S.A.H.B.'s earliest concerts, but which reached its zenith when the group toured Germany in early 1976. "We did it in Hamburg. It was great!"

The band made one album without Alex. He returned to them in 1977 for the frankly disappointing ROCK DRILL, and then quit to make one more album without them. The next few years, however, saw Harvey's star fade dramatically. He worked with a succession of musicians, and occasionally even alone, but after a solo deal with RCA collapsed in early 1980, it was clear that Harvey was running out of steam. He was also dogged by health problems, and on February 4, 1981, having just completed a four week tour of Europe, he suffered a fatal heart attack, while waiting for a ferry home from Zeebrugge.

The Sensational Alex Harvey Band was a unique combination, its music the product of a chemistry which even the band members themselves could not guarantee to produce every time. That they succeeded in doing it as much as they did was an achievement of miraculous proportions. That they scored even a handful of hits bucked a bucketful of long odds. And though their inclusion in the glam bag remains a matter of timing as much as anything else, it's still true that the era itself was beautified no end by their existence.

Vambo still rules.

Sensational Alex Harvey Band Glam Years Discography:
UK Original Singles
  ○ *There's No Lights On The Christmas Tree, Mother / Harp* (Vertigo 6059 070, 1972)
  ○ *Jungle Jenny / Buff's Bar Blues* (Vertigo 6059 075, 1973)

- *Giddy Up A Ding Dong / Buff's Bar Blues* (Vertigo 6059 091, 1973)
- *Faith Healer / St. Anthony* (Vertigo 6059 098, 1974)
- *Sgt. Fury / Gang Bang* (Vertigo 6059 106, 1974)
- *Anthem pt 1 / Anthem pt 2* (Vertigo 6059 112, 1974)
- *Delilah / Soul In Chains* (Vertigo ALEX 1, 1975)
- *Gamblin' Bar Room Blues / Shake That Thing* (Vertigo ALEX 2, 1975)
- *Runaway / Snake Bite* (Vertigo ALEX 3, 1975)
- *Boston Tea Party / Sultan's Choice* (Mountain TOP 12, 1976)
- *Amos Moses / Satchel & The Scalp Hunter* (Mountain TOP 19, 1976)
- *Cheek To Cheek / Jungle Jenny* (Vertigo 6059 173, 1977)
- *Mrs. Blackhouse / Engine Room Blues* (Mountain TOP 32, 1977)

US Original Singles
- *Swampsnake / Gang Bang* (Vertigo 113, 1974)
- *Sgt. Fury / Tomahawk Kid* (Vertigo 200, 1974)
- *Delilah / Soul In Chains* (Atlantic 3293, 1975)

UK Original Albums
- FRAMED (Vertigo 6369 081, 1972)
- NEXT (Vertigo 6360 103, 1973)
- THE IMPOSSIBLE DREAM (Vertigo 6360 112, 1974)
- TOMORROW BELONGS TO ME (Vertigo 9102 003, 1975)
- LIVE (Vertigo 6360 122, 1975)
- THE PENTHOUSE TAPES (Vertigo 9102 007, 1976)
- SAHB Stories (Mountain TOPS 112, 1976)

    Note: All S.A.H.B. albums have been reissued on CDs with bonus material drawn either from PENTHOUSE TAPES or S.A.H.B. WITHOUT ALEX.

UK Important Archive Albums
- BIG HITS AND CLOSE SHAVES (Vertigo 6360 147, 1977)
- LIVE IN CONCERT (Windsong WIND 002, 1991)
- LIVE ON THE [OLD GREY WHISTLE] TEST (Windsong WHIS 004, 1994)

    Note: Both IN CONCERT and LIVE ON THE TEST are BBC recordings. IN CONCERT was reissued in 1998 as one half of THE GOSPEL ACCORDING TO (New Millennium), paired with a sub-bootleg recording of S.A.H.B.'s 1977 Reading Festival show.

US Original Albums
- NEXT (Vertigo 1017, 1973)
- THE IMPOSSIBLE DREAM (Vertigo 2000, 1974)
- TOMORROW BELONGS TO ME (Vertigo 2004, 1975)
- LIVE (Atlantic 18184, 1975)

☆ **13** ☆
Elton John

— *Crocodile Rock* —

His first Glam hit, *Crocodile Rock*, entered the UK chart on November 4, 1972.

Chart Hits		
	UK	US
Singles	75+ (1971 --)	70+ (1970 --)
Albums	35+ (1970 --)	35+ (1970 --)

The magic that Marc Bolan promised was delivered not only through his music, but across every level on which he operated. Even a simple photograph captured it — Bolan was quite ridiculously photogenic, a trait which, above all others, was to be aspired to by all the glam rock flotsam that surfaced in his wake.

Not for the first time in rock history could the music come a poor second to the packaging, but in the past only a privileged few ever got away with it. Bolan, however, liberated the halt, the lame, the ugly and the hopeless, until a sprinkling of glitter and a pair of platform boots were really all you needed to bring a hint of glamour to the most disparate of careers. And when Van Der Graaf Generator vocalist Peter Hammill, in the guise of nihilistic pop iconoclast Rikki Nadir, condemned "all those jerks in their tinsel glitter suits, pansying around …" he bemoaned not the handful of names who actually enlarged upon Bolan's original vision, but those who emerged from stage left, simply to borrow a handful of stardust.

When the Strawbs went on TOP OF THE POPS with false cheekbones, they created Glitterfolk. When Edgar and Johnny Winter took to smothering themselves in rhinestones, they were no longer bluesmen, they were Glitterbluesmen. Labelle patented Glittersoul, Parliament created Glitterfunk, Silverhead forged Glittermetal. But in every instance, the Glitter was nothing more than a visual aid, a convenient peg upon which to hang a career or two, a gravy train to leap on or off, the moment something more opportune came along.

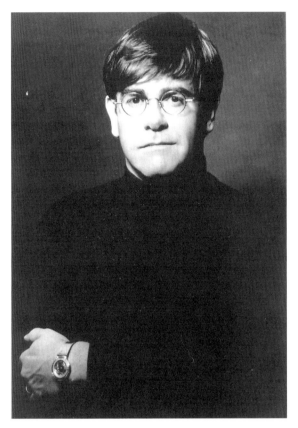

And to all but the most dedicated progenitors, that was the beauty of it. Glam rock functioned on a level so transparent that you could indulge it to whatever extent you liked — lifestyle, image, or simply a couple of neat promo tricks with which to beef up a rotting carcass.

Thus Rod Stewart, a 60's club veteran for whom the spangles were nothing more than a cheap shot — aimed at keeping peoples' minds off the fact that it had been folks like the hitherto unrepentantly bedenimmed Rod who had made glam rock so necessary in the first place.

Thus Geordie, a middling northern hard rock band with a friend who worked in a platform boot factory (or so it seemed at the time — the band was actually worth a bit more than that, though.)

And thus Elton John.

A short balladeer with medium paunch and severe myopia, Elton had been kicking around the British club scene since the mid-1960's, and gaining in appeal ever since. Tied to song writing partner Bernie Taupin, Elton had already got a fair career off and running — the first time Slade went on TOP OF THE POPS with *Shape Of Things To Come*, in March 1970, Jim Lea remembers, "another chap was doing his first T.O.T.P. — a pianist called Elton John. He sang a song called *Lady Samantha* and looked very serious."

Both records flopped, and in Elton's case, that was why. He looked too serious, and when, a few months later, he did score with the plaintive *Your Song*, he really hadn't learned his lesson. But he was willing to try. Sessions for his TUMBLEWEED CONNECTION album in May 1970, began with John and producer Gus Dudgeon attempting to weld the pianist's muse to a more extravagant backing, with the recruitment of folkie Michael Chapman's band — a line-up which included bassist Rick Kemp and guitarist Mick Ronson. And though Ronson himself was still in the early days of what would eventually prove a devastating partnership with the unknown David Bowie, his guitar style was already in place — indeed,

Elton's label head, Dick James, dismissed the entire session as "too psychedelic," and consigned it to the archive for another 20+ years (one cut, a truly inspired *Madman Across The Water*, later emerged on Elton's RARE MASTERS compilation.) Elton returned to the drawing board, and history — which surely came as close as Christmas to being utterly rewritten — breathed a massive sigh of relief.

It was two years more before Elton stuck even a tentative toe back into the waters, by which time, of course, the glam explosion was in full flower. But he'd dropped the serious business almost altogether. Now he was just being cruel.

Talking about *Space Oddity*, the single which had given him a solitary hit in 1969, David Bowie remarked how flattered he was that "Elton John took so much out of it" — and so he had, with *Rocket Man*, an April 1972 hit that offered a vicious reminder of even the rising Ziggy's humble origins. And Elton had the last laugh as well. Portraying himself as the lonely spaceman of both songs' fame, he warned: "I'm gonna be high as a kite by then . . ." It took Bowie another eight years before he discovered how Major Tom had been occupying his lonely orbit: "Ashes to ashes, fun to funky / We know Major Tom's a junkie" (neither did this rivalry end any time soon. In 1974, Bowie got John Lennon into the studio to record a couple of songs with him. Three months later, Elton got him onto a stage for the first time in two years. Bowie got a US No. 1 out of his collaboration — Elton ended up with three.)

Rocket Man gave Elton his first hit since *Your Song*. The knockabout *Honky Cat* followed, and just when the world was already convinced that the fat boy was never going to be anything more than another pleasant singer-songwriter, the worm turned. In fact, it exploded.

Elton had always had an eye for fashion — in April, again, US customs had impounded four pairs of platform boots in the belief that the only people who needed eight inch heels were drug smugglers. But a Hollywood optician supplied the singer with his first pairs of spectacular spectacles, and over the next couple of months, the boots got taller, the glasses grew wider, and when the mood took him, he'd crown the creation with an ostrich feather head-dress. It was cabaret, Liberace with a jungle-beat, but Elton never pretended it was anything but.

"It's Glamour. I'm sending show business up. I'm so bloody clumsy, and there's nothing graceful about me with a pair of flying boots on. I just like to get up and have a lark. I do it tongue in cheek, with an 'up yours' sort of attitude. It's a reaction against everything I wasn't allowed to do as a kid. I wasn't allowed to wear winklepicker shoes in case they hurt my feet. I wasn't even allowed to wear Hush Puppies, can you imagine that? Not having had a real teenage life, I'm living all those 13 to 19 years now. Mentally I may be 25, but half of me is still 13."

The image predated the music by maybe six months, but by fall 1972, the two had been reconciled with devastating style. *Crocodile Rock*, ostensibly a tribute to the American juke joint scene of the late 1950's, was glam rock stomp of the first degree. Elton biographer Philip Norman described it as an unashamed paean to Bill Haley, Eddie Cochran, Neil Sedaka, the old Rock And Roll crew, and Don McLean noted a resemblance between it and *American Pie*. But if *Crocodile Rock* had any parentage to speak of, it was Gary Glitter's *Rock'n'Roll*.

Neither was it a fluke. Although Elton would never allow either his music or his reputation to wholly submerge itself within the glam rock milieu, over the next couple of years he unleashed at least a handful of unashamed glitter classics — the driving *Saturday Night's Alright (For Fighting)* and *Bennie And The Jets*, the camp tongue in cheeky *The Bitch Is Back*, the rollicking novelty *Ho! Ho! Ho! Who'd Be A Turkey At Christmas*.

Funeral For A Friend, the somber pomp piano and guitar duet which opened 1973's deliriously extravagant GOODBYE YELLOW BRICK ROAD album, was an evocative blend of rock and emotional theater even before a young Polish ice skater took it for a mid-1980's championship bout. Elton even turned in one of those vast stately dirges which the likes of Cockney Rebel and Roxy Music alone had managed to nail to the glam flag, the supremely maudlin and painfully autobiographical *Someone Saved My Life Tonight*.

It was his last release with the Elton John Band which served him in such good stead throughout his rise to fame. It was also his good-bye to the era that made him ... and to the era that made it possible for him to write the self-fulfilling prophecy which, on first examination, was as absurd as the monster spectacles which now accompanied him everywhere, *I'm Gonna be A Teenage Idol*.

Like Paul Gadd behind him, Reginald Dwight (as Elton started life) was the last person on earth you'd expect to be served up as weenybait. But add a few sparkles, and a neat change of name ... and anything was possible.

Elton John Glam Rock Discography:
UK Original Singles
- *Crocodile Rock / Elderberry Wine* (DJM DJS 271, 1972)
- *Daniel / Skyline Pigeon* (DJM DJS 275, 1973)
- *Saturday Night's Alright / Jack Rabbit / When You're Ready* (DJM DJX 502, 1973)
- *Goodbye Yellow Brick Road / Screw You* (DJM DJS 285, 1973)
- *Step Into Xmas / Ho Ho Ho, Who'd Be A Turkey* (DJM DJS 290, 1973)
- *Candle In The Wind / Bennie And The Jets* (DJM DJS 297, 1974)
- *Don't Let The Sun Go Down On Me / Sick City* (DJM DJS 302, 1974)
- *The Bitch Is Back / Cold Highway* (DJM DJS 322, 1974)
- *Lucy In The Sky With Diamonds / One Day At A Time* (DJM DJS 340, 1975)

- ○ *Philadelphia Freedom / I Saw Her Standing There* (DJM DJS 354, 1975)
- ○ *Someone Saved My Life Tonight / House Of Cards* (DJM DJS 385, 1975)

US Original Singles
- ○ *Crocodile Rock / Elderberry Wine* (MCA 40000, 1972)
- ○ *Daniel / Skyline Pigeon* (MCA 40046, 1973)
- ○ *Saturday Night's Alright / Jack Rabbit / When You're Ready* (MCA 40105, 1973)
- ○ *Goodbye Yellow Brick Road / Young Man's Blues* (MCA 40148, 1973)
- ○ *Step Into Xmas / Ho Ho Ho, Who'd Be A Turkey* (MCA 65018, 1973)
- ○ *Bennie And The Jets / Harmony* (MCA 40198, 1974)
- ○ *Don't Let The Sun Go Down On Me / Sick City* (MCA 40259, 1974)
- ○ *The Bitch Is Back / Cold Highway* (MCA 40297, 1974)
- ○ *Lucy In The Sky With Diamonds / One Day At A Time* (MCA 40344, 1975)
- ○ *Philadelphia Freedom / I Saw her Standing There* (MCA 40364, 1975)
- ○ *Someone Saved My Life Tonight / House Of Cards* (MCA 40421, 1975)

UK Original Albums
- ○ DON'T SHOOT ME, I'M ONLY THE PIANO PLAYER (DJM 2100, 1973)
- ○ GOODBYE YELLOW BRICK ROAD (DJM DJE 2/4 9001, 1973)
- ○ CARIBOU (DJM DJH 0439, 1974)
- ○ CAPTAIN FANTASTIC AND THE DIRT BROWN COWBOY (DJM DJX 1, 1975)

UK Important Archive Albums
- ○ GREATEST HITS (DJM DJH 0442, 1974)
- ○ HERE AND THERE (live) (DJM DJH 0473, 1976)
- ○ HERE AND THERE (expanded edition) (Rocket 314 528 164 2, 1995)
- Note: Each of Elton's key albums was reissued on CD through 1994-96 with bonus material, taken from the RARE MASTERS collection. HERE AND THERE, however, was upgraded to include two complete concerts.

US Original Albums
- ○ DON'T SHOOT ME, I'M ONLY THE PIANO PLAYER (MCA 2100, 1973)
- ○ GOODBYE YELLOW BRICK ROAD (MCA 10003, 1973)
- ○ CAPTAIN FANTASTIC AND THE DIRT BROWN COWBOY (MCA 2142, 1975)

US Important Archive Albums
- ○ GREATEST HITS (MCA 2128, 1974)
- ○ HERE AND THERE (live) (MCA 2197, 1976)
- ○ TO BE CONTINUED (boxed-set) (MCA 10110, 1991)
- ○ RARE MASTERS (Polydor 314 514 139, 1992)

☆ **14** ☆
Geordie

− Don't Do That −

Their first Glam hit, *Don't Do That*, entered the UK chart on December 2, 1972.

	Chart Hits	
	UK	US
Singles	4 (1972-73)	—
Albums	—	—

Brian Johnson's been part of AC/DC so long — twenty years, since he replaced the late Bon Scott in 1980 — that it's difficult to believe he did anything of note beforehand. Just a couple of nowhere pub bands, and prior to that, a schoolboy group that played Beatles covers. Right? Wrong.

In February 1972, Johnson joined a Newcastle based band called USA, alongside guitarist Vic Malcolm, bassist Tom Hill and drummer Brian Gibson. They changed their name to Geordie a few months later, and in December 1972, British television viewers watched aghast, and then agape, as Geordie tore down from the English north, and told the whole world, *Don't Do That*. No matter that the band members hailed from the precise same neck of the woods as Bryan Ferry, and spoke with the same kind of accent as well, Geordie was the antithesis of all that was cool, calm and sophisticated in glam.

Flat caps, big boots, belting blues . . . that first time on TV, they did affect a more contemporary look, flared trousers, stacked heels, armless tunics, colorful vests. But there the comparisons with anyone — including Slade and The Jook, the only bands around with anywhere near as much fiery commitment — ended. Geordie was meaty fists pounding in the air, hey-hey, drums that drove tanks across the muddy fields of the Somme, guitars that scythed, a bass that atom bombed, and Johnson's vocals had a range, a pitch and, most of all, a volume which both defied and decried simple pop stardom.

If Geordie had any antecedent, it was Eric Burdon's original Animals. If they had any rivals, it was Nazareth, the similarly blues-based Scots quartet who emerged on the chart scene just five months after *Don't Do That*. But whereas Nazareth never ventured any deeper into glitter pastures than Dan McCafferty's taste in tank tops, if the kids wanted hard hitting glam rock, Geordie was willing to give it to them. The new year brought Geordie's second — and biggest — hit single, *All Because Of You*, and again, it was the clothes and just maybe a hint of glitter (that's Glitter) round the drums that fed the illusion, because when Geordie came to cut their first album, the ambiguously titled HOPE YOU LIKE IT, they plugged it full of wailing blues rock.

Can You Do It (No. 13 in June) and *Electric Lady* (No. 32 in August) rounded out a remarkable nine months for the band, and when the hits stopped, so did the pretense. Geordie's second album, in 1974, was called DON'T BE FOOLED BY THE NAME, and pictured our heroes as Chicago style gangsters. Inside, of course, the music remained much the same, that patent Geordie crash and bang, an exhilarating cacophony which took savage originals and established classics alike (*House Of The Rising Sun* and *St. James Infirmary* were both primal Geordie fodder)

and made magic mincemeat of any preconceptions anyone ever had of them. Indeed, a third, and final, album, 1976's SAVE THE WORLD, passed unnoticed by almost everyone, but anyone finding their way in by accident could never emerge from the experienced unchanged.

Certainly Bon Scott never forgot them. Scottish born, he was still in the UK when he first encountered Geordie, when his own band, Fraternity, opened a show for them. AC/DC guitarist Angus Young recalled, "the first night, [Bon] went to check out Geordie because all he could hear was this yelling and screaming coming from the stage. Bon looked up, and he saw this guy — Brian — on the floor, legs going all over the place." The singer had been stricken with appendicitis, but Scott thought it was part of the show. "Bon was on the table yelling 'more! more!' He thought it was all part of the act."

Geordie Discography:
UK Original Singles
  ○ *Don't Do That / Francis Was A Rocker* (Regal Zono 3067, 1972)
  ○ *All Because Of You / Ain't It Just Like A Woman* (EMI 2008, 1973)
  ○ *Can You Do It? / Red Eyed Lady* (EMI 2031, 1973)
  ○ *Electric Lady / Geordie Stomp* (EMI 2047, 1973)
  ○ *Rock'n'Roller / Geordie's Lost His Liggy* (EMI 2100, 1973)

US Original Single
  ○ *All Because Of You / ?* (MGM 4539, 1973)

UK Original Albums
  ○ HOPE YOU LIKE IT (EMI EMC 3001, 1973)
  ○ DON'T BE FOOLED BY THE NAME (EMI EMA 764, 1974)
  ○ SAVE THE WORLD (EMI EMC 3134, 1976)

US Original Album
  ○ HOPE YOU LIKE IT (MGM 4903, 1973)
      Note: Geordie reformed, with Terry Schlesser replacing Johnson, for a 1983 album,
          NO SWEAT (Neat 1008.)

☆ 15 ☆
Wizzard

– Ball Park Incident –

Their first Glam hit, *Ball Park Incident*, entered the UK chart on December 9, 1972.

	Chart Hits	
	UK	US
Singles	9 (1972-84)	—
Albums	2 (1973-74)	—

In late 1972, on the run from the Electric Light Orchestra he had invented less than a year before, Roy Wood created what should — and indeed could — have been a most dubious combination of 50's revivalism and old Phil Spector chops, then turned the whole thing upside down by donning wild man wig and a lavish supply of grisly face paint. He looked like a psychedelic witch doctor, and Wizzard, the band of gypsies which inhabited the nightmare reaches behind him, might actually have been quite horrifying if only the mood of the times had been a little less flippant.

Because it was a very flippant time. Even the darkest of fantasies could be defused without the slightest effort. It was only later, when pocket book psychology returned to rock with the flowering of a new, pretentious wave of glam rockers, that the dividing line between Good and Bad Clean Fun was drawn. And even then, it was clear that the process was, for the most part, little more than a safety valve by which an ego could justify appreciating something so ultimately frivolous as Glitter music.

Wizzard, though, had no time for such shenanigans. A multi-colored collision of visual outrage and vaudeville, pumping out a string of irresistible teen anthems — both *Angel Fingers* and *See My Baby Jive* topped the British chart — Wizzard actually had their fingers in so many pies that it was impossible to ignore them.

Wood himself had once led the Move, that most beloved of 60's psych-pop successes, and all the magic that went into their music had followed him into this new group. The still burgeoning Rock And Roll revival tapped by Gary Glitter and Elton John absorbed Wood's own patent love for American Graffiti. Wizzard's respect for the classicisms that

Wood had introduced to ELO ensured that the prog rock crowd wasn't going to stray too far. And half a dozen Top 10 hits in just two years kept the pop kids happy. Oh, and Wood could play so many different instruments that he made Mike Oldfield look like an underachiever. Even with eight other musicians in the Wizzard line-up, Wood still played twelve instruments himself on the band's debut album, including 14 minutes of sundry brass bits on the closing *Meet Me At The Jailhouse*. "Da first side's weird," bassist Rick Price remarked. "And da second side's weirder."

"I formed the Wizzard sound from a couple of tracks on my solo album," Wood admitted in 1973. "They were *Locomotive* [a sax led novelty dance song] and *Rock Down Low* [rollicking rock'n'horns a-go-go]. The idea I had for Wizzard was a modern John Barry Seven, or Lord Rockingham's XI, but since the lads all got together, the sound's changed a bit from that."

Most of Wizzard had previously plied their trade with a Birmingham rock band called Mongrel, but such a pedigree did not impact on Wood. Blithely he had them executing everything from Edwardian parlor songs (*Jolly Cup Of Tea*) to classic ballads (*Wear A Fast Gun*.) But Wizzard's raison d'etre were the Spector-esque rockers that brought them the hits, and the necrophilic revisionism which was the band's second album, the astonishing EDDY AND THE FALCONS.

Painstakingly, and with a skill which even the Rutles would be hard pressed to echo, Wood recreated a string of favorite 50's oldies, then changed them just enough to earn himself the song writing credit. But Wood's mood was shifting even before the album had run its course. First he returned to the solo career he'd put on hold when Wizzard took off, then he unleashed Wizzard's next single, almost 18 months after their last one, the swing inflected *Indiana Rainbow*, a new album, WIZZO, was canned, and that was the end.

Wood, of course, would resurface in late 1977 with a new band named after that abortive final Wizzard album, and Wizzard themselves resurface periodically, every time their 1973 holiday hit, *I Wish It Could be Christmas Every Day*, is reissued.

There's some great footage of that one as well, Wood and the band surrounded by a choir of angelic children, piping the chorus in time-honored kiddie style, and getting kisses and cuddles from Uncle Roy in reward. But is it just one's imagination, or is that little girl at the end of the clip scared out of her wits? She went along, after all, expecting to see jolly old St. Nick. Instead, she's wrapped in the arms of . . . wild man wig, grisly face paint . . . it's Santa Psychedelia, and he's not a pretty sight.

Wizzard Discography:

UK Original Singles

- ○ *Ball Park Incident / Carlsberg Special* (Harvest 5062, 1972)
- ○ *See My Baby Jive / Bend Over Beethoven* (Harvest 5070, 1973)
- ○ *Angel Fingers / Got The Jump* (Harvest 5076, 1973)
- ○ *Wish It Could Be Xmas / Rob Roy* (Harvest 5079, 1973)
- ○ *Rock And Roll Winter / Dream Of Unwin* (WB K16357, 1974)
- ○ *This Is The Story Of My Love (Baby) / Nixture* (WB K16434, 1974)
- ○ *You've Got Me Running / Just My Imagination* (WB, 1974)
- ○ *Are You Ready To Rock / Marathon Man* (WB K16497, 1975)
- ○ *Rattlesnake Roll / Can't Help My Friends* (Jet 758, 1975)
- ○ *Indiana Rainbow / The Thing Is This* (Jet 768, 1976)
  - Note: *I Wish It Could Be Xmas* was simultaneously released by Warners (K16336) who held Roy Wood's solo contract. *Indiana Rainbow* is credited to Roy Wood's Wizzard.

UK Original Albums

- ○ WIZZARD'S BREW (Harvest 4025, 1973)
- ○ INTRODUCING EDDIE & THE FALCONS (WB K52029, 1974)

UK Important Archive Albums

- ○ SEE MY BABY JIVE (compilation) (Harvest 4034, 1974)
- ○ 16 GREATS OF ROY WOOD AND WIZZARD (Emporio EMPR 573, 1995)
- ○ THE BEST OF (Disky 865962, 1996)

US Original Albums

- ○ WIZZARD'S BREW (UA 042, 1973)
- ○ INTRODUCING EDDIE & THE FALCONS (UA 219, 1974)

☆ 16 ☆
Mud

— Crazy —

Their first Glam hit, *Crazy*, entered the UK chart on March 10, 1973.

Chart Hits		
	UK	US
Singles	16 (1973-85)	—
Albums	4 (1974-75)	—

Of all The Sweet's compatriots in the Chinnichap camp, Mud was undoubtedly dearest to the songwriters' hearts, at least in terms of the material they were given. Cut in a similar mold to The Tremoloes and The Marmalade of the 60's, the south London band had been working England's club circuit for almost half a decade without any reward, living in the back of a Transit van and recording sporadic — and none-too-notable — soul-inflected singles for whichever label would have them. But when producer Mickie Most caught their show one night, he was immediately impressed. "I thought they had something 'tomorrow' about them. They had what every other band didn't have, they bridged the gap between Sweet and Slade."

With barely a pause for breath, Most alerted Nicky Chinn and Mike Chapman to the quartet's potential. They traveled up to Nottingham to see them play, and signed them on the spot. A deal with Most's RAK label followed. Chinnichap, of course, would keep the band in new songs.

"They were incredibly prolific writers," Mud vocalist Les Gray recalled. "We had our ups and downs with them, but they were very talented and we had great respect for them." Mud's appeal to the duo, on the other hand, was plain. First and foremost, they were directionless, a Top 40 covers band, very professional, very polished, but beyond that, totally without ambition.

Two singles helped acquaint the partners: *Crazy*, in March 1973 and *Hypnosis* in June. Mud wasn't allowed to play on either of them. But it was *Dyna-Mite*, a song which Chinnichap originally wrote for The Sweet, and then offered to Hello, that would see Mud move into the major league. "The first couple of records were all arranged for us, which was a bit restricting," Gray recalled. "But once the band had proven themselves capable of coming up with ideas in the studio, Mike [Chapman] said we could go ahead and progress, and that's when we did *Dyna-Mite*."

THE SINGLES '67-'78

"Normally, Mike would play the songs to us with an acoustic guitar, then we'd go away and Rob (Davis, guitarist) would do a musical arrangement. We'd then go into the studio and build up the basic idea in conjunction with Mike."

Years of crowd-pleasing had seen Gray develop a more than adequate Elvis Presley routine, and *Dyna-Mite* — although not the kind of thing the *Hound Dog* singer would have fancied, even in his prime — was a perfect vehicle for Gray. Particularly when his energies were allied to his bandmates' visual prowess. Mud's sense of image was every bit as strong as their musical output. When *Tiger Feet*, a rousing pop-rocker which meant nothing more than you wanted it to, took them all the way to No. 1 at the beginning of 1973, the band's nifty footwork went straight from the television studio to the dance floor. When *Rocket* gave them their fourth Top 10 hit in eight months, the high kick which introduced the guitar solo was responsible for more bruised chins than any other dance step of the year.

"We gradually developed things so that there was a different dance for every record," Gray explained. "And different clothes for every TV show. There was no video in those days, so we had to do a live TV show every time. Of course it was meant to be tongue in cheek. The music was as good as we could get it, but everything else was absolute mayhem. It was rehearsed to look like chaos."

At a time when flared trousers were already growing to absurd dimensions, Mud delighted in donning bell bottoms which matched their waist measurements. At a time when most men still felt self-conscious wearing an earring stud, guitarist Rob Davis took to dangling bracelets from his lobes. And when that grew passé, he simply clipped a couple more on and ended up walking with a permanent stoop.

Like The Sweet, Mud's principle stomping ground was BBC TV's TOP OF THE POPS. Both bands, in concert, put on an adequate, but by no means memorable performance, but in the controlled environment of T.O.T.P., they were at the mercy of nothing. For Mud's first appearance, clad in violently mismatched check suits, Davis spent the entire performance locked in the lotus position, while drummer Dave Mount furiously aped Groucho Marx from behind his kit. Six months later, with *Tiger Feet* at No. 1, Mud appeared dressed as 60's instrumental darlings the Shadows, with Davis an imperfect Hank Marvin clone. "Well, I did have the glasses, and for that added touch I tied a piece of string them."

Vivid greens and putrid pinks ensured that their stage outfits would clash violently with whatever fixtures bedecked the T.O.T.P. studios that week, and even Chinnichap were to express surprise at how adept the band had become. "Sweet will be the group to provide us with the No. 1 hits," Mike Chapman had said shortly after the release of *Crazy*. "Mud will have plenty of Top 10 successes, but they aren't really in quite the same league." In the event, Sweet had but one No. 1, the anthemic *Blockbuster*. Mud hit the top three times.

But just like The Sweet in their hit making prime, Mud, too, broke away from Chinnichap as soon as they thought their reputation was so great that it would take a miracle to bring them back to earth. They had already taken to recording other people's material, although the string of old Rock And Roll hits which made up the bulk of their two RAK albums was intended as nothing more than party-time filler. Similarly, their chart-topping reworking of Buddy Holly's *Oh Boy*, and the less momentous *One Night*, were both recorded with Chinnichap's blessing, vital components in a half-realized scheme to out-Showaddywaddy Showaddywaddy, Bell Records' pet Rock And Roll revivalists. Chapman admits that at one point, he and Chinn were concerned only with writing songs which would allow Les Gray to trot out his Elvis Presley routine one more time. "Once I'd discovered what he could do, it was like a red rag to a bull."

Sadly, it was also to spell the beginning of the end for Mud. From a rumbustious combo bent on raising hell at every available opportunity, they took their role first as revivalists, second as romantics, very seriously indeed. With the exception of the *Wig-Wam-Bam*-alike *Moonshine Sally* (itself one of the first recordings Mud made with Chinnichap, held back because at the time, it wasn't considered good enough!) the band's later releases were to see a new, mature-sounding Mud going all out to capture the trendy parents' vote.

They broke with Chinnichap and linked instead with producer Phil Wainman, and their taste in songs remained solid — ironically so. It was, after all, Mud who unearthed *Under The Moon Of Love*, the song which was to give Showaddywaddy a late 1976 chart-topper — at the same time as Mud themselves were barely scratching the Top 10 with a weak-kneed cover of *Lean On Me*. By the time Mud finally broke up in 1980, even the tiger feet seemed arthritic. Les Gray reflected, "We went to RCA . . . in 1979, but the management team who actually signed us were all cleared out of the company. They had a big shake up and the new people that came in didn't seem to be interested in us at all. We were left by the wayside, and when that contract ran out, I left the band. It didn't seem to be developing any further." Rob Davies followed. He joined the Darts. Ray Stiles joined the Hollies, but today, Mud live on as a shamelessly nostalgic act fronted by Gray, and huge in Holland. "We have a good time," Gray told writer Chris Welch in 1997. "And I promise — we're all still crazy."

Mud Glam Years Discography:

UK Original Singles
- *Crazy / Do You Love Me* (RAK 146, 1973)
- *Hypnosis / Last Tango In London* (RAK 152, 1973)
- *Dyna-Mite / Do It All Over Again* (RAK 159, 1973)
- *Tiger Feet / Mr. Bagatelle* (RAK 166, 1974)
- *The Cat Crept In / Morning* (RAK 170, 1974)
- *Rocket / Ladies* (RAK 178, 1974)
- *Lonely This Christmas / I Can't Stand It* (RAK 187, 1974)
- *Secrets That You Keep / Watching The Clock* (RAK 194, 1975)
- *Oh Boy / Moonshine Sally* (RAK 201, 1975)
- *Moonshine Sally / Bye Bye Johnny* (RAK 208, 1975)
- *One Night / Shake Rattle & Roll / See You Later Alligator* (RAK 213, 1975)
  Note: Following *One Night*, Mud broke with both Chinn and Chapman, and Mickie Most's RAK label.

US Original Singles
- *Crazy / Do You Love Me* (Bell 415, 1973)
- *Tiger Feet / Mr. Bagatelle* (Bell 602, 1974)

UK Original Albums
- MUD ROCK (RAK 508, 1974)
- MUD ROCK VOLUME TWO (RAK 513, 1975)
- GREATEST HITS (RAK 6755, 1975)

UK Archive Important Album
  ○ THE SINGLES 1967-78 (Repertoire REP 4657, 1997)

☆ 17 ☆
Lou Reed

— Walk On The Wild Side —

His first Glam hit, *Walk On The Wild Side*, entered the UK chart on May 12, 1973.

Chart Hits		
	UK	US
Singles	2 (1973-87)	1 (1973)
Albums	12 (1973 --)	20+ (1972 --)

Despite all that was exploding around the UK, there was only a handful of albums squeezing into Christmas stockings that winter of 1972 that excited much in the way of dramatic comment. ZIGGY STARDUST, after all, was already eight months old, and even the most disapproving parent had got a handle on that by now. Slade and T. Rex had been more or less accepted; Elton's HONKY CHATEAU and DON'T SHOOT ME were mild mannered singer-songwriter stuff, a million miles from the spectacle of his spectacles; and nobody else had really got the hang of the long-playing business just yet. Nobody, that is, except for Lou Reed, and a little thing he called TRANSFORMER.

TRANSFORMER. Its very title suggested some kind of heavy deviation. The sailor with the salami down his pants on the back cover was only the first stop on the trip David and Lou had planned for the kiddies. Dismissed by many of Reed's own fans as a mere caricature of what Velvet Lou was supposedly capable of, TRANSFORMER emerged as a lush, almost impeccably delivered catalog of permutations and perversions. It has been described as one of the most decadent albums of its time. It was certainly one of the campest, hustling its way through the soft white underbelly of New York and pulling back exactly the same curtains as the Velvet Underground used to, but looking in from a very different angle.

The sordid degradation, the hopeless wandering through a twilight world of sex change kittens and midnight cowboys were the same as they always were. But for the first time, Lou wasn't taking things so seriously. Or at least his audience wasn't — and in the halls of legend, it all amounts to much the same thing.

"Did you say something about being cheap?" Reed asked. "God, I've always been cheap and decadent. But I don't think TRANSFORMER is a decadent album. Singing about hustlers and gay people isn't decadent ... the only song I'd put in that category would be *New York Telephone Conversation*. But something like *Vicious* — the only motivation for that was because Warhol asked me to write a song called *Vicious* — 'it would be so faahbulous, y'know?' So I said 'what kind of vicious?' and he said, 'oh, 'vicious, you hit me with a flower.' That's outasight, y'know?"

Reed, of course, was new to the solo game in 1972. He'd spent six years spent leading the Velvet Underground through the stinking intestines of American psychosis until it finally collapsed under its own weight. A tentative solo debut had shattered under its maker's own inexperience. Rumor insists that until David Bowie wandered in and offered to produce Reed's next record, his label (RCA) was going to drop him. The execution was stayed — and Lou Reed stayed as well.

Recording in London through that summer of 1972, Reed made a special guest appearance at a Bowie gig, then dropped by the studio where Mott The Hoople was recording his *Sweet Jane* for their ALL THE YOUNG DUDES album, also under Bowie's supervision. Of course, Bowie couldn't resist bringing his two protégés together — a tape exists (but has never been released) of Reed singing along with Mott's backing track, a combination which was as great as it should have been. And though Mott's Ian Hunter later admitted that he never really liked the song, *Sweet Jane* remained in the band's live set for a good year thereafter, segueing out of *Roll Away The Stone*, and working wonderfully there as well.

Bowie and Reed sparked continually — tantrums and depression haunted the TRANSFORMER sessions like a vengeful ghost, and once the album was complete, Bowie barely mentioned Lou's name again. But still it was a masterpiece, as Reed himself was quick to admit. "TRANSFORMER is easily my best produced album. That has a lot to do with Mick Ronson. His influence was much stronger than David's — but together, as a team, they're terrific." Ronson alone arranged the album's most beautiful moment, the tender *Perfect Day* (revived 20+ years later for an all-star charity No. 1.) But Bowie is largely credited with writing *Wagon Wheel*, one of the most playful songs in sight, and overall Reed is right. TRANSFORMER is still his best produced record, and Bowie and Ronson together were a terrific team.

Lou Reed

"We are concentrating on the feeling rather than the technical side of the music," Ronson said. "He's an interesting person, but I never know what he's thinking. However, as long as we can reach him musically, it's alright."

The album's piece de resistance, of course, was *Walk On The Wild Side*. Released as a single with a bravado which few record companies would ever dream of emulating, *Wild Side* hit the streets in May 1973, some six months after the LP itself. Already, then, the song's scurrilous, circuitous tour of the Warhol Factory had been heartily discussed in every forum from the music press to the drag circuit.

Respected and respectable Brit DJ Tony Blackburn ("the poor deluded fool," one observer remarked) made the song his Record Of The Week, and its ascension to No. 10 on the British chart was achieved without any censorship whatsoever — in the US, where the lyric's meaning was even less of a secret, RCA took the precaution of issuing radio stations with a cleaned up version of the song, only to have their goodwill flung back in their faces when the DJ's went with the album version regardless. The song made No. 16.

Still Reed was uncertain about where to take this new direction. Attempts to form a new band called the Tots fizzled out when the glamour refused to stay glued together, and the gay angle bothered him as well — not because he disliked it, but because he disliked the connotations which accompanied it. "These kids can pretend to be as gay as can be, but when it comes down to it, they just won't be able to make it. You just can't fake being 'gay.' That line 'everybody's bisexual' — that's a very popular thing to say right now. I think it's meaningless."

Instead, he began tinkering with a concept album, a maggoty saga of divorce called BERLIN; put together a gonzo metal live band around the screaming twin guitars of Steve Hunter and Dick Wagner; and announced that the TRANSFORMER backlash was not far away. "Maybe I'll write a song," he threatened, "called *Get Back In The Closet, You Queers.*"

He didn't.

Lou Reed Glam Years Discography:
UK Original Singles
  ○ *Walk On The Wild Side* / *Perfect Day* (RCA 2303, 1972)
  ○ *Vicious* / *Satellite Of Love* (RCA 2318, 1973)

US Original Singles
  ○ *Walk On The Wild Side* / *Perfect Day* (RCA 0887, 1973)
  ○ *Vicious* / *Satellite Of Love* (RCA 0964, 1973)

UK Original Album
  ○ TRANSFORMER (RCA 4807, 1972)

US Original Album
  ○ TRANSFORMER (RCA 4807, 1972)

☆ **18** ☆
Suzi Quatro

− *Can The Can* −

Her first Glam hit, *Can The Can*, entered the UK chart on May 19, 1973.

	Chart Hits	
	UK	US
Singles	16 (1973-82)	7 (1974-81)
Albums	2 (1973-80)	6 (1974-80)

The first time Britain saw Suzi Quatro, she was already on TOP OF THE POPS, five foot nothing of leather-soaked dynamite, stomping through *Can The Can* the very same weekend as David Bowie was launching his latest (last) British tour, and the contradiction screamed out at everyone. "The guys in my band don't wear glitter," she snarled. "They're REAL men." It didn't take an Einstein to figure out what that made everyone else.

Suzi Quatro, Chinnichap's third major signing, was a native of Detroit. The erstwhile Suzi Soul was in a fast disintegrating band called Cradle at the time, meeting Mickie Most when he was in Motor City recording the Jeff Beck Group at the Tamla Motown studios. Impressed by her ambition and aggression, the producer told her to look him up if she was ever in England. A year later she took him up on the offer.

"I put her in a hotel and kind of Anglicized her," Most later recalled, but her first single for Most, *Rolling Stone*, co-written by Errol Brown of Hot Chocolate, went nowhere. Which is when the producer decided to pair the Divine Miss Q with Chinnichap.

According to Chapman, Suzi was one of those rare artists who Most knew ought to be a star, he just didn't have any idea how to make her one. And why? Because he saw her as a singer-songwriter, while the English press simply saw her as a freak. "If you knew Suzi like the tattooist knows Suzi" was a typical headline, and while it was comforting to know that even without a hit to her name, Suzi was already building a certain image, Most needed a song that would translate that image into direct action. *Can The Can* was that song.

"They saw the aggression in Suzi," Most says of Chinnichap's first song for the singer, while Chapman adds, "It was a classic example of a record creating an artist, because *Can The Can* certainly created Suzi. It made her a superstar everywhere in the world except America."

The basic premise of *Can The Can*, and the follow-up efforts, *48 Crash* and *Daytona Demon*, was to project Suzi as a leather-clad man-eater, a role model for the girls rather than the boys. "You don't have to lie back and think of England," was the message. "But he might want to."

"Put your man in a can, honey, get him while you can," she roared in *Can The Can*, and later, in *Daytona Demon*, "he's a souped-up, heavy-hung, he-man." It didn't even matter that the songs were written by a pair of guys — in so effectively, and unsubtly, dehumanizing the male of the species, Quatro completely reversed the traditional Sex Object roles.

Men were nothing more than Super-Studs, and in an age when sexual liberation was supposedly at the forefront of everybody's mind, it was refreshing that women were finally being permitted to get in on the act — even if it did take two men and a mouthful of gum to give them the platform from which to do it.

The demon unleashed in these early Quatro 45's, however, was not to hang around for long. No less than with The Sweet and Mud, Chinnichap, it transpired, were also hell bent on a quest for rock credibility. Chapman admits, "the criticism of our music was wearing us down. The culmination came when I was in the studio with Suzi and we picked up the New Musical Express, which contained a review of the latest Suzi Quatro single by Charles Shaar Murray. It said something like Nicky and I were misrepresenting the artist by making such banal music, that Suzi would be better off without us, that we were both fakes, that we didn't know what we were doing, and so on.

"I took it pretty well I guess, but Suzi broke down in tears, so I got angry. We sent a roadie out to buy some pig's brains, some wrapping paper and a card, and I wrapped it all up with a big bow and wrote on the card something like 'Dear Charles, If you are bent on becoming as ...'" and I thought of all the egotistical words I could ." as I am, then perhaps you could do with some of these."

The brains sat stinking in their wrapper on Murray's desk all weekend. "When he got in and opened it up, the thing stunk the place out. I think they cut off my subscription the next week. But that's when the critics got to me. I'd had enough, Suzi had had enough, and when I told Nicky about it, he'd had enough too. We needed credibility, we were tired of being put down."

They began to make amends immediately, and Quatro undoubtedly began to make "better" records. She did not, however, make better pop records, and *The Wild One*, a No. 7 in November 1974, effectively ended her career as the Queen of Glam. By the time she returned to the Top 10 — the ONLY barometer of glam success that really mattered — three years and several musical bridges had been passed, and she was duetting soppy love songs with Chris Norman of latter-day Chinnichap starlets, Smokey.

THE ESSENTIAL
Suzi Quatro

Featuring Suzi's biggest hits

Can The Can
Devil Gate Drive
Wild One
Stumblin' In

Ghosts of her past, of course, abounded. Half the women bursting through from Britain's punk rock explosion had one eye on the lessons they'd learned from Quatro, while in America, her appearance in the ratings-ruling HAPPY DAZE TV series brought her a whole new appreciative audience.

But it's no coincidence whatsoever that Suzi's final American hit, 1981's *Lipstick*, was followed in less than a year by Joan Jett's first — *I Love Rock'n'Roll*, nor that Jett's favored wardrobe of black leather and sneer owed more to early Quatro than a visit to the same tailor. Suzi opened a whole new can the can of worms when she emerged in 1973. And no-one has succeeded in closing it since.

Suzi Quatro Glam Years Discography:

UK Original Singles
- *Rolling Stone / Brain Confusion* (RAK 134, 1972)
- *Can The Can / Ain't Ya Something* (RAK 150, 1973)
- *48 Crash / Little Bitch Blue* (RAK 158, 1973)
- *Daytona Demon / Roman Fingers* (RAK 161, 1973)
- *Devilgate Drive / In The Morning* (RAK 167, 1974)
- *Too Big / I Wanna Be Free* (RAK 175, 1974)
- *The Wild One / Shake My Sugar* (RAK 185, 1975)
- *Your Mama Won't Like Me / Peter Peter* (RAK 191, 1975)

US Original Singles
- *Can The Can / Ain't Ya Something* (Big Tree 16053, 1973)
- *48 Crash / Little Bitch Blue* (Bell 401, 1973)
- *Can The Can / Don't Mess Around* (Bell 416, 1974)
- *All Shook Up / Glycerine Queen* (Bell 477, 1974)
- *Devilgate Drive / In The Morning* (Bell 609, 1974)

○ *Keep A Knockin' / Cat's Eye* (Bell 615, 1974)
○ *Your Mama Won't Like Me / Peter Peter* (Arista 0106, 1975)

UK Original Albums
○ SUZI QUATRO (RAK 505, 1973)
○ QUATRO (RAK 509, 1974)
○ YOUR MAMA WON'T LIKE ME (RAK 514, 1975)

UK Important Archive Albums
○ ROCK TILL YA DROP (Biff 4, 1988)
○ THE ESSENTIAL (EMI 33346, 1998)
   Note: ROCK TILL YA DROP concentrates exclusively on Quatro's primal glam years.
   THE ESSENTIAL offers a 2 CD overview of her career.

US Original Albums
○ SUZI QUATRO (Bell 1302, 1973)
○ QUATRO (Bell 1313, 1974)
○ YOUR MAMA WON'T LIKE ME (Arista 4035, 1975)

☆ 19 ☆
David Essex

– Rock On –

His first Glam hit, *Rock On*, entered the UK chart on August 18, 1973.

Chart Hits		
	UK	US
Singles	26 (1973-94)	2 (1973-74)
Albums	16 (1973-93)	1 (1974)

On record, it's a heartbeat, but on film, that's already ceased. And it's the final slamming of the hospital doors which ushers in the funereal beat that runs through the national anthem of rock — *Stardust*, the most sobering reflection yet on that most clichéd of glorious Rock And Roll ambitions, "live fast, die young . . . and leave a beautiful corpse."

Jim MacLaine, the hero both of STARDUST and its predecessor, THAT'LL BE THE DAY, did all three, and in so doing, he dragged British cinema out of a rut it had been riding for half a decade (in the late 1990's, the similarly themed VELVET GOLDMINE would have a similar effect to American art houses.) No longer tethered to the twin bankable gods of

Hammer horror and sit-com spin-offs, the mid-1970's saw British pop music movies explode into a focus unseen since they heyday of Merseybeat. Glam rock was a visual extravaganza even before the cameras started rolling, but still its screen test took a lot of folks by storm.

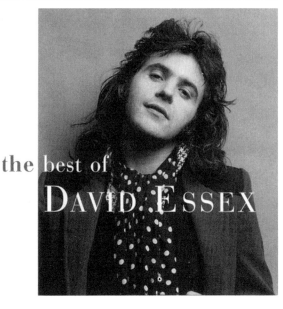

Unfortunately, that's about as far as it got. Bolan's BORN TO BOOGIE seems quaint today, Slade's IN FLAME merely dated, Glitter's REMEMBER ME THIS WAY was never anything less than absurd, and Bowie's much delayed ZIGGY STARDUST — THE MOTION PICTURE had all the guts and guitars mixed out of it to try and make its tenth anniversary release sound more "80's."

THAT'LL BE THE DAY and STARDUST, though . . . celluloid really doesn't get much better than this.

THAT'LL BE THE DAY, based upon a slice of rampant literary nostalgia by author Ray Connolly, starred the recently risen star of David Essex as a typical English teen, doing typically English teenaged things, in the typically English late 1950's. Thrill as Jim Maclaine greases his hair! Swoon as he plays silly buggers at the funfair! Laugh as he trots out a script's worth of incomprehensible colloquial dialogue.

Plotwise, then, it was a dead ringer for AMERICAN GRAFFITI, with one minor twist. Few of the fictional figureheads of AMERICAN GRAFFITI seemed to exist outside of the period costumes into which they were thrust. Jim Maclaine, however, was a believable would-be rock star long before his own attention began to stray in that direction. It was only natural, then, that a sequel should place him in precisely that position — even as the Bolanically good-looking Essex's own star rode roughshod over Maclaine's cinematic achievements.

Rock On, Essex's debut hit, arrived after almost a decade of trying, and of course it benefited from its placement on the chart-topping movie soundtrack. But there Essex's twin careers split in defiant twain. He began the decade playing Jesus in GODSPELL, and he ended it as Che Guevara in EVITA. And in between times, he blended the two roles so perfectly that it didn't even matter that a pair of flares was his only real concession to the demands of his audience. If glam really was about creating an image, then sustaining it till it took on its own life, Essex came as close to perfection as anyone.

Record Mirror fans voted him the year's best newcomer (ahead of Suzi Quatro, Barry Blue and Marie Osmond.) *Lamplight*, a semi-sound-alike follow-up single (all pseudo dub echo and yearning, sly, vocals), made the UK Top 10 in late 1973. And by the time STARDUST hit the cinema circuit, Essex had already notched up two more stand-alone singles, *America*, and the rollicking, cynical show biz bravado of *Gonna Make You A Star*. Poking fun at his own critical stature, Essex ran through a shopping list of his own perceived failings ... "is he more than just a pretty face?" ... then answered them for the nay-sayers ... "I don't think so." He was rewarded with his first No. 1, and the song was still hanging round the Top 30 when *Stardust* rode out with the movie's premiere.

As a movie, STARDUST cannot be praised too highly. Its soundtrack cannot be beaten. As with its predecessor, the two album set essentially followed the biggest hits of the decade on display, replacing the late 1950's with the early-mid 60's, and then padding out the vinyl action with a few custom made classics of its own. THAT'LL BE THE DAY prompted fresh performances out of former Bonzo Dog Band vocalist Viv Stanshall. STARDUST roped Dave Edmunds into the brew.

The greatest British producer of the era — even if he did squander most of his talent on pub rock bands — and one of the finest guitarists as well, Edmunds arrived with a clutch of tracks which sounded suspiciously like out-takes from his own latest album, SUBTLE AS A FLYING MALLET, and instructions to back Essex on a few decidedly Cavernesque rockers.

But it was Essex who prevailed, with his title track not only granting him his fifth successive hit single, but also offering a requiem for every Rock And Roller who has ever climbed too high, and fallen too hard. Plus it boasts a Chris Spedding guitar solo to die for — literally, in Jim Maclaine's case.

It was a powerful performance — too powerful, maybe, for the pop kids to absorb. Inextricably bound as it was to the heartbreaking conclusion to the movie, and certainly too gloomy to set the Christmas charts afire, it did well to hit No. 7, and it was nine months more before Essex was back at the top, with another slice of good time Cockney mocking, *Hold Me Close*, and the last hurrah of his days as a true teenage idol.

By the end of 1975, IF I COULD had revealed him to be a singer songwriter of astonishing balladic prowess. By 1978, he had developed enough to give the almighty *Stay With Me Baby* a good run for its money. His reading of *Oh! What A Circus*, from EVITA, proved him the only viable (and still the only worthwhile) contender for the Guevara role in the Argentinean soap cycle, and subsequent singing actor roles, in SILVER DREAM MACHINE and MUTINY ON THE BOUNTY, have since established him as one of Britain's best loved all-round performers.

His 1994 version of Buddy Holly's *True Love Ways*, performed with actress Catherine Zeta Jones, however, proved that such an accolade doesn't necessarily foreshadow a descent into full-blooded mawkishness, any more than a 1989 Shep Pettibone revision of *Rock On* proved that he'd run out of ideas for new songs. But still, David Essex made his greatest record in late 1974, for the closing moments of the closest thing Rock And Roll has ever come to the perfect self-abusing movie. And for that . . . rock on.

David Essex Glam Years Discography:
UK Original Singles
- *Rock On / On And On* (CBS 1693, 1973)
- *Lamplight / We All Insane* (CBS 1902, 1973)
- *America / Dance Little Girl* (CBS 2176, 1974)
- *Gonna Make you A Star / Window* (CBS 2492, 1974)
- *Stardust / Miss Sweetness* (CBS 2828, 1974)

US Original Singles
- *Rock On / On And On* (Columbia 45940, 1973)
- *Lamplight / We All Insane* (Columbia 46041, 1973)

UK Original Albums
- ROCK ON (CBS 65823, 1973)
- DAVID ESSEX (CBS 69088, 1974)
- STARDUST (original soundtrack) (Ronco RG 2010, 1974)

US Original Albums
- ROCK ON (Columbia 32560, 1973)
- STARDUST (original soundtrack) (Arista AL 5000, 1974)

☆ **20** ☆
Bryan Ferry

– A Hard Rain's A-Gonna Fall –

His first Glam hit, *A Hard Rain's A-Gonna Fall*,
entered the UK chart on September 23, 1973.

Chart Hits		
	UK	US
Singles	25+ (1973 --)	2 (1976-88)
Albums	10+ (1973 --)	6 (1976 --)

It was during the hiatus initiated by Eno's departure from Roxy Music, in the summer of 1973, that Bryan Ferry's ambitions as a solo performer, dormant throughout Roxy Music's rise to ascendancy, finally emerged — first via a revolutionary reading of Bob Dylan's *Hard Rain*, truly the most scarifying single to hit the British chart that fall, then by THESE FOOLISH THINGS, an album's worth of pop standards given the distinctive Ferry vocal touch.

With its contents ranging idiosyncratically from *Sympathy For The Devil* and *Hard Rain* (of course), through to *The Tracks Of My Tears* and *It's My Party*, Ferry created an album which remains one of the weirdest records ever cast towards a rock audience, even one as enlightened as the British glam scene. As versatile in his arrangements as he ever was as a songwriter, Ferry paralyzed the most innocuous lyric with a sense of genuine menace, and when that failed, with a heartache which was almost palpable. His version of *It's My Party* alone is sheer genius, although Ferry saved his best performance for the title track.

Writing in the book THE LIVES OF THE GREAT SONGS (Pavilion UK, 1994), journalist Robert Cushman surveyed almost sixty years' worth of recordings of *These Foolish Things*, including performances by the likes of Billie Holiday (1936), Bing Crosby (1955) and Frank Sinatra (1961.) He found Ferry's version superior in virtually every department. High praise indeed — even if Ferry's enunciation still makes "Garbo" sound like gargoyles, and the evening's "sinvitation" seem even more sinister than that.

No sooner was the album complete, than Ferry was contemplating its follow up. "It seems a pity not to do another solo," he smiled. "There are thousands of other songs I'd like to have a crack at destroying." 1974's ANOTHER TIME ANOTHER PLACE, then, painstakingly duplicated its predecessors' format (and again came up trumps both in performance and content. Ferry's version of *You Are My Sunshine* must be heard to be believed), and unleashed another murderous single, Dobie Grey's mod classic *The In*

Crowd, with a scything guitar which — unbeknownst to most listeners — actually painted a picture of what Roxy Music might have become.

Davy O'List, dropped from the band the moment they signed a deal, was listening to a Bryan Ferry interview on the radio one day, when the singer said he'd like to work with him once again. "I called his management and said 'here I am,'" O'List laughed, and days later, he was whisked into the studio. The result made No. 13 in the spring of 1974.

Like Eno, Bryan Ferry continued releasing solo albums throughout the lifetime of Roxy Music, and indeed, way beyond it. Not all of them have been as sensational as Ferry's own reputation would demand — 1995's MAMOUNA even boasted a reunion with Eno, and still couldn't cut it. The mid-1980's' BOYS AND GIRLS mingles lightweight soundscapes with a handful of genuinely seductive opuses. And the late 1970's IN YOUR MIND was distinguished by one song alone, the rambunctious *This Is Tomorrow*.

But even with that in mind, it's sometimes worth remembering just how far ahead of the pack Bryan Ferry's career has consistently been. THESE FOOLISH THINGS, for instance, beat David Bowie (the generally accepted market leader of the era) to the "covers album" concept by a clear three months. The often-apocalyptic STRANDED had a similar head start over Bowie's doom-laden DIAMOND DOGS.

Indeed, both with and without Roxy Music, Ferry was to both outlast and outsell Bowie, at least in terms of glam rock. While Bowie moved from the delicious, spiraling tease of ALADDIN SANE to the hard rock of DIAMOND DOGS and on to the plastic soul of

YOUNG AMERICANS, Roxy, Ferry (and, in his early solo career, Eno), were all to continue along the lines laid down by their first tentative attempts to cross teenage revolution with Fritz Lang's METROPOLIS.

Even after the glam genre itself had run its course, and Ferry was flirting with a succession of new styles and images (including the Gaucho look, which single-handedly inspired the New Musical Express' long running LONE GROOVER cartoon strip), he continued to signpost the direction things might have gone had only the rest of the pack not drifted off in search of other, safer, harbors.

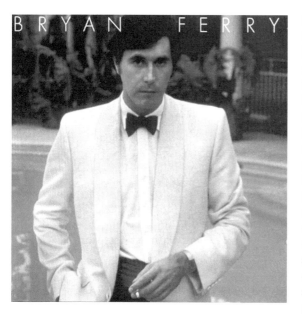

Ferry's solo cover of the Velvet Underground's *What Goes On*, in 1978, did something which nobody had done before, and took Lou Reed's best known band onto the British chart — and that at the height of punk rock, when everyone was singing the Velvets' rancid praises. MANIFESTO, Roxy Music's 1979 comeback album, effortlessly sign posted the first manifestations of what would emerge as the post-punk movement. And Ferry's appearance at 1985's Live Aid concert was generally regarded as the only truly genuine performance of the entire bloated festival — and the only one which remembered that, at the end of the day, it's only Rock And Roll.

He couldn't help it. Even today, with Roxy Music long dead and buried, Bryan Ferry wears a Hollywood Glamour sheen, a veneer as captivating as it is flimsy. And even at his safest, he gives the impression of being out on the edge. The only man who can make *Will You Love Me Tomorrow* sound like a threat, or *You Are My Sunshine* sound like a dirge, he's also quite possibly the coolest man alive — and the sexiest dancer on earth. Plus, he redefined the meaning of decadence at a time when most people were still trying to find out what it used to mean.

Bryan Ferry Glam Years Discography:
UK Original Singles
- A *Hard Rain's A-Gonna Fall* / *2 HB* (Island WIP 6170, 1973)
- *The In Crowd* / *Chance Meeting* (Island WIP 6196, 1974)
- *Smoke Gets In Your Eyes* / *Another Time Another Place* (Island WIP 6205, 1974)
- *You Go To My Head* / *Remake Remodel* (Island WIP 6234, 1975)
- *Let's Stick Together* / *Sea Breezes* (Island WIP 6307, 1976)

UK Original EP
  ° EXTENDED PLAY (Island IEP 1, 1976)

UK Original Albums
  ° THESE FOOLISH THINGS (Island ILPS 9249, 1973)
  ° ANOTHER TIME ANOTHER PLACE (Island ILPS 9284, 1974)

UK Important Archive Album
  ° LET'S STICK TOGETHER (Island ILPS 9367, 1976)

US Original Albums
  ° THESE FOOLISH THINGS (Atlantic 7304, 1973)
  ° ANOTHER TIME ANOTHER PLACE (Atlantic 18113, 1974)

US Important Archive Album
  ° LET'S STICK TOGETHER (Atlantic 18187, 1976)

☆ 21 ☆
Jobriath

— JOBRIATH —

His first Glam album, JOBRIATH, was released in October 1973.

Perhaps the saddest of all the glitter / glam casualties was Jobriath. Described by manager Jerry Brandt as being as different from Bowie as "a Lambourghini is from a Model A Ford (they're both cars, it's just a question of taste, style, elegance and beauty)," Jobriath was projected as some kind of missing link — the intellect of Bowie, the craziness of Slade, the joy of Bolan, the theater of Alice, and the mystery of Garbo.

Even after the singer's debut album, JOBRIATH, was released in October 1973, Brandt steadfastly refused to let the boy be interviewed. And while Tony DeFries had put Bowie through a similar period of invisibility, he only did it once he was certain people wanted to talk to his charge in the first place. Brandt did not give people that option, and the rock press retaliated by labeling Jobriath a hopeless, hapless hype before he'd even opened his mouth. Jobriath never stood a chance.

Bruce "Jobriath Boone" Campbell was born in 1946 in King Of Prussia, Pennsylvania, smack in the heart of Amish country. He appeared in the original LA run of HAIR, recorded one album with a long-forgotten group called Pidgeon, and spent some time under the aegis of former Hendrix manager Mike Jeffries. And then Columbia Records president Clive Davis spoke the words which alerted the world to the fact that Jobriath was somehow different: that Jobriath was "mad and unstructured, and destructive to melody." Jerry Brandt, Carly Simon's manager, signed the singer on the spot.

Brandt's enthusiasm was contagious — as Elektra Records chief Jac Holzman later confessed. "I made two errors of judgment in my days at Elektra, and Jobriath was one of them." Some $80,000 were poured into Jobriath's eponymous debut album, with close to half of that going on promotion. Full page ads in Vogue, Penthouse and the New York Times targeted Jobriath far beyond the reach of the traditional pop music audience. They had to make do with an almost 50 foot square billboard in Times Square, and the singer's image on the front of buses from London to New York.

Although Jobriath has since become something of a byword for overblown promotion and tacky hype, JOBRIATH itself was critically well received. Produced by Eddie Kramer, and featuring Led Zeppelin bassist John Paul Jones and Peter Frampton, it landed rave reviews in both Cash Box and Rolling Stone ("Jobriath has talent to burn"), earned the singer a memorable showing on TV's Midnight Special, and boded well for the singer's proposed live debut, at the Paris Opera House.

That show never happened. Almost as soon as the album was out, Elektra seem to have begun regretting their profligacy, all the more so since a second Jobriath LP was already underway. The problem, Jac Holzman said, was that "the music seemed secondary to everything else. It was . . . lacking in any sense of reality. It's an embarrassment." By the time Jobriath's sophomore album, CREATURES OF THE STREET, was ready, Elektra had all but washed their hands of him. The record appeared to zero promotion, barely a handful of reviews (all scathing), and when the band toured the US that spring of 1974, they were roundly booed off almost every stage.

It was only towards the end of an increasingly miserable, and apparently drug-dazed, outing, that Jobriath and his band, the Creatures, began winning audiences over — indeed, their last ever show together, at Tuscaloosa University, ended with five encores and a near riot. Had the group only had the chance to regroup, they might indeed have fulfilled a lot of the early prophecies. Instead, Jobriath announced his retirement, and remained true to his word for the rest of his life. He was apparently working in lounge cabaret in New York when he died, from AIDS, in July 1983.

Today, Jobriath is closer to success than he ever was in life. The first openly gay pop star in American music history, Jobriath's admirers range from Morrissey to the Pet Shop Boys, while the expected internet web sites dedicated to Jobriath have been joined by one dedicated to his cat, Chaplin. The last word, however, goes to a British customs officer, who stopped Jobriath at the airport the first time the singer flew into London. Looking him up and down, and casting his mind back to his journey into work that morning, the officer finally spoke.

"Hey! Didn't I see you on the Number 11 bus?"

The star's reply has not been recorded.

Jobriath Discography:
UK Original Singles
  ◦ *Take Me I'm Yours* / ? (Elektra K12129, 1974)
  ◦ *Street Corner Love* / ? (Elektra K12146, 1975)

US Original Single
  ◦ *Liten Up* (mono) / (stereo) (Elektra E45210, 1974)

UK Original Album
  ◦ CREATURES OF THE STREET (Elektra K42163, 1975)

US Original Albums
  ◦ JOBRIATH (Elektra 75070, 1973)
  ◦ CREATURES OF THE STREET (Elektra 71010, 1975)

☆ 22 ☆
Alvin Stardust

− *My Coo Ca Choo* −

His first Glam hit, *My Coo Ca Choo*, entered the UK chart on November 3, 1973.

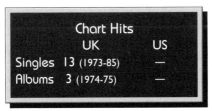

	Chart Hits	
	UK	US
Singles	13 (1973-85)	—
Albums	3 (1974-75)	—

Like Gary Glitter, Alvin Stardust had been kicking around the outskirts of British Pop for a decade of so before he re-emerged on the elder side of glam rock. As Shane Fenton, he led the Fentones to chart success with *I'm A Moody Guy* and *Cindy's Birthday* in 1961-62, but from there sank into the obscurity of the nightclub circuit until a meeting with songwriter Pete Shelley was suddenly to bring him out of his shell for keeps.

The in-house producer at Magnet Records, Shelley had recently written a song called *My Coo Ca Choo*, a cunning blend of *Spirit In The Sky* and Gene Vincent. "I was looking for someone who could sing rock'n'roll, but who looked pretty mean," Shelley later said. "Everyone else was into glitter music, and I thought the time was right for someone who was the complete opposite of all that, (but) who could still thrill an audience. As mean as Mick Jagger with the appearance of Elvis Presley. And Shane's manager said I should meet him."

Fenton's own name, of course, could not be revived. As Alvin Stardust, however, he seemed unrecognizable, and Shelley's vision of *My Coo Ca Choo*'s coo-er ensured that he would probably remain that way.

Alvin's first TV appearance was on LIFT OFF WITH AYSHEA, a children's' TV staple, and a proven testing ground for up and coming pop stars. It was not a particularly notable showing. Alvin looked old, moved old, and positively dazzled everyone with his impersonation of a pink and blue Slush Puppy. With the more important TOP OF THE POPS just around the corner, Shelley felt something far more drastic was in order.

"I wanted him to look like a Teddy boy. I got him to dye his hair black, then we hit on the idea of black leathers, and Alvin said he would sing the number with a stance almost like a boxer." The whole thing came together, Shelley added, "in a round-about way," But it was to succeed beyond their wildest hopes. Black hair, black boots, black gloves bedecked with rings, heavy bangles and a permanent glower, Stardust looked like a cross between a leather fiend and a child molester. He was "The Man In Black," "The Untouchable," "The Star Who Is Forbidden To Smile," he might even, said the New Musical Express, be "The Son of Gary Glitter." Quite honestly, he was evil.

Children's television seriously contemplated banning him. One show did forbid him to appear — "They thought I'd frighten the kiddies," Alvin told chat show host Russell Harty moments after mortifying his host by saying, "When I was told I was doing the RUSSELL HARTY SHOW, I thought it was a talk-in version of BASIL BRUSH. I thought you were a little dog or something, which surprised me because . . . I'm not supposed to do children's television."

Surprisingly, *My Coo Ca Choo* rose only to No. 2, held off the top spot by fellow veteran Gary Glitter. *Jealous Mind*, which did make it all the way, was a far inferior number, virtually a rewrite of its predecessor, but still sounding like nothing else on earth. In fact, defying every imaginable law of averages, Stardust and Shelley wrangled another four hits out of much the same song before his appeal started to wane. And by that time, the singer had carved out another career anyway, as an all-round family entertainer par excellence.

Alvin Stardust's basic achievement was to seize upon one of society's most hysterical calculations — that Leather equates with Trouble — garnish it with a hint of mystery (it was some time into *Coo Ca Choo*'s run before people began realizing just who this moody old geezer really was — DJ Tony Blackburn is generally recognized as the first person to catch him out), and allow schoolboy imagination to do the rest.

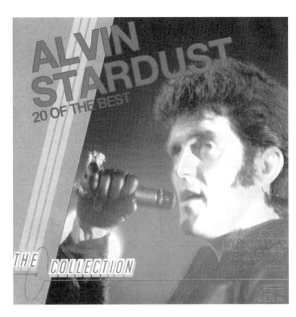

He was peculiarly asexual and that alone had him marked. But playground rumor took things a lot further. Behind the bike shed after TOP OF THE POPS, the knowledgeable kids would hold triumphant court. Alvin, they swore, owned a roomful of whips, a boxful of handcuffs, and the world's largest collection of hand-crafted nipple clamps — indeed, before you knew it, he had a fully-equipped torture chamber in his basement, paid for out of the royalties from *Coo Ca Choo*, where he would take stage-door yummies every night after the show. And there . . . well, no-one was really sure what happened after that, but one thing was certain. He didn't "do it" like normal people.

It was total rubbish, of course. In reality, Stardust was happily married, with a four year old son. But legends aren't built around stories like that, because if they were, pop would be more toothless than most of its so-called stars are already. So when the truth began to emerge, it came out slowly, just a bit at a time. First, familiarity with Stardust's image and stance somehow made him seem less of a threat. When he gripped the microphone in that funny upside down way of his, it was as much a trademark as Gary Glitter's idiot smile and Dave Hill's "Superyob" guitar.

Then the savage hypnotic guitar of *Coo Ca Choo* was slowly distilled. When Alvin glowered through *Red Dress*, why, there was almost a melody there. He started communicating with the audience, still glaring at them of course, but there was a warmth in his eyes. One day, he even smiled. Children's television let him back into the room, parents found other pop stars to complain about, and by the time *Good Love Can Never Die* and *Sweet Cheatin' Rita* gave him hits six and seven, in the spring and summer of 1975, his audience contained as many moms as daughters.

He dropped the leather around the same time as he dropped out of the chart, but he was never out of work, and never far from the public heart. The early 1980's even saw him back on top for a while . . . for five years, in fact, which was a longer run than both of his past successes put together. And into the 1990's, he continued packing out shows, a little bit older, a little bit slower, and a little more unsteady on his platforms as well. But he was still an entertainer, and *My Coo Ca Choo* still cooks.

Alvin Stardust Glam Years Discography:
UK Original Singles
   ° *My Coo Ca Choo / Pull Together* (Magnet 1, 1973)
   ° *Jealous Mind / Guitar Star* (Magnet 5, 1974)
   ° *Red Dress / Little Darling* (Magnet 8, 1974)
   ° *You You You / Come On* (Magnet 13, 1974)
   ° *Tell Me Why / ?* (Magnet 19, 1974)

UK Original Albums
   ° THE UNTOUCHABLE (Magnet 5001, 1974)
   ° ALVIN STARDUST (Magnet 5004, 1975)

☆ **23** ☆
Leo Sayer

– *The Show Must Go On* –

His first Glam hit, *The Show Must Go On*,
entered the UK chart on December 15, 1973.

Chart Hits		
	UK	US
Singles	17 (1973-93)	—
Albums	—	—

It's a joke, right? One of those odd chronological quirks by which budget glam CD compilations, and journalists who missed the boat first time round, justify saddling anyone with the tag, simply because they were around at the time.

Metal drummer Cozy Powell scored a couple of percussion-crunching hits for Mickie Most's RAK label. Stick him on a glam compilation. Guitarist Chris Spedding took the same route to stardom . . . stick him on a Glam comp. And he used to be in the Wombles . . . so stick them on one as well. Of course, Leo Sayer — whose period of greatest chart impact unquestionably coincided with the great glam explosion — belongs. And if that's the only criteria that matters, let's sling Lieutenant Pigeon in as well.

Ah, but then the mind's eye rolls back to December 1973 and the world's first glimpse of a young Leo Sayer, fresh from a pub band with the evocative name of Patches, dressed as a pierrot, and bemoaning the fact that no matter how bad things got, the show had to go on. Twenty years later, a dying Freddie Mercury would draw similar conclusions from his own worst nightmare, and give Queen their most affecting hit record in years. Sayer, who wrote the song about "an important gig that goes wrong," would be the first to admit that his inspiration was somewhat more mundane. But

with the song performed to piano and banjo, and Sayer's saddened clown alone on the stage, it was a powerful image regardless. And image, lest we forget, was everything back then.

The Show Must Go On rocketed to No. 2, and the pierrot won a lot of young fans, entranced by the look, and the funny, quirky, record — Sayer sang with an almost desperate choke in the back of his throat, on the verge of tears, on the edge of delirium. It was, quite simply, one of the performances of the year. NME readers even elected Sayer their No. 1 Most Promising New Name in the end of year poll, beating out Queen and Mike Oldfield for the honors.

But the joke — and what a calculated, and calculatedly cruel joke it was — was on them. Sayer, whose day job involved co-writing yearning ballads with David Courtney, then palming them off on Roger Daltrey, wasn't really a twisted, broken funny man — he wasn't even particularly twisted. Step into the SILVERBIRD album which followed hot on the single's footsteps, and the clown was gone once you threw away the cover.

And though Sayer did, eventually, come good (1975's *Moonlighting* remains THE greatest elopement song ever written, and 1977's chart-topping *When I Need You* brought genuine pathos to a somewhat mawkish Carole Bayer Sager ditty), at the time, it was hard not to feel cheated by the whole affair. Cheated, and made to look just a little bit silly in front of all the school friends who'd not been impressed by Sayer's song in the first place. Clowns scare a lot of people, you know. And now you know why.

Leo Sayer Glam Years Discography:

The records are meaningless. It's the TV appearance which counts. But the show went on regardless.

☆ 24 ☆
Queen

− *Seven Seas Of Rhye* −

Their first Glam hit, *Seven Seas Of Rhye*, entered the UK chart on March 9, 1974.

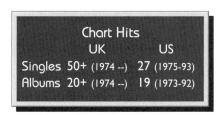

Chart Hits		
	UK	US
Singles	50+ (1974 --)	27 (1975-93)
Albums	20+ (1974 --)	19 (1973-92)

The problem with Queen is knowing how seriously to take them.

Actually, that's not as much of a problem as it used to be. The death of Freddie Mercury in 1991 did more than rob the world of one of the most provocative performers in Rock And Roll, it also deprived it of one of the most enthralling games people could play, namely: how seriously should we take Queen?

Not too seriously, say the writers and cast of WAYNE'S WORLD, who single-handedly returned all six minutes of the multi-layered *Bohemian Rhapsody* to the top of the worldwide charts on the strength of three rather amusing moments in the back of a car. Not too seriously, say an army of detractors whose hatred of Fat Freddie and his mock operatics was sufficient to send them scurrying every time someone said "Scaramouche" at them.

Not too seriously, say fans of vintage Sweet records, for whom Queen's blending of complex harmonies and heavy guitars had already been done before.

And not too seriously, said Queen themselves, for how could you do anything but laugh along with a band who could write a song about fat-bottomed girls riding bicycles?

But get onto the campuses of middle America and laugh at Queen at your own peril, because all the girls have fat bottoms out there and besides, any band that can write *We Will Rock You*, the alternative National Anthem of Major Sporting Events (Gary Glitter's *Rock'n'Roll*, of course, is the other one) must have something heavy going for it.

Track through the first four Queen albums, and essentially the entire history of modern music is distilled therein. Even without the mega-conceit of *Bohemian Rhapsody*, which was little more than The Sweet's *Action* rendered into cod-Italian, Queen knew no shame. They stole from here, they stole from there, and in the magpie's nest of their scintillating best we find, vintage Rock And Roll, classic rockabilly, glam rock, sham rock,

copyright Rock Classics

shock rock, schlock rock. Only Queen could get away with the 50's schmaltz of *Good Old Fashioned Lover Boy* because only Queen would have wanted to, and an hour in the company of their greatest hits brings up a dozen other, similar, sentiments. Is this the real life, indeed?

And camp! They made a tent manufacturer look like an underachieving seamstress. Other glam era bands couched their delicious double entendres in intellect and poetry. Freddie Mercury wore his on the outside of his trousers, which themselves were so tight they left little to the imagination. "Come on, Mr. Feller," he coaxes on the second album's *Fairy Feller's Master Stroke*, "crack it open if you please." And a nation's worth of juvenile minds spluttered over their breakfast corn flakes.

The band's most peerless phase began in 1973 with QUEEN I, shortly after Mercury launched an ill-fated career as the immortally named Larry Lurex, and shortly before Queen staked their claim on the future on tour with Mott The Hoople. Crossing first Britain, then America (a saga retold in *Now I'm Here*), with Mercury growing in opulent confidence every night, Queen's own vision of glam rock — that which was so succinctly summarized in 1975's *Killer Queen* — was on open display even before their first hit single, *Seven Seas Of Rhye*, gave them the chance to strut the stuff on TV, and long before the rest of the world figured out what they were up to. That secret, after all, was the magic behind the next three years' worth of LP's.

copyright 1980 Phil Anderson / KAOS2000 Magazine

Each new release seized upon a different aspect of the band's personality, then took it as far it would go. From the hard rockin' glitter dudes of QUEEN I, to the mystic sorcerers of II; from the uninhibited glam pop poachers of SHEER HEART ATTACK, to the tentative metal muthas of A NIGHT AT THE OPERA, Queen's genius lay in their ability to forge so many points of interlocking contact that not one of them stepped outside of the Queen fan's own reference points. And once that was done, they could get away with anything.

Whether it was drummer Roger Taylor, rhapsodizing his car (*I'm In Love With My Car*); guitarist Brian May playing a thousand notes a minute (*Brighton Rock*); or even bassist John Deacon funking everyone over (*Misfire* — a purebred progenitor of his later *Another One Bites The Dust*), Queen was big enough for everything, and reveled in their magnanimity. Mercury himself was utterly shameless, a breathless virgin through one song, a knowing curmudgeon in the next, multilingual, multisexual, and possessed of an innate pretentiousness so natural that it was impossible to object.

Or, if not impossible, it was certainly futile.

Queen Glam Years Discography:
UK Original Singles
- *Keep Yourself Alive / Liar* (EMI 2036, 1973)
- *Seven Seas Of Rhye / See What A Fool I've Been* (EMI 2121, 1974)
- *Killer Queen / Flick Of The Wrist* (EMI 2229, 1974)
- *Now I'm Here / Lily Of The Valley* (EMI 2256, 1975)
- *Bohemian Rhapsody / I'm In Love With My Car* (EMI 2375, 1975)

US Original Singles
- *Keep Yourself Alive / Son And Daughter* (Elektra 45863, 1973)
- *Liar / Doin' Alright* (Elektra 45884, 1973)
- *Killer Queen / Flick Of The Wrist* (Elektra 45226, 1974)
- *Keep Yourself Alive / Lily Of The Valley* (Elektra 45106, 1975)
- *Lily Of The Valley / Keep Yourself Alive* (Elektra 45268, 1975)
- *Bohemian Rhapsody / I'm In Love With My Car* (Elektra 45297, 1975)

UK Original Albums
- QUEEN (EMI 3006, 1973)
- QUEEN II (EMI EMA 767, 1974)
- SHEER HEART ATTACK (EMI 3061, 1974)
- A NIGHT AT THE OPERA (EMI EMC 103, 1975)

UK Important Archive Album
- QUEEN AT THE BEEB (Band Of Joy CD 001, 1989)

US Original Albums
- QUEEN (Elektra 75064, 1973)
- QUEEN II (Elektra 75082, 1974)
- SHEER HEART ATTACK (Elektra 71026, 1974)
- A NIGHT AT THE OPERA (Elektra 1053, 1975)

US Important Archive Album
- QUEEN AT THE BEEB (Hollywood, 1993)

☆ 25 ☆
Brian Eno

— HERE COME THE WARM JETS —

His first Glam album, HERE COME THE WARM JETS,
entered the UK chart on March 9, 1974

Chart Hits		
	UK	US
Singles	—	—
Albums	5 (1974-92)	—

Brian Eno's role within Roxy Music was one which few people could ever have described. A deliberate non-musician, he originally came on as their sound engineer, advancing from that occupation's customary position behind the mixing desk when it became apparent that he didn't so much mix the band's sound, as mix it up.

Featured in much the same role as Hawkwind's Del Dettmar, feeding the instruments through a variety of electronic devices, then doing things to them, he rapidly became as integral a part of the band's music as anyone on stage, as witnesses to Roxy Music's maiden OLD GREY WHISTLE TEST performance will testify. Long after the song itself had finished, Eno continued playing with the instruments, treating the show's viewers to a sound extravaganza that still amazes today.

Ill-defined musically, he was even more obscure in person. Towering squatness, beautiful ugly, flamboyant, fey, freakish, there were more rumors in the air than there were hairs on his head . . . he was heir to a vast pharmaceutical fortune (Eno's was a well-known indigestion remedy.) He was gay, he was glam, he was an alien, he was a Heaven sent emissary from the Lord God Himself . . . Eno, of course, is an anagram of One. In fact, he was plain old Brian Peter George St. Baptiste de la Salle Eno, an East Anglican Catholic whose only real claim to fame was that he was destined to bear the longest name in rock history. As a youth, he dreamed of painting, first with oils on canvas, but then with sounds on ears. So he studied electronics, and published a book, MUSIC FOR NON-MUSICIANS. Then he met saxophonist Andy Mackay in a London tube station, and was enrolled into Roxy as their technical adviser.

Eno's summer 1973, departure for a solo career left outside observers aghast, and totally oblivious to the irony of that emotion. A mere year before, Eno's presence had been regarded as just another gimmick in Roxy Music's bag of tricks. It's indicative of the sheer power of the band that, just twelve months later, people didn't even remember their original hostility towards the man.

It has since become apparent, of course, that Eno was never cut out for the life of a pop star, and had even less intention of making pop music. At the time, however, there was very much a sense that if Eno had not quit, vocalist Bryan Ferry would have been forced to. Two such powerful personalities simply could not exist side-by-side in one band, particularly as Eno himself was not averse to donning the increasingly outlandish costumes which in other bands would have suited the front man alone.

"It was a very interesting combination of people that got together," guitarist Phil Manzanera says of the early Roxy Music. "We all had our own agendas, and when any one of those agendas got out of sync with the other peoples', like Eno's did with Bryan, then they sort of jumped ship." Indeed, Manzanera and saxophonist Andy Mackay almost followed Eno out of the band at this same time. "I was very good friends with Brian, and it did affect me a lot when he left. I almost left, I came very, very, close. But in the end, at that point, I still wanted to be in a pop band that was being successful. It would have been perverse to quit, and that's when I realized there was an avenue to do both, to be in Roxy Music and to work with Eno."

In fact, Eno did set himself up, at least briefly, as a genuine competitor for Roxy Music's core audience. His bizarre electronic collaboration with Robert Fripp, NO PUSSYFOOTING, notwithstanding, Eno's debut single, *Seven Deadly Finns*, would not have sounded too out of place in Roxy Music's own repertoire. A second non-album single, a so-straight-it's-camp (or vice versa!) version of *The Lion Sleeps Tonight*, wouldn't have been too incongruous turning up on a Bryan Ferry album. And HERE COME THE WARM JETS and TAKING TIGER MOUNTAIN BY STRATEGY, Eno's first two solo albums, can almost be classed as Proxy Music.

Not only are Roxy's Andy Mackay, Phil Manzanera and Paul Thompson numbered among the guest musicians, but these jarring collections of jagged, ragged first-take pop also offer a glimpse into the parallel development Roxy Music might have taken had Eno challenged Ferry's own song writing dominance, as well as his visual prominence.

When he played the London Rainbow on June 1, 1974, on a bill which co-starred Kevin Ayers, John Cale and Nico, Eno's slight, beréted figure filled the stage with the power of *Baby's On Fire* and *Driving Me Backwards*. When Record Mirror reviewed HERE COME THE WARM JETS, they described it as "one of the finest British albums in months." And when Eno linked with the Winkies, guitarist Phil Rambow's devilishly styled glam pub rock band, Roxy Music themselves must have quaked just a little.

An ingrained dislike of touring, however, scuppered any notions Eno might have had of hammering home his advantage. Though he was happy to work with sundry friends and old bandmates in the ad-hoc union that was 801, his record company's need for him to hit the road in earnest required more than a simple "no" in response.

Brian Eno

So, Eno and the Winkies played a few bars, recorded a stunning John Peel session . . . and five days into their headlining British tour, the singer was rushed into hospital when his right lung collapsed.

"It was the only project I've been involved in during the last few years that I would say was abortive," Eno reflected from his hospital bed. "But I decided that I didn't want to be a star — the kind of figure Bryan [Ferry] became. I knew that becoming that would only inhibit what I really wanted to do, because my ideas are so diverse and frequently apparently unrelated that I need a low profile position from which to produce them."

Over the past 25 years, he has lived up to that manifesto with staggering gusto.

Brian Eno Discography:
UK Original Singles
- *Seven Deadly Sins / Later On* (Island WIP 6178, 1974)
- *Backwater / On Some Faraway Beach* (Island ENODJ 1, 1974)
- *The Lion Sleeps Tonight / I'll Come Running* (Island WIP 6233, 1974)

UK Original Albums
- HERE COME THE WARM JETS (Island ILPS 9268, 1974)
- JUNE 1 1974 (Island ILPS 9291, 1974)
- TAKING TIGER MOUNTAIN BY STRATEGY (Island ILPS 9309, 1975)
- 801 LIVE (Island ILPS 9444, 1976)

US Original Albums
- HERE COME THE WARM JETS (Island ILPS 9268, 1974)
- TAKING TIGER MOUNTAIN BY STRATEGY (Island 13001, 1975)
- LIVE (Polydor 6178 801, 1976)

US Important Archive Albums
- RARITIES (EG ENOX 1, 1983)
- DALI'S CAR (live / BBC.) (Griffin, 1994)

☆ **26** ☆
Mick Ronson

— SLAUGHTER ON 10TH AVE —

His first Glam album, SLAUGHTER ON 10TH AVE,
entered the UK chart on March 16, 1974.

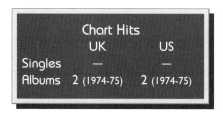

	Chart Hits	
	UK	US
Singles	—	—
Albums	2 (1974-75)	2 (1974-75)

Mick Ronson, of course, was best known as David Bowie's lead guitarist throughout his years of greatest influence, the figurehead for a thriving fan club (as were Bowie's wife Angie, and son Zowie), but a musical icon as well. And following Bowie's on-stage retirement in July 1973, Ronson told writer Michael Benton, "I can tell you, Mick Ronson will continue. He may even go out on the road as Mick Ronson one day, and a solo album is pretty likely." And no sooner were Bowie's PIN-UPS sessions complete than Ronson, and the rest of the band — bassist Trevor Bolder, drummer Aynsley Dunbar and pianist Mike Garson — were sequestered in Trident Studios recording that solo set.

"And David was furious," Wayne County claims. "Although he helped Mick on that album (he wrote one song, co-wrote another and supplied an English lyric to a third), he didn't want Mick to do the solo thing. He was really frightened that Mick on the road, Mick with a record out, would detract from him. But of course he couldn't do anything about it because Tony DeFries had made up his mind that this was what Mick should be doing."

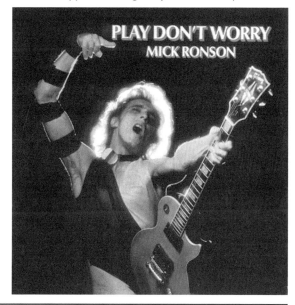

Sketched out with former SRC mainstay Scott Richardson who co-wrote both *Only After Dark* and *Pleasure Man*, (songs originally intended for a joint Ronno / Richardson project, Fallen Angels), SLAUGHTER ON 10TH AVENUE, Ronson's first solo set, was released on March 1, 1974, a solidly excellent set which was nevertheless greeted with a decidedly luke-warm response. A tour embarked upon at the same time went down even worse. Thirteen shows were arranged — an omen in itself! — with the opening night coming almost suicidally at the Finsbury Park Rainbow, a baptism of fire and a veritable lion's den as the nation's press poured out to cast their eye over the man already being touted as a surrogate Bowie.

The build-up to the show began in the foyer. Blow-ups of Ronson's photograph, posters and album sleeves littered the area. Specially recruited flunkies handed out fan club membership forms, photos and an address to which members of the audience could send their own carefully considered opinion of the show in 200 words or less.

It was, in a way, a microcosmic recreation of the stunts used to publicize Bowie during his early days. The slick way in which the audience was led to believe they were part of the family, encouraged to participate in the carnival and generally assist Mainman in launching Ronson as . . . once again, the term Surrogate Bowie raised its head. David wasn't touring, so his guitarist was instead. Ten years before, it would have been his car that pulled in the punters.

Bowie was actually in the audience that first night, scant consolation for Ronson, who looked decidedly unhappy as first, the stalls continually erupted with calls for the singer, then when the evening's biggest response was reserved for *Moonage Daydream*. In fact, according to Bowie's personal assistant of the time, Sue Fussey (the future Mrs. Mick Ronson), The Artist Formerly Known As Ziggy would have been quite willing to make an appearance. He had been sick of touring, she says, but within a week of retiring, he was sick of not touring. Only the fiercest exhortation prevented Bowie from running out on stage, exhortations born of DeFries' knowledge that if Ronson was to cut it as a solo artist, he would have to do it unaided.

Mick Ronson

What went wrong with the show and, to a lesser degree, the album, was Ronson's inexperience. He was being launched as a superstar, with only three years' service as a superstars' lieutenant for credentials. Few doubted his technical skills, and few doubted he could cut it as a producer / arranger. He was, unquestionably, the finest British guitarist to emerge since the halcyon days of Beck and Clapton. But a few backing vocals aside, it wasn't until the Rainbow show that most people had even heard him sing!

Charles Shaar Murray of the New Musical Express, summed it all up best. Ronson, he decreed was "an exceptionally gifted man. His album proves [that] he has a coherent and convincing musical identity of his own, and his live work with Bowie demonstrated that he is an exciting and original guitarist as well. But . . . he can not hope for super stardom by divine right, which is what all Mainman's hype and flummery were trying to set him up for."

The album was a success, however, making the UK Top 10, and by late 1974, Ronson was putting the finishing touches to his second album, PLAY DON'T WORRY. Drawing from sessions as far back as Bowie's PIN-UPS album (a storming version of the Velvets' *White Light White Heat*, with Ronson's vocals replacing Bowie's own), and covering songs from a Pure Prairie League album that Ronson had arranged the year before that (*Angel No. 9* and *Woman*), PLAY DON'T WORRY was a considerably more assured, and mature album than its predecessor. Ronson, however, was uncomfortable, both with the record and with the prospect of returning to the road to promote it. His recruitment into Mott The Hoople as replacement for Ariel Bender, then, was a Godsend — at least for a few days.

"It seemed real good for about a week . . . no, I'm kidding, ten days," Ronson told Circus magazine. "It all seemed like everybody was enthusiastic, but after a few days it was a drag really. People would lay in bed or not bother to turn up and nobody would speak to each other. They were together for a long time and then, when they got a little bit of money, they didn't want to pour any of it back into the band. What they wanted at that stage was everything out of the business, but nothing in the business. They didn't want to gamble — to them it was a steady job."

This final incarnation of Mott The Hoople lasted one single, the elegiac *Saturday Gigs*, before Ronson and Hunter split shortly before Christmas 1974. By the time PLAY DON'T WORRY was released in the spring, they had already pieced together a new band, Hunter-Ronson.

Mick Ronson Glam Years Discography:
UK Original Singles
  ○ *Love Me Tender / Only After Dark* (RCA 0212, 1974)
  ○ *Slaughter On 10th Avenue / Leave My Heart Alone* (RCA 5022, 1974)
  ○ *Billy Porter / Seven Days* (RCA 2482, 1975)

UK Original Flexidisc
  ○ *Slaughter On 10th Avenue* (RCA 11474XST, 1974)

UK Original Albums
  ◦ SLAUGHTER ON 10TH AVENUE (RCA 0353, 1974)
  ◦ PLAY DON'T WORRY (RCA 0681, 1975)

US Original Albums
  ◦ SLAUGHTER ON 10TH AVENUE (RCA 0353, 1974)
  ◦ PLAY DON'T WORRY (RCA 0681, 1975)

UK/US Important Archive Albums
  ◦ SLAUGHTER ON 10TH AVENUE (Snapper SMMCD 503, 1998)
  ◦ PLAY DON'T WORRY (Snapper SMMCD 504, 1998)
    Note: Both include copious bonus live / out-take material

☆ 27 ☆
The Glitter Band

– Angel Face –

Their first Glam hit, *Angel Face*, entered the UK chart on March 23, 1974.

Chart Hits		
	UK	US
Singles	7 (1974-76)	—
Albums	3 (1974-76)	—

Back in the wake of *Rock'n'Roll*'s initial breakthrough, with a concert tour looming and success still fresh, Gary Glitter and producer Mike Leander began piecing together a backing band, the Glittermen. It was an old idea in new sparkling trousers. Back in the mid-1960's, the pair had hatched a similarly show band-esque combo, dominated by the unique inclusion of a two drum / two sax core.

Adapting that approach to the new sound, and with Mike Leander Show Band baritone saxophonist John Rossall established as the leader, the newly named Glitter Band swiftly gathered almost as devoted a following as Gary himself. It was inevitable, then, that by late 1973, Leander was launching the Band on its own parallel career, and that despite the fact that they never actually played on any of Gary's records!

"Mike Leander played all the instruments on the records," Gary revealed two decades later. "Sometimes I'd help out a bit, and between us, we did it all. They were like garage records. Occasionally, they would overdub a few things, but generally it was easier for Mike and I to get on with it, because we were writing it as we were doing it."

Angel Face, The Glitter Band's first single, was cut straight from the Glitter mold, regimental pounding drums, meaty fists waving in the air, choruses of "Hey!," and a tentative lyric as pure as any of the boss man's. *Just For You* and *Let's Get Together Again* followed, in style and success. But no less than the Leader, The Glitter Band was agonizingly alert to the limitations of this approach. Early in 1974, while Gary turned everything down with the dirge-like *Remember Me This Way*, the Band made its own concessions to musical maturity and scored its biggest hit yet with *Goodbye My Love*, a soft-rock lullaby for everyone who has ever lost a loved one at the airport.

For a group that most people had written off as a bunch of hack session workers, it was a surprisingly powerful vision, and while the same standard was not to be adhered to over subsequent releases, still the band prospered. All but one of their seven successive UK chart entries (1975's *Love In The Sun*) made the Top 10. And maybe that was the problem. Suddenly sensing musical credibility, the band abandoned working with Gary, and in 1976, changed their name to the G Band.

Of course it was a daft idea, a hopelessly misguided attempt to break away from their past, and a pomposity which would backfire with a vengeance. They kept the "G," but the kids still wanted the "Litter." And when they covered the Stones' *Sympathy For The Devil*, they probably thought they were being radical. Everyone else called them silly.

Glitter Band Glam Years Discography:
UK Original Singles
- *Angel Face / You Wouldn't Leave Me* (Bell 1348, 1974)
- *Just For You / I'm Celebrating* (Bell 1368 n / r, 1974)
- *Let's Get Together Again / Jukebox Queen* (Bell 1383, 1974)
- *Goodbye My Love / Got To Get Ready* (Bell 1395 (-), 1975)
- *The Tears I Cried / Until Tomorrow* (Bell 1416 n / r, 1975)
- *Love In The Sun / I Can Hear Music* (Bell 1437, 1975)
- *Alone Again / Watch The Show* (Bell 1462, 1975)
- *People Like You, . . . Like Me / Makes You Blind* (Bell 1471, 1976)
- *Don't Make Promises / If You Go Away* (Bell 1481, 1976)

US Original Single
- *Goodbye My Love / Got To Get Ready* (Bell 107, 1975)

UK Original Albums
- ○ HEY! (Bell 241, 1974)
- ○ ROCK'N'ROLL DUDES (, 1975Bell 253 n / r)
- ○ LISTEN TO THE BAND (Bell 259, 1976)
- ○ GREATEST HITS (Bell 264, 1976)

UK Important Archive Album
- ○ HITS COLLECTION (Biff GRAB 1, 1990)
  Note: HITS COLLECTION includes both original and alternate takes of several tracks, plus previously unreleased *Everybody Needs Somebody To Love.*

US Original Album
- ○ MAKES YOU BLIND (Bell 207, 1976)

☆ 28 ☆
KISS

– KISS –

Their first Glam album, KISS, entered the US on chart April 20, 1974.

Chart Hits
	UK	US
Singles	10+ (1979 --)	25+ (1974 --)
Albums	15+ (1976 --)	20+ (1974 --)

Alice Cooper's comic rock horror show aside, glam rock meant little in the United States. Primal sleaze balls the New York Dolls scarcely escaped from New York, while Flash Cadillac And The Continentals were more concerned with reviving mom and dad's memories of their own Senior Proms, going so far as to excise any reference to glittered jackets from their cover of Barry Blue's *Dancing On A Saturday Night*, and replace it with faded denim.

Brownsville Station made a gallant, but fairly ponderous, stab at Gary Glitter's *Leader Of The Gang*, and lifted some neat wardrobe tips from The Sweet for a short time. And while Grand Funk's mogadon plod through Little Eva's *Locomotion* itself owed more to Gary than it did to being an American band, and Black Oak Arkansas' *Jim Dandy To The Rescue* worked until you actually saw a picture of Dandy himself, the majority of the action was confined to the handful of Anglophiliac strongholds scattered up and down the east and west coasts.

Joan Jett talks nostalgically of Rodney Bingenheimer's glam rock discos in LA, where she grew up on a diet of Glitter, Bolan, Bowie and Slade. Joey Ramone was almost beaten up when he tried to buy the first Gary Glitter album from a tough neighborhood record store; and Iggy Pop had a great pair of shiny silver trousers. But aside from that . . .

The reason for the music's Stateside failure was simple. Americans hate having fun. At least, that's what the Brits would say, when they came home from another desultory tour, although maybe it wasn't as simple as that.

Glam rock was a singles oriented phenomenon, revolving around one classy song, one classy line, one classy lick. Just as the American bubblegum scene was born out of the songwriter's struggle to sound sharper, snappier, than the competition (and with the Beatles out of the way, the competition was never that awesome), so in Britain the

KISS

Government-appointed BBC Radio One and the imported Radio Luxembourg became a battleground in which the first 30 seconds of a song were all that mattered, and a handful of hook lines worth more than the most profound of philosophies.

Of course the bands made albums — Slade and T. Rex even made good ones — but still they revolved around a handful of singles. They'd never have cut it on American FM, and with AM having followed up the universal appeal of the Osmonds and Cassidy by venturing even further into the realms of adult-oriented soft rock, there was no room at that inn either.

But people did still like dressing up, and did still want their idols to put on a show for them. And while the British side of things was just too weird looking (and faggy) for middle-American tastes, the only real answer was to go back to the comic books and see what developed there. Which is where KISS entered the equation.

Perhaps the story that best sums up KISS was related by producer Bob Ezrin. He'd already worked with Alice, so he knew what it was all about. And when he first saw KISS, he knew what they were all about as well. But one day, his curiosity was aroused during a conversation with a high school kid. "KISS? Oh man, they're great. The kids at school love them. The only problem is, their records are so shitty. But we buy them anyway, simply cos they look good."

That was KISS' secret. Musically they were little more than another stultifying heavy metal band singing about sex, sex and partying all night. Nothing special there. But visually they were the tops . . . they were Over The Tops.

No-one knew what they really looked like, they never appeared in public in anything less than full performance drag — disfiguring face paint, heels, padding, the lot. The guitarist fired sky rockets from his guitar, the bassist breathed fire, the drummer levitated. In

copyright 1982 Phil Anderson / KAOS2000 Magazine

between times, flash bombs like atom bombs would detonate across the stage, and the dry ice would choke the first fifteen rows. Manager Bill Aucoin claimed it cost $10,000 a week simply to keep the band on the road. But they sold a million with every record, and there was barely a critic in the country who would even stay in the same room as them.

The KISS operation was marketed on three fronts. While Aucoin hyped the media and KISS hyped the kids, backstage sat Neil Bogart, the crown prince of bubblegum and president of KISS' record company, Casablanca. As his track record suggests, he'd never been that keen on heavy metal.

But KISS, he said, was different. "I am dedicated to them," he said once. "They are everything I've ever looked for in a rock band." He paid $15,000 for KISS' signatures. By the end of the first year he and Aucoin had sunk over a quarter of a million bucks into them. "We put in everything we had. We undertook what was to become one of the most exciting promotions of my career. We believed in KISS, so we crossed our fingers and hoped that the money would hold out. At the time, KISS were Casablanca. We were trying to establish the label at the same time as trying to establish the group."

"The whole concept of KISS is unlikely," singer Gene Simmons said later. "The fact that we started in 1972 when the glam-glitter rock scene was dead [sic] was crazy. So was the fact that we wanted to grow our hair at a time when everybody else wanted to look like Patti Smith. Everybody became 'hey, we're just like you.' We didn't want to be just like you ..."

KISS Glam Years Discography:
UK Original Singles
- *Nothin' To Lose* / *Love Theme From Kiss* (Casablanca 503, 1974)
- *Rock And Roll All Night* / *Getaway* (Casablanca 510, 1975)
- *Shout It Out Loud* / *Sweet Pain* (Casablanca 516, 1976)
- *Beth* / *Detroit Rock City* (Casablanca 519, 1976)

US Original Singles
- *Nothin' To Lose* / *Love Theme From Kiss* (Casablanca 0004, 1974)
- *Kissing Time* / *Nothin' To Lose* (Casablanca 0011, 1974)
- *Strutter* / *100,000 Years* (Casablanca 0015, 1974)
- *Hotter Than Hell* / *Let Me Go Rock'n'Roll* (Casablanca 823, 1975)
- *Rock And Roll All Night* / *Getaway* (Casablanca 829, 1975)
- *Rock And Roll All Night* (live) / *Rock'n'Roll* (Casablanca 850, 1975)
- *C'mon And Love Me* / *Getaway* (Casablanca 841, 1975)
- *Shout It Out Loud* / *Sweet Pain* (Casablanca 854, 1976)
- *Flaming Youth* / *God of Thunder* (Casablanca 858, 1976)
- *Beth* / *Detroit Rock City* (Casablanca 863, 1976)

UK Original Albums
- KISS (Casablanca 4003, 1974)
- DRESSED TO KILL (Casablanca 4004, 1975)
- HOTTER THAN HELL (Casablanca 7007, 1977)

- ° ALIVE (Casablanca 2008, 1977)
- ° DESTROYER (Casablanca 2009, 1977)

US Original Albums
- ° KISS (Casablanca 7001, 1974)
- ° HOTTER THAN HELL (Casablanca 7006, 1974)
- ° DRESSED TO KILL (Casablanca 7016, 1975)
- ° ALIVE (Casablanca 7020, 1975)
- ° DESTROYER (Casablanca 7025, 1976)

☆ 29 ☆
Sparks

— This Town Ain't Big Enough —

Their first Glam hit, *This Town Ain't Big Enough*,
entered the UK chart on May 4, 1974.

Chart Hits		
	UK	US
Singles	13 (1974-96)	2 (1982-83)
Albums	4 (1974-79)	6 (1974-83)

The original, glam era, Roxy Music enjoyed a remarkable batting average. They released six singles, all six were hits. They released five albums, all five, too, were hits. Ferry launched a simultaneous solo career, that also did well. When Eno left, he also went solo, and while he had no hits, there are few souls in Britain who don't have one or the other of his earliest, pre-ambience, albums.

It was the heyday, too, of Island Records. Scarcely looking at the glitter rock market, once past the big leaguers, they dominated it regardless. For Roxy was only one string on their bow. The second was Sparks.

Sparks were two brothers from California. Russell Mael was the youngest, boyishly good-looking, all cuteness, curls and ethereal falsetto. Ron was older, an undernourished Charlie Chaplin, slicked back hair and gonky eyes. They had a British hit with *This Town Ain't Big Enough For Both Of Us* and their greatest ambition was to become as big as General Motors. They had another hit with *Amateur Hour*, and by God, they nearly were as big as General Motors.

Something For The Girl With Everything, Never Turn Your Back On Mother Earth, Get In The Swing and *Looks Looks Looks* followed — outside of the Bolan / Glitter / Chinnichap triumvirate they were probably the best singles band of the era, maybe even better because their albums were good as well.

And yet all the while, there was something strange about them. Like 10cc, Rod and the Faces, the *Only Rock'n'Roll* era Stones, Leo Sayer, Cozy Powell . . . they fit into glam rock primarily because they were around at the time. In another lifetime, a few years back or forth, they would have looked and sounded exactly the same, but one wonders, would they have made it? At a time when motive was as important as music, Sparks had a superficial appeal that meshed perfectly with the period. It's also worth noting that, like Roxy and the Dolls, Bob Harris insulted them on screen.

Forming their first band, Halfnelson, in 1969, the Maels released two albums on Bearsville, an eponymous debut (confusingly reissued, equally eponymously, when the band changed its name to Sparks) and the monochromatic A WOOFER IN TWEETER'S CLOTHING. Neither sold (although a single from HALFNELSON, *Wonder Girl*, was a hit in Alabama), and when a spring 1973 tour of America opening for Todd Rundgren fell through, Sparks were left much to their own devices.

While management and label continued to express faith in Sparks' quirky visions, it was fast becoming obvious that neither really knew what to do with them. For manager Roy Silver, the group was simply another curio to add to an already bizarre stable of acts (Fanny, Tiny Tim and Bill Cosby numbered among his other clients.) For Bearsville, there simply wasn't enough money in the company coffers to truly do Sparks justice.

Finally, the Maels decided to make their own move. According to their own legend, they were penniless, living on food stamps and had even been banned, for some long-forgotten transgression, from the one LA venue which had been booking them at all regularly, the Whisky. Meanwhile, their parents had just moved to London, so, breaking up the existing band, the brothers called one of Silver's British business friends, former John's Children bassist John Hewlett, to ask if he would be interested in taking over their affairs. He was, and on production of a legal document

ending the band's relations with both Silver and Bearsville, Hewlett approached Island records for the necessary moneys to fly the Maels alone over to England.

Island offered 500 pounds, and with the brothers safely entrenched on English soil, "young, good-looking and out-of-work" musicians were beseeched from the classified pages of Melody Maker to make themselves known.

One such young, good-looking and out of work musician was bass player Martin Gordon. "Actually, I wasn't out of work," he admits. "I was currently employed as a technical author, writing manuals about how to stop oil tankers from blowing up." It was busy work as well, which meant he hadn't had a haircut in months at the time of the audition. And Ron and Russell, who are nothing if not punctilious, were not impressed.

"For eight weeks I was back with my manuals and Melody Makers, until one day they just called me up out of the blue and asked me to go along again, by which time I'd had my hair cut and was able to make a far better impression."

Accepted into the band, Gordon was promptly placed in charge of the auditions from which the final two band members were drawn, drummer Norman "Dinky" Diamond, who had previously been playing on the German cabaret circuit, and guitarist Adrian Fisher, formerly with Gary Moore's Skid Row, and ex-Free bassist Andy Fraser's Toby. Before that, he'd been a tea boy at Robert Stigwood's RSO.

A technical author, a cabaret drummer and a tea boy. It was hardly the "unknown band" which the Maels maintained they discovered at a party thrown by their biggest fans, the Kennedy family, but the brothers, with their astute knowledge of the power of the media, were more than aware that a good story could sell as many records as a good song. It was also a lot more glamorous than the truth, and in England, as 1973 slipped into 1974, glamour still held a lot of appeal for the kids.

Compared with its predecessors, 1974 was swiftly shaping up to be a year of almost startling mediocrity. Along with the handful of worthwhile breakthroughs, there was a bucket load of thoroughly dispensable ones. The sudden rush of new faces, if not new talents, that had begun in the summer of '72, had quite painfully dried up. The Sweet were already embracing democracy, Marc Bolan's reign was over, Slade had softened their sound beyond recognition, Bowie was into disco, Gary Glitter was into ballads, and Mud thought they were Elvis Presley. Alongside them, the Wombles had emerged from the nursery to become the year's best selling singles artists, the Bay City Rollers were close behind them, and bringing up the rear were television soaps, the perennial Eurovision Song Contest and the long running Opportunity Knocks talent contest. It was left to a sudden national obsession with the Martial Arts to challenge the seemingly eternal chart residence of aged French balladeers, country and western singers, and *Y Viva Espana*.

"Without drawing overworked comparisons," announced Island's first Sparks press release, "We believe that Sparks, with their music and unique visual identity, will capture the imagination and affection of roughly the same audience sector which has made Roxy Music such an overwhelming success." With John Hewlett adding that the band was trying "to recapture the excitement of the Small Faces and the Who," two very different sets of expectations were carefully being nurtured — only to be shattered when the band's first single, *This Town*, was released and ended up sounding like nothing on earth.

Marvelously produced by Muff Winwood, and backed by an equally phenomenal non-album cut, *Barbecutie*, *This Town Ain't Big Enough* was poised for a chart entry within days of its first radio play. It entered at No. 48 in the first week of May. According to legend, Winwood himself was so enthused by the project that he bet Elton John that *This Town* would make the Top 5. Elton listened to the song and lay his money down — "no way will that be a hit!" He lost.

A video for the single, directed by Rosie Samwell-Smith (wife of ex-Yardbird Paul) was shot, but it wasn't needed. On May 9, 1974, Sparks appeared in person on TOP OF THE POPS. Seven days later, *This Town* had leaped 21 places, to No. 27. By the end of the month, Sparks were No. 2, held off the top spot by fellow chart debutantes the Rubettes.

Even today, 21 years later, *This Town* remains a remarkable record, quite unlike any of its (or maybe any other!) time. Siouxsie and the Banshees released their own version of the song on 1987's THROUGH THE LOOKING GLASS album, and Siouxsie reflects, "I found the contrast between the two brothers really appealing. I think it was really important to see them on television, they were one of the few bands you'd see, and say 'thank God there's something good on, in amongst all this idiocy.'

"In 1974, 1975, there weren't a lot of lulls in the tedium. There was Roxy, but Bowie was past it, Lou Reed was . . . losing it, so there was Sparks, *This Town Ain't Big Enough*, Ron with his mustache, and — thank goodness for them!"

"Our music is a weird combination of a gutsy backing and Russell's falsetto," Ron explained, while Russell elaborated, "the singing is dictated by the way the songs are written. When Ron writes, he happens to use the right hand a lot on keyboards, and he comes up with songs without any regard as to whether they can be sung like that."

Ron himself claimed the song developed out of an evening spent playing Bach etudes on his piano at home, but Russell continued, "he'll go from high notes to low notes without singing it himself, so he doesn't even know if a person can possibly sing like that. But it's quite interesting occasionally, to force yourself to sing like that, and not transpose it to a key that's easier. The result is, I sing whatever's there. Actually, my voice hasn't changed since I was 12. It hasn't broken yet, and I'm keeping my fingers crossed that it doesn't, otherwise we're going to be in for a lot of trouble."

Sparks' third album, KIMONO MY HOUSE, was released to almost unprecedented acclaim, and unprecedented confusion, two weeks after *This Town Ain't Big Enough*. The title was debated endlessly — what did it mean? School yards echoed with increasingly surreal (and often obscene) explanations, some so convincing that it was actually disappointing to learn, a decade later, that it was all quite innocuous. "It was just a pun," Russell explained. "Kimono my house, come on over to my house."

Ian MacDonald, in the New Musical Express, proclaimed the album an "instant classic," and few listeners disagreed. From the opening fade of *This Town Ain't Big Enough* to the closing sax and squawk driven *Equator*, a song which still boasts one of the greatest endings in recorded history, it was an astonishing record. By the end of May, KIMONO had joined *This Town Ain't Big Enough* in the UK Top 10. Yet, within days of that first TOP

OF THE POPS appearance, the whole thing had changed. Martin Gordon was fired, and promptly replaced by one half of John Hewlett's other clients, Jook guitarist Trevor White, and bassist Ian Hampton.

The new Sparks line-up debuted on TOP OF THE POPS on May 23, with the performance that pushed *This Town Ain't Big Enough* up to its peak of No. 2. And while the single slipped from the Top 20 with unprecedented haste, from No. 9 to nowhere in the space of a week, Island lost no time in following it up. Just two weeks after its predecessor left the chart, *Amateur Hour* entered the chart at No. 42. The following week, this beginners' guide to adolescent sex was No. 17. It ultimately crested at No. 7.

"The first gig we did," White remembers, "was in Cleethorpes, and it was just incredible, total pandemonium. I spent the entire gig in a daze, trying to relate to the fact that I was on stage with all these screaming kids out front, and thinking, 'two months ago, I was playing to total apathy with The Jook, at some Top Rank place. Now look at it.'"

Even as the tour wound on, talk turned to Sparks' next album, and according to White, the Maels had no intention whatsoever of trying to capitalize on KIMONO's success. "The way they looked at it was, the last album had been a success, but everyone had heard it, so now we had to do something completely different, that they won't have heard. They felt that they always had to be one step ahead of what people expected from them, so they would just veer off in a new direction whenever they felt like it."

And if they could drop a few bombshells while they were at it, all the better. "I remember when I joined," says White, "I thought it a bit strange that they should want two guitarists, especially as they already had one as good as Adrian Fisher. But I think it had been on their minds for a long time to get rid of him, they were just looking for the right moment." That moment came just as the new album, PROPAGANDA was completed. First the brothers erased all the guitarist's solos. Then they erased the guitarist.

The hits kept coming. PROPAGANDA reached the stores in November, to an instant chart placing. *Never Turn Your Back On Mother Earth* and the maniacal *Something For The Girl With Everything* kept them on the singles chart, and the band's second British tour, if anything, was even more successful than its predecessor. And the brothers were hatching their master plan.

White continues, "the places they seemed most at home were in places like Paris, trolling up and down the Champs d'Elysees, that was really where they were at. Or even in England, they were really into the English way of life. They used to get up in the morning, have a cup of tea, then look up an Egon Ronay restaurant to have lunch in. That whole upper-class, sophisticated decadence thing that they tried to put over on the records, that's what they were really like. That's what Sparks was all about" — and that's what their next album was all about.

In July 1975, a new single, *Get In The Swing*, previewed the new record with a riotous celebration of a cocktail set whose relentless pursuit of the ultimate Good Time had led them to reject all but the most materialistic of values. Producer Tony Visconti explained, "Russell and Ron are true avant-gardists. They are both ex-art students, like so many rock

stars, but they really are artists, and they wanted to make a completely left-field, bizarre, album. With all due respect to Muff Winwood, he's very straight ahead and down the line, 'let's double track this, put harmonies there, mix it and get it out.' He's very singles-oriented, and he helped immeasurably in the beginning. But they still had all these weird ideas in mind, and they were looking for someone like me to help them put them across."

"There were a lot of bizarre things on that album, and a lot of tangents from the mainline way of recording." Over a decade later, Visconti was still impressed by INDISCREET. "It's one of my favorite albums. Totally uncommercial, but so creative. We did everything under the sun and I learned a lot." And besides, "there was nothing on it that was remotely like *This Town Ain't Big Enough*." Which meant, that in the Maels' vision of the future, there was no need for the kind of musicians who could play that song.

Sparks toured Europe through the spring of 1975, then split. The Maels were returning to America to work, concentrating solely on that market, and using session men as and when required. In a widely quoted remark which today, he puts down to "a case of stomach flu or something," Ron informed the media, "we'd got sick of England. The weather was disgusting, the food was terrible and we got tired of the provincial atmosphere. What at first seemed quaint later got really annoying."

"Actually, the weather's still disgusting," he smiled, looking out of his hotel window almost two decades later. "But the food's got much better."

Home in Los Angeles, the Maels' first stop was Mick Ronson's house. They had already co-opted drummer Hilly Michaels and bassist Sal Maida, from Milk'N'Cookies, into a new Sparks' line-up. According to Russell, Michaels knew Ronson, and over the next few weeks, he and Ron were regular visitors to the guitarist's house. "We thought of Ronson as a producer," Ron says, "but then we recorded some demos with him and Hilly, and they were so good that we asked him to join Sparks." Ronson declined. "I would have liked to do it, but I was still involved with Ian [Hunter], and the Dylan thing (Ronson was a part of Rolling Thunder until April 1976). There just wasn't time." In his stead, the Maels recruited Jeffrey Salem.

Three songs were demoed with Mick Ronson, *I Wanna Be Like Everybody Else*, *Big Boy* and *Everybody's Stupid*, recorded on a tiny mono cassette recorder in one corner of the room. "And it must have been awful for Jeffrey," recalled Joseph Fleury, manager Hewlett's assistant. "Ron and Russell would play him the Ronson tape, and say 'play like that!'" Of course he couldn't, and though it would unfair to say that the resultant album (1976's BIG BEAT) suffers accordingly, it does lack something. A certain spark, perhaps.

The Sparks story continues to this very day, a tumultuous story which commenced with a period of disco success (as great as any they enjoyed during the early 1970's), was followed by the subjugation of the US on the crest of the early 1980's new wave, and which today sees them still selling prodigiously in mainland Europe. Recent years even brought a string of born-yet-again UK hits, while 1997's PLAGIARISM album stands among their finest works ever, a thorough updating of Sparks' biggest hits, and the Maels' own tribute to the band they love the most — themselves.

Sparks Glam Years Discography:
UK Original Singles
  ○ *This Town Ain't Big Enough / Barbecutie* (Island WIP 6193, 1974)
  ○ *Amateur Hour / Lost And Found* (Island WIP 6203, 1974)
  ○ *Never Turn Your Back / Alabamy Right* (Island WIP 6211, 1974)
  ○ *Something For The Girl / Marry Me* (Island WIP 6221, 1975)
  ○ *Get In The Swing / Profile* (Island WIP 6236, 1975)

○ *Looks Looks Looks* / *Marriage of Jacqueline Kennedy to Russell Mael* (withdrawn) (Island WIP 6249, 1975)
○ *Looks Looks Looks* / *Pineapple* (Island WIP 6249, 1975)
○ *I Want To Hold Your Hand* / *Under The Table With Her* (withdrawn) (Island WIP 6282, 1976)
○ *I Want To Hold Your Hand* / *England* (Island WIP 6282, 1976)
○ *Big Boy* / *Fill 'Er Up* (Island WIP 6337, 1976)
○ *I Like Girls* / *England* (Island WIP 6377, 1976)

US Original Singles
○ *This Town Ain't Big Enough* / *Barbecutie* (Island IS 001, 1974)
○ *Talent Is An Asset* / *Lost And Found* (Island IS 009, 1974)
○ *Achoo* / *Something For The Girl* (Island IS 023, 1974)
○ *Looks Looks Looks* / *Marriage of Jacqueline Kennedy to Russell Mael* (Island IS 043, 1975)
○ *I Want To Hold Your Hand* / *England* (Island 8282, 1976)

UK Original Albums
○ KIMONO MY HOUSE (Island ILPS 9272, 1974)
○ PROPAGANDA (Island ILPS 9312, 1974)
○ INDISCREET (Island ILPS 9345, 1975)

UK Important Archive Albums
○ THE BEST OF SPARKS (Island ILPS 9493, 1977)
○ MAEL INTUITION (Island IMCD 88, 1990)
○ IN THE SWING (Karussell 5500652, 1993)
○ HELL (Columbia 473516, 1993)

US Original Albums
○ KIMONO MY HOUSE (Island 9272, 1974)
○ PROPAGANDA (Island 9312, 1974)
○ INDISCREET (Island 9345, 1975)

US Important Archive Album
○ PROFILE: THE ULTIMATE SPARKS COLLECTION (Rhino 70731, 1991)

☆ **30** ☆
Cockney Rebel

– *Judy Teen* –

Their first Glam hit, *Judy Teen*, entered the UK chart on May 11, 1974.

Chart Hits		
	UK	US
Singles	11 (1974-95)	—
Albums	5 (1974-77)	—

Drawing up similar battle lines to Roxy Music, and at one point threatening to rival both Ferry and Eno in terms of chart and critical applause, was Steve Harley. A former journalist who certainly knew a thing or two about manipulating the news, he came on like a Rock And Roll Cassius Clay, insisting he was the greatest, and doing so with such conviction that before long, an awful lot of people were believing him.

His group was Cockney Rebel, a name which conjured up visions of a Pearly King jollity á la the Small Faces, Joe Brown, Tommy Steele, any artist who made a million from dropping his aitches (and even David Bowie had tried that from time to time.) But the songs which were to make up Cockney Rebel's first two albums, THE HUMAN MENAGERIE in 1973 and PSYCHOMODO in '74, painted a totally different picture.

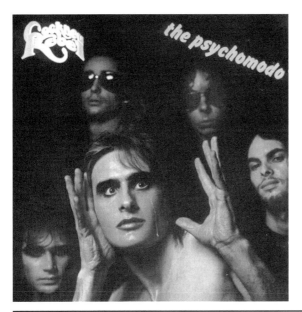

A media darling a full year before the band's sophomore single, *Judy Teen*, brought Cockney Rebel their commercial breakthrough in June 1974, neither Harley's appeal nor his success owed anything to what had gone down before. But the sight of his gaunt frame done up in grease paint and bowler hat, swaying on a cane and lamenting some long lost paradise of low-burning candles and children at war, was enough to force you to take a step beyond anything Bowie was to achieve once his own success had been masterminded.

Cockney Rebel

It mattered not that Harley's lyrics were, for the most part, random sketches thrown together in the hope that they might rhyme, nor that his greatest musical achievements were a wealth of meaninglessness. They worked because Harley worked, late at night, conjuring up images of smoke-filled passageways, flickering firelight and don't worry about that, it's only a shadow-dance on the tapestries. "Come to a strange place, we'll talk over old times, we never smile."

Songs like *Sebastian* — even on the cabaret comeback circuit, Harley's signature tune to this very day, *Death Trip, Sling It* and *Cavaliers* were a heaving, seething, maggoty mass, rock'n'rancor with a painted smile, a pretty tune and a nest of rattlesnakes at the bottom of the cookie jar. Echoing, as Record Collector magazine put it, the "glitzy chic of Roxy Music", and certainly drawing upon the same literary and cultural references as both Roxy and Bowie, Cockney Rebel epitomized the strain of glam which — were one to pursue it in terms of historical

chronology — ricochets smartly off Be Bop Deluxe, the Doctors Of Madness, London Suede . . . the cerebral side of sleaze, the doomed decadence which lurches between Christopher Isherwood's Berlin cabarets and the love scenes in Orwell's 1984.

It was a tense arrangement, and that tension which finally caused the band to implode, following a massively successful tour through the summer of 1974. By the time *Mr. Soft* gave the band its second hit single, it was no more — Harley went on TOP OF THE POPS to perform the song with only drummer Stuart Elliot surviving from the original line-up (Curved Air's Francis Monkman, and B.A. Robertson completed this impromptu band.) He subsequently formed a new Cockney Rebel, and plunged headlong into the pop fantasy which culminated in 1975's chart-topping *Make Me Smile (Come Up And See Me)*. Of the remainder of the band, violinist Jean Paul Croker moved into session work, while bassist Paul Jefferies and guitarist Milton Reames James were briefly members of Be Bop Deluxe, before forming their own band, Chartreuse, in 1976. Jefferies was killed in the Lockerbie air disaster in 1988.

Harley himself loathed the glam tag. The satin and tat that draped the band's line-up on the HUMAN MENAGERIE cover, he swore, lasted "for about five minutes. You never saw me or anyone in my band wearing platform shoes. You've got *Death Trip* and *Sebastian*, I've . . . sung *Sebastian* in Belgium with an 80 piece orchestra, a 200 piece choir, to 20,000 people. There's nothing glam about that. THE PSYCHOMODO was wild, there was nothing glammy about that at all."

He is, of course, utterly wrong.

Cockney Rebel Glam Years Discography:
UK Original Singles
- *Sebastian / Rock And Roll Parade* (EMI 2051, 1973)
- *Judy Teen / Spaced Out* (EMI 2128, 1974)
- *Mr. Soft / Such A Dream* (EMI 2191, 1974)
- *Bed In The Corner / Big Big Deal* (EMI 2233, 1974)

US Original Singles
- *Sebastian / Rock And Roll Parade* (EMI 3846, 1973)
- *Tumblin' Down / Singular Band* (EMI 4023, 1974)

UK Original Albums
- THE HUMAN MENAGERIE (EMI 759, 1973)
- THE PSYCHOMODO (EMI 3033, 1974)

UK Important Archive Album
- LIVE AT THE BBC (Windsong WINCD 073, 1995)

US Original Albums
- THE HUMAN MENAGERIE (EMI 11294, 1973)
- THE PSYCHOMODO (EMI 11330, 1974)

☆ 31 ☆
Showaddywaddy

— *Hey Rock'n'Roll* —

Their first Glam hit, *Hey Rock'n'Roll*, entered the UK chart on May 5, 1974.

Chart Hits		
	UK	US
Singles	23 (1974-82)	—
Albums	10 (1974-87)	—

Gary Glitter and The Glitter Band, Mud, the Rubettes, Alvin Stardust — glam rock was the music of the 1970's, but sometimes it was simply the sound of the 50's, updated with some spangles and maybe a few extra drum beats. Across early albums by each of them, the past was resurrected again and again for a generation that barely even knew the songs as oldies — in March 1974, Bill Haley's original *Rock Around The Clock* actually returned to the UK top 20, while David Essex's THAT'LL BE THE DAY movie only tugged the nostalgia strings even harder.

It was into this climate of unabashed reinvention that Showaddywaddy sashayed. An English Sha Na Na with none of the problems, the band formed in 1973 in Leicester, England, around the nuclei of two local groups, The Choice and the Hammers. Both regulars at the Fosse Way pub, jam sessions swiftly became the union of Baby Face Jagger-ish vocalist Dave Bartram, fellow singer Buddy Gask, guitarists Russ Field and Trevor Oakes, twin bassists Al James and Rod Deas, and twin drummers Malcolm Allured and former Black Widow percussionist Romeo Challenger.

Throughout this early period, the Hammers and the Choice continued gigging in their own right, often on the same bill and occasionally supporting Showaddywaddy! Eventually, however, Showaddywaddy took over completely and, after winning a local talent contest, the group entered and won television's NEW FACES show.

Signing to Bell records, and immediately earning a support slot on David Cassidy's latest British tour, Showaddywaddy launched itself with a string of original recordings — the Glitteresque *Hey Rock'n'Roll* and *Rock'n'Roll Lady*, and the seasonally slowed down *Hey Mr. Christmas* — but quickly turned its hit making attention to the material that went down the best in concert ... Cochran (*Three Steps to Heaven*), Holly (*Heartbeat*), and Cooke (*Chain Gang*.) "We do a lot of writing," Bartram acknowledged, "but there are so many great old songs from the 50's and 60's and we love bringing our own flavour to them — and that's what our audience have come to expect from us."

Decked out in full 50's drag — drape coats, quiffs, brothel creeper sneakers, the lot — Showaddywaddy made few overt claims to the glam crown. They wore it simply because it fit. Overtly visual, excessively photogenic, they started out playing Rock And Roll revival shows, and after fame hit, they simply kept on. It was just that the revival shows were getting bigger and bigger.

Produced, with devastating authenticity, by Mike Hurst, *Hey Rock'n'Roll* gave Showaddywaddy a gold disc straight out of the traps, and soared to No. 2. A year later, *Three Steps To Heaven* reached the same dizzy heights, and though the three singles released in the interim all stalled in the upper teens, it was clear from the outset that Showaddywaddy's success was in no way dependent upon current fads. That much was proven when *Under The Moon Of Love* (a song originally recorded by Mud, and foolishly passed over as a single) took Showaddywaddy to No. 1 before Christmas 1976.

Superstar dilettantes like Bowie and Elton John not withstanding, not one of Showaddywaddy's glam rocking contemporaries was still even hoping to have regular hits by then. In any event, Showaddywaddy continued racking up the smashes well into the early 1980's, even presiding over (and outliving) a whole new generation of rocking revivalists — Darts, Rocky Sharpe — and really only relinquishing their hold on the 50's market when the similarly pop-inclined Shaking Stevens came along in 1983.

Yet they remain a going concern. Five of the founding octet still gig constantly as Showaddywaddy, and were a headline attraction during the 1995 Isle Of Man TT motorcycle race, while the band remain in the sporting headlines with the English soccer success of guitarist Trevor Oakes' sons Stef and Scott. Of the remainder of the original line-up, Allured and Gask (plus a later band member, Ray Martinez) perform as the Teddys.

Showaddywaddy Glam Years Discography:
UK Original Singles
- *Hey Rock 'n' Roll* (Bell 1357, 1974)
- *Rock 'n' Roll Lady* (Bell 1374, 1974)
- *Hey Mr. Christmas* (Bell 1387, 1974)
- *Sweet Music* (Bell 1403, 1975)
- *Three Steps To Heaven* (Bell 1426, 1975)
- *Heartbeat* (Bell 1450, 1975)
- *Heavenly* (Bell 1460, 1975)
- *Trocadero* (Bell 1476, 1976)
- *Take Me In Your Arms* (Bell 1489, 1976)
- *Under The Moon of Love* (Bell 1495, 1976)

UK Original Albums
- SHOWADDYWADDY (Bell BELLS 248, 1974)
- STEP TWO (Bell BELLS 256, 1975)
- TROCADERO (Bell SYBEL 8003, 1976)

UK Important Archive Album
- GREATEST HITS (Arista ARTY 15, 1976)

☆ 32 ☆
Fancy

— *Wild Thing* —

Their first Glam hit, *Wild Thing*, entered the US chart on June 15, 1974.

Anyone who was anywhere near a radio through the summer of 1974 will doubtless remember it well. A lascivious bass line throbbing obtrusively through the ether, a scythed guitar hacking one of rock's most memorable riffs, a synthesizer line that sounded like Jello dripping from vertiginous heights, and over it all, a young lady in a seemingly serious state of sexual arousal moaning, "wild thing, I think you . . . move me?"

Oh, Donna Summer had nothing on Helen Court, and Helen Court, it swiftly transpired, simply had nothing on. A former Penthouse Pet, and therefore presumably well versed in the vicarious manipulation of juvenile male hormones, Ms. Court turned in what remains one of the most pointedly sexual vocal performances ever to transfix an American radio audience. No wonder her band was called Fancy.

Producer Mike Hurst explains, "one night back in [summer] 1973, I thought the time was right to do a new, rocked up version of the Troggs' classic *Wild Thing*. I knew a great many good musicians, but my favorite guitarist by far was Ray Fenwick . . ." who Hurst had, in fact, known since Fenwick replaced Steve Winwood in the Spencer Davis Group, some six years before. Since that time, Fenwick had become one of Britain's most in-demand session men (Jon Lord's GEMINI SUITE was one of his more adventurous efforts), and had even released his own solo album.

Hurst continues, "Ray immediately went for the idea of using a female vocal for *Wild Thing* . . . it made it sound more raunchy, especially when we found Helen . . . to sing, or perhaps I should say breathe, the words."

Fenwick introduced former Linda Hoyle's Affinity bassist Mo Foster to the proceedings, enticing him away from an equally rewarding sessions career which included work with the likes of Jimmy Helms, Joan Armatrading and Olivia Newton-John. Then, with Henry Spinetti adding drums and Alan Hawkshaw supplying keyboards, they got to work on *Wild Thing*. Needlessly, perhaps, Hurst reiterates the track's best remembered qualities:

"it was a dirty, low-down track, with all the heavy breathing and suggestive orgasmic guitar and bass work."

Hopes to have their creation storm the UK charts were dismissed when Hurst couldn't find a single label in the land willing to unleash this smorgasbord of squelchiness upon the innocent ears of the public. The American Big Tree label, however, was nowhere near as squeamish, and in June 1974, *Wild Thing* thrust a tentative toe into the Billboard Top 100.

It eventually peaked at No. 14 in America, and won the group an utterly unexpected gold disc. But its antics were only just beginning. In short order, *Wild Thing* crossed the Pacific to charm the Australian Top 20, charted across most of Europe, and became one of the biggest hits of the year in Holland and Belgium. It even, in the end, impacted in Britain in an odd sort of way, when the Goodies comedy trio released their own take on *Wild Thing*, taking Fancy's original sexiness to its ultimate conclusion. "Come on, hold me tight," breathes vocalist Bill Oddie. And then . . . "uuurrgggh, not THAT tight."

A spectacular success, then, and Fancy's thoughts turned towards a follow-up. The question was, what sort of follow-up? The initial idea was simply to get nasty with another much-beloved classic, but musicians of Fenwick and Foster's caliber really weren't cut out for a career in pop-porn, no matter how rewarding it might be. The solution, then, was to take Fancy out of the realms of the studio imagination, and into reality.

For a drummer, Fenwick looked no further than one of his own past collaborators. Les Binks had been on the verge of joining the Spencer Davis Group when it folded. Since that time, he had worked with Taste's Charlie McCracken in Headstone and won the admiration of no less than Billy Cobham. In September 1974, he was extracted from Alvin Stardust's band and transplanted into Fancy.

Securing a suitable vocalist was harder. Helen Court wasn't interested in continuing, and may in any case have proven a little more limited, vocally, than what her bandmates were now looking for. Nevertheless, legend insists that the trio auditioned some 200 singers in their search for a replacement, including Carole Grimes and Curved Air's Sonja Kristina. They settled, however, on Annie Kavanagh, a Londoner who had spent 10 of her 23 years living in Australia. It was there that she had joined the local cast of the rock musical HAIR, for tours of Australia and New Zealand, following which she was invited to Britain to join the show's London chorus. In summer 1972, she moved across to the newly opened JESUS CHRIST SUPERSTAR, and around the same time, she did some vocal sessions with Steely Dan.

Kavanagh joined Fancy in October, just in time to accompany them into the studio to record a new single. And that fall of 1974, the reconstituted Fancy returned to the US Top 20 with the utterly dissimilar, but really rather good, *Touch Me*. They toured the country as well, making their first ever live appearance at a theological college in Grand Rapids, Michigan on November 8, then marching on for another month, to land some extraordinarily encouraging reviews.

Far from regaling the kids with a battery of novelties, which of course is what most grizzled rock journalists expected, Fancy emerged as a fine, funky rock band, as adept at getting down'n'dirty with *Wild Thing*, as in revising Elvis' *One Night* as a slow blues stomper. Kavanagh in particular was a revelation, an amazingly powerful vocalist, looking good, moving well . . . if any band deserved to just keep on rising, it was Fancy.

The band's debut album, WILD THING, followed early in the new year. The two hit singles (and *Wild Thing*'s original B-side, the Pretenders-esque *Fancy*) notwithstanding, it was a solid slice of blues rock, with Kavanagh effortlessly proving why she got the nod over even her better known fellows at the auditions. Indeed, WILD THING was as deserving as most every other hit album of the new year, the difference being, it did not come even close to actually being a hit.

Undeterred, Fancy continued gigging, hitting the Far East and Europe before they returned to England and started work on a new album, the hopefully titled SOMETHING TO REMEMBER. Signing to the fledgling Arista label (RCA in America), Fancy turned in another remarkable record, highlighted by dynamic remakes of Stevie Wonder's *I Was Made To Love Him* and Mose Allison's *Everybody's Crying Mercy*, and leading off with what amounted to Kavanagh's own autobiography, the persuasively funky *She's Riding The Rock Machine*.

Within days of their London showcase at Ronnie Scotts, Fancy headed out for their first full tour, opening for 10cc — themselves promoting their newly released THE ORIGINAL SOUNDTRACK album. It was, appearances aside, a fairly compatible billing — just like the headliners, Fancy were no slouches when it came to making the studio work for them. And just like the headliners, they also adhered to that most revered of all great rock clichés — when in doubt, BOOGIE. And Fancy sure could boogie.

Opening at Leeds University on March 5, the tour crisscrossed Britain for the rest of the month, reaching London on March 21, and Fancy swiftly proved themselves capable of standing in the same room as 10cc — who were, of course, the only reason most people were there. Despite taking out fair-sized ads in the UK music press, Arista had singularly failed to get behind *She's Riding The Rock Machine*, while the music press seemed equally unimpressed.

SOMETHING TO REMEMBER was canned as "pretty thin gruel" in Melody Maker, while the only decent review the single landed was for its B-side, a reprise of the A-side minus

Annie Kavanagh. "Doubtless lovely and talented, I have nothing against her at all," the review explained. "It's just that the band are so good that she gets in the way of my enjoyment."

A second single, *I Was Made To Love Him / Tour Song*, followed *Rock Machine* into the basement, and when a third, Ray Fenwick and Mike Hurst's *Music Maker* duet, rocketed off in the same ignoble direction, Fancy's attention turned towards the land where they had already made it . . . or had they? In fact, things were turning out even worse in America than they had been in Britain. For reasons which were doubtless clear to anybody touched by *Wild Thing*, RCA retitled the album FANCY TURNS YOU ON, then sent it out to fend for itself, an invitation to funk despatched to an audience which was apparently expecting something a little less carefully spelled.

Fancy split in the summer of 1975. Kavanagh remained in Britain for a while, turning in spirited performances on albums by Ray Russell and Neil Innes, before finally returning to Australia. Fenwick and Foster went back to session work, and Binks eventually turned up in Judas Priest. It was a sad end to what should have been a satisfying saga — even *Wild Thing*, throbbing little beast that it was, had considerably more musical merit than most "novelty" records are usually saddled with, while Fancy's two albums still sound remarkably fresh today — a little mid-70's funk heavy, naturally, but considerably brighter, braver and less self-conscious than many better feted bands of a similar ilk.

Fancy Discography:
UK Original Singles
  ○ *Wild Thing / Fancy* (Atlantic, 1974)
  ○ *Riding The Rock Machine parts 1/2* (Arista 3, 1975)
  ○ *I Was Made To Love Him / Tour Song* (Arista, 1975)
  ○ *Music Maker / ?* (Arista, 1975)

US Original Singles
  ○ *Wild Thing / Fancy* (Big Tree 15004, 1974)
  ○ *Touch Me / I Don't Need Your Love* (Big Tree 16026, 1974)

UK Original Albums
  ○ WILD THING (Atlantic K51502, 1974)
  ○ SOMETHING TO REMEMBER (Arista 102, 1975)

US Original Album
  ○ WILD THING (Big Tree 89502, 1974)
  ○ TURNS YOU ON (RCA 1482, 1975)

☆ 33 ☆
Pandora

− Pandora −

Their first Glam recording, flexidisc *Pandora*, was released in July 1974.

Talk about obscure — Pandora are so unknown that even their record company didn't know they existed until 20 years after they broke up. No-one seems to know who they were . . . exactly where they came from . . . where they are now . . . their very names and credits are lost in the mists of time. But the seven track flexidisc that they recorded in a Cleveland warehouse under the supervision of Granicus drummer Joe Battaglia in 1974, which went unheard for almost 20 years (then resurfaced in a desk drawer in the mid-1990's) stands today as the pre-eminent slice of American glam rock, the kind of record which — if it had only been heard at the time — could have wiped the smirk off a lot of foreign faces. The Brits still believe they had the glam market sewn up, and faced with the likes of KISS and the Dolls, they probably did. But then Pandora come screaming out of the speakers, and all bets are off. Forever.

The easiest point of reference for Pandora was the New York Dolls, at least in terms of the trash aesthetic. But they were deeper than that, and darker. If the Spiders From Mars had been invaded by Badger, then forced to play extemporized Silverhead jams, if the Alice Cooper Band found a singer who sounded like Roger Wootton of Comus, if Jobriath had joined Led Zeppelin instead of Robert Plant, and if *Whole Lotta Love* had been written by Marc Bolan — Pandora played glam rock, but it was glam with a decidedly demented bend in the middle, a harbinger of all that would be

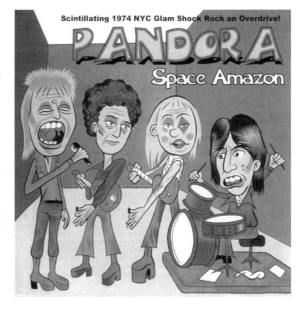

perpetrated in that name during the mid-late 1980's, but so utterly a child of its own time that the comparison itself falls down flat.

Which in turn simply lends literally oodles of mystique to what became Pandora's deeply posthumous debut album. Passions inflamed by the rediscovery of the flexidisc, the producer then unearthed the full Pandora session, a ten track collection which was finally released in 1997. Comprising all seven of the tracks on that original flexidisc, plus three more (*Crack Your Skull, Don't Put Me,* and *Daze Of Madness*), SPACE AMAZON was in turns, freaky, frenzied and frantically fey, and it withstood the test of obscurity better than pretty much any other album of its ilk. And whether or not anyone ever find out who Pandora were … well, sometimes the image just speaks for itself. Which is what KISS was banking on all along.

Pandora Discography:
US Original Flexidisc
  ○ *Pandora* (Eva-Tone [no catalog No.], 1974)

US Important Archive Single
  ○ *Space Amazon* (Arf Arf AA 064, 1997)

☆ 34 ☆
Brett Smiley

— *Va Va Va Voom* —

His first Glam recording, *Va Va Va Voom,* was released in October 1974.

He was, to put it bluntly, beautiful. Pouting, blonde, and so pretty in pink, 19 year-old Brett Smiley exploded out of British TV one evening in fall 1974, and if the country had not already been deeply in love with glam rock, he would have started it off right there and then.

At a time when David Bowie was still most people's vision of androgynous perfection, Smiley made Ziggy look like a bricklayer — and a particularly coarsely, unshaven one at that. Later, something called Lief Garrett would hijack much the same look and make way too much money, but Smiley did it first, and Smiley did it best. Besides, he could write his own songs and sing them well, too.

Everything about Brett Smiley screamed "pay attention!" — including the fact that Brett Smiley really is his name. Radio Luxembourg took a shine to the effervescent *Va Va Va Voom*, Smiley's breathtaking first single, and played it half to death. The English weekly rock paper Disc splashed Smiley across its October 12, 1974 front cover in vivid, living color (headline: "BEAUTIFUL BRETT".) And he made his UK television debut on the top-rated weekend interview program, RUSSELL HARTY PLUS, a pink gabardine suited vision breathily lisping through the B-side *Space Ace*, and scarcely flinching when the tape operator played the wrong backing track.

What really caught the eye, though, was the expression of absolutely exquisite detachment with which Smiley regarded the entire proceedings. Asked a question he

didn't fancy answering, he'd take his sunglasses off. Asked another one, he'd put them back on.

Later, Smiley would admit that he was out of his head on sleeping pills and tranquilizers, but it was languor, not lethargy, that shone through his performance. That, and an almost Noel Cowardesque air of decadence which, for even the most casual viewer, made the act of watching television almost painfully raw and personal, like gate crashing the inaugural meeting of Narcissists And Social Butterflies Anonymous, just as they realize that anonymity is the last thing they crave. Russell Harty thought he was interviewing just another would-be pop star. In fact, he was greeting a Greek God.

Smiley had been in London less than a week when the call came through to appear on RUSSELL HARTY PLUS, and it didn't phase him in the slightest. Why should it? He was 19

Brett Smiley

and gorgeous, he was an American in England, he had an enormous deal with Anchor Records, the UK wing of ABC, and he had been discovered by Andrew Loog Oldham, the man who put the sex in the Stones, the greatest star maker / image creator in British — dammit, Western — pop history.

A previous manager had already tried launching the teenager in England, in 1972, at the height of the country's fascination with the teenybop dreams of Cassidy and the Osmonds. The Indiana born Smiley's credentials were already impressive: a four year stint in the Broadway production of OLIVER, which saw him rise from the chorus to the lead role (and only just lose out to Mark Lester for the movie), and a clutch of television ads, had long since groomed him for stardom.

But a handful of recordings with future Knack supremo Doug Fieger's band Sky, proved insufficient to land him a deal, and Smiley returned to the US, first to the family home in Seattle, doors away from what would later become famous as the Kurt Cobain residence, and then to Hollywood, where he leaped headlong into the Glitter scene revolving around Rodney Bingenheimer's English Disco.

"There was a whole crowd of us that sat around in velvet and boots and make-up. We weren't really from wealthy families, but you could always get by, and if you were cute you could get by real easy."

Va Va Va Voom tapped effortlessly into that mood, a manic amalgam of vintage Bolan and playful Bowie, brought to a shattering three minute climax by a brilliant Stevie Marriott guitar solo, and a characteristically dramatic Oldham production. "His favorite record was *River Deep Mountain High*, by Ike and Tina Turner," Smiley reasons, but even that doesn't explain it all. Oldham may have learned his craft at the altar of Spector, but he was never content to remain a mere pupil. *Va Va Va Voom* was more than a pop single. It was a pulsating statement of demented intent.

Smiley recalls, "I wrote *Va Va Va Voom* here in New York, and I thought it was just a throwaway. But I was playing some songs for Andrew and he loved it. At the time, I couldn't for the life of me understand why, but later I did. He loved it because it's simple, and it doesn't say that much." Neither was *Va Va Va Voom* the end of the duo's ambitions. Armed with Anchor's staggering $100,000 recording advance (plus another $100,000 for publishing), they headed down to Nashville to record the basic tracks for a Smiley album. "Then we took them to New York and added more, then Andrew would take the tapes to Olympic Studios in London, and come back with something totally different."

And then it all went sour. *Va Va Va Voom* barely registered a flicker on the sales-o-meter. Brett himself was just one more pretty face on a scene which, quite frankly, already had more pretty faces than it knew what to do with.

A projected US release on Sire fell through, despite the unabashed support of New York DJ Scott Muni's ENGLISH HOUR, and to crown it all, says Oldham, Anchor got cold feet and pulled the plug on everything before the album had even been paid for.

Smiley returned to the States, where he now lives in New York, still writing, still playing, and still recording some monumental music — proof that the audacious brilliance of *Va Va Va Voom* was not a fluke, but that its failure, and Smiley's subsequent silence, certainly were.

Brett Smiley Discography:
UK Original Single
  ○ *Va Va Va Voom* / *Space Ace* (Anchor ANC 1004, 1974)

☆ 35 ☆
Hello

– *Tell Him* –

Their first Glam hit, *Tell Him*, entered the UK chart on November 9, 1974.

Chart Hits		
	UK	US
Singles	2 (1974-75)	—
Albums	—	—

Hello was four North London teenagers with a Chuck Berry fixation, discovered in 1971, by Argent songsmith Russ Ballard and the Zombies' old road manager David Blaylock — then working as a plugger for Chappell Music.

Lining up as vocalist Bob Bradbury, lead guitarist Keith Marshall, bassist Vic Faulkner and drummer Jeff Allen, the band started life as a youth club covers band called The Age, and the original plan was for Hello to become an outlet for Ballard's non-Argent song writing output. At their first ever recording session, Hello recorded what became the demo for *Can't Let You Go*, a Ballard song that gave 60's superstar Barry Ryan his first hit of the new decade. At their second, they cut *You Move Me*, the Ballard rocker which would become their debut single (for Bell Records) in early 1972.

It was not the most memorable song Ballard had ever written, particularly at a time when the British chart was overflowing with the glam / pop confections of T. Rex, The Sweet and Slade. So when a second Ballard composition, *C'mon*, followed it into the dumper, Blaylock began casting further afield for the elusive breakthrough — starting at the top.

Nicky Chinn and Mike Chapman, the masterminds behind both The Sweet and New World's recent run of smashes, were at the top of their profession, and in March, Hello unleashed a murderous version of the duo's *Dyna-Mite*, some months before either The

Sweet or Mud got their hands on it.

What happened next is open to debate. According to some accounts, the songwriters reclaimed the song before Hello could get round to releasing it. According to others, either the band, or producer Mike Leander, rejected it in favor of Hello's own *Another School Day*. Either way, history would never forgive them, because if they had released the single, Hello would have been enormous, no questions asked.

The band was astonishingly photogenic, particularly vocalist Bradbury, a willowy sprite with soulful, saucer-like eyes and an angelic mane of brownish-blonde hair. They were also surprisingly adept at turning everything they played into a souped up Chuck Berry bubblegum anthem. In its subsequent, chart-topping, form, *Dyna-Mite* was an insubstantial boogaloo of unrestrained foot-stomping meaninglessness. In Hello's hands, it was a little bit slower, a little bit sultrier — it even made sense in a funny sort of way.

Not that *Another School Day* didn't have "smash hit" written all over it, but the record did nothing regardless, and that despite Hello making its TV debut to perform it on LIFT OFF WITH AYSHEA. "They appeared on the same show as David Bowie, who had just released *Starman*," recalls manager David Blaylock. "It was Hello's first ever TV, they were very nervous (and very young — 15 if they were a day), and before they went on, Bowie took the time to give them a few tips about how to present themselves. I always thought that was great of him."

Superstar tutoring or not, Hello was to wait until 1975 before they released another single and, bolstered by the band's utterly unexpected showing as seventh most promising new name in the annual NME readers poll, they promptly chalked up their first hit with a magnificent reworking of the Exciters' *Tell Him*. Another of Leander's clients, The Glitter Band, had recently recorded the song for their HEY album, but Leander was convinced that their rendition could be infinitely improved upon. He was right as well: *Tell Him* slammed into the British chart at No. 6, and convinced that lightning could very easily strike twice, the band returned to The Glitter Band's catalog for their follow-up, *Game's Up*. Inexplicably, for it, too, was a great record, it bombed.

So did Blaylock's choice for the next release, a spangle-drenched cover of Amen Corner's 1968 hit *Bend Me Shape Me*, and in early 1976, Hello returned to Russ Ballard to see if he could extract them from their trough. He could. *New York Groove* stands as one of the classic singles of 1976, a glitter rock monster which remains a favorite on the Glam

Slam compilation circuit, and which effortlessly gave Hello its second chart entry, a full eleven months after their first. It even earned the band a role in a new movie, Australian comedian Barry Humphries' SIDE BY SIDE. Appearing alongside Mud, the Rubettes and the newly launched superstar songbird Stephanie de-Sykes, Hello star as one of several bands roped into a comical tale of gangland club rivalries, and the accompanying soundtrack (released on the budget Pickwick label) features reprises of *Game's Up* and *Bend Me Shape Me*, alongside hit offerings from Fox, Disco Tex, Billy Ocean and Gary Glitter.

Hello followed *New York Groove* with another Ballard composition, the equally powerful *Star Studded Sham*. An immediate Top 20 hit in Germany, where the band had recently completed a sell-out tour with Smokie, it failed to make any chart inroads whatsoever in Britain, an astonishing lapse on the behalf of the local singles-buying public, and one which was only compounded when the band's long-awaited debut album, KEEPS US OFF THE STREETS (eye-catchingly packaged in a mock denim sleeve), went the same way.

Even more bizarrely, tracks which outside observers still believe would have given the group the hits they needed — *Teenage Revolution* and the raucous *Christmas Day In The* festive offering — were withdrawn from the singles schedules at times when an immediate plunge back into the pond would certainly have given Hello the British break they needed. Copies of *Teenage Revolution* were, in fact, pressed and distributed to the trade before the release was canceled, to be replaced by the distinctly less-appropriate (but jolly catchy) *Love Stealer*.

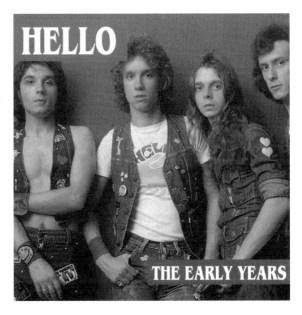

Love Stealer was to be Hello's last British release of any note. Shortly after, Bell was absorbed into the Arista label, and with Hello simultaneously transferring their allegiance to the German and Japanese markets (a move which would pay enormous dividends), their UK presence slipped off the register.

According to Blaylock, the basic problem was that both Bell and RAM, the band's management, were spoiled for choice when it came to unleashing new talent. Gary Glitter, The Glitter Band and the Bay City Rollers all took precedence over Hello in the marketing department, and when they had run their course, Slik came along to bang another nail into Hello's UK coffin.

Neither did Ace Frehley's patronage help. *New York Groove* failed to register whatsoever in Britain, while the guitarist actually turned down the perfect follow up in a second Hello song, *Good Ol' USA*. And so his career, too, fizzled to a halt.

Hello finally broke up in 1979, with a beltful of German hits to their credit: *Dean*, *Shine On Silver Light*, and dynamic covers of *Hi Ho Silver Lining* and the Turtles' *Eleanor* included. In later years, guitarist Keith Marshall had a world-wide hit with *Only Crying*, his first solo effort, while Bob Bradbury also attempted a late 1980's comeback with the sizzling *Crazy About Dyna*.

Even more recently, Hello has returned to the racks via a career-spanning retrospective on manager Blaylock's own Biff! label, and an 18 cut summary of their British singles (and most legendary demos), THE EARLY YEARS. Clearly, the band's memory lingers on with considerably greater tenacity than their hit making career.

Hello Glam Years Discography:
UK Original Singles
- *You Move Me / Ask Your Mama* (Bell 1238, 1972)
- *C'mon / The Wench* (Bell 1265, 1973)
- *Another School Day / C'Mon Get Together* (Bell 1333, 1973)
- *Tell Him / Lightning* (Bell 1377, 1974)
- *Game's Up / Do It All Night* (Bell 1406, 1975)
- *Bend Me Shape Me / We Gotta Go* (Bell 1424, 1975)
- *New York Groove / Little Miss Mystery* (Bell 1438, 1975)
- *Teenage Revolution / Keep Us Off The Streets* (Bell 1479, 1976)
- *Star Studded Sham / ?* (Bell, 1976)

US Original Single
- *New York Groove / Little Miss Mystery* (Bell 166, 1975)

UK Original Album
- KEEP US OFF THE STREETS (Bell 263, 1975)

UK Important Archive Albums
- STAR STUDDED GLAM (Biff 1CD, 1988)
- THE EARLY YEARS (Dojo EARL D17, 1993)

☆ **36** ☆
Kenny

— *The Bump* —

Their first Glam hit, *The Bump*, entered the UK chart on December 7, 1974.

Chart Hits
	UK	US
Singles	4 (1974-75)	—
Albums	1 (1976)	—

Having sprung to song writing superstardom as the brains behind the Bay City Rollers' record breaking run of hits, Bill Martin and Phil Coulter were far from dismayed when their association finally ended. Indeed, they'd already started grooming the Rollers' replacements, even before the Tartan horrors' urge for artistic fulfillment exploded into the open, and in December 1974, those replacements were finally unveiled, touting a song which had passed by all but unnoticed when first aired on a Rollers B-side.

That was *The Bump*, the starting point for a whole new dance craze, the sole purpose of which seemed to be to knock your partner flying with one burlesque-like sideways swing of the hip. *The Bump* was a Christmas No. 3 that took Martin-Coulter out of 1974 with at least as great a commercial success as they had ever had with the Rollers. Indeed, for a few weeks that festive season, bruised hips weren't simply an occupational hazard for devoted disco dancers, they were a fashionable prerequisite.

According to legend, Kenny was discovered rehearsing in a banana warehouse in Enfield, North London, although no-one ever thought to ask what two such renowned songwriters as Bill and Phil were doing in a North London banana warehouse in the first place. Or the band, come to that — Chuff, as they were then known, was a prog rock regular at sundry early 70's free festivals, and when first confronted by their new suitors' dreams of teen scene domination, their initial response was disdain.

Still, once assured of stardom — *The Bump*, their debut single, was already recorded, and chart bound, before Kenny was even discovered — the group quickly got into the swing of things. Unfortunately, quotes along the lines of, "our image is better, more clean cut than the Rollers'," were not exactly guaranteed to endear Kenny to its intended audience, particularly once it became known that not only was Kenny absent from *The Bump*, they never got to play on any of their records. Pop as artifice was one thing, but even the dumbest pop kids don't like their idols made to look like complete buffoons.

They had already retaliated against the Rock And Roll revivalists Rubettes for not singing on their first hit, by giving the real vocalist as big a smash as the Rubettes themselves were ever to manage without him. Kenny was to be punished with a career which stretched to just three further hits, with attempts to push two of their own number, Rick Driscoll and Yan Stile, as capable songwriters, ignored even by the band's own mentors. Kenny recorded just one of the duo's own songs, *Happiness Melissa* (the B-side of their first flop, *Nice To Have You Home*), and by late 1976, Kenny was traveling down the same road as any number of other former pop sensations, hankering for independence, and fighting to escape their puppet masters.

It took a week in court for Kenny to wrest its destiny away from Martin and Coulter, by which time the hits had already dried up. Still, Polydor was more than happy to snatch them up, and in 1977, a new album, RICOCHET, and single, *Hot Lips*, died a death. When a serious road accident put Stile out of action shortly after, Kenny folded. They have never reformed.

Kenny Glam Years Discography:
UK Original Singles
   ○ *The Bump* / ? (RAK 186, 1974)
   ○ *Fancy Pants* / ? (RAK 196, 1975)
   ○ *Baby I Love You OK* / ? (RAK 207, 1975)
   ○ *Julie Ann* / ? (RAK 214, 1975)

US Original Single
   ○ *The Bump* / ? (RAK 49032, 1974)

US Original Album
   ○ THE SOUND OF SUPER K (RAK SRAK 518, 1974)

☆ 37 ☆
Jet

– JET –

Their first Glam album, JET, was released in March 1975.

Jet suffered from a similar malaise to Jobriath, only in reverse. Whereas Jobriath had no past, Jet had too much of one. They were to be the best of everything — bassist Martin Gordon and, very fleetingly, pianist Peter Oxendale had both served time in Sparks. Singer Andy Ellison and drummer Chris Townson were a little bit of Bolan in John's Children clothing (Townson had also starred in The Jook.) Davey O'List, of course, was a founding member of Roxy Music and, more recently, had provided the devastating guitar intro to Ferry's solo reworking of *The In Crowd*.

Producer Roy Thomas Baker was best known for his work with Queen. Jet's clothes were designed by Elton John's tailor. Their career was handled by Gary Glitter's management. Everything was calculated to harness all the disparate threads which made up the best of the glitter / glam scam, and deliver them as a cohesive whole. And everything fell apart with almost predictable haste.

In reality, Jet was considerably more original than most folk were to give them credit for. In Gordon they had a truly gifted, if somewhat erratic, songwriter — he claims even to have come close to breaking Ron Mael's dominance of the Sparks' song writing quota when the band rehearsed his *Cover Girl* during the KIMONO sessions. Ellison had long since earned the reputation as one of rock's most exciting visual performers. O'List, of course, still thrived on his reputation from his days with the Nice, when he and Keith Emerson had effortlessly topped the instrumentalist polls, and fans had fought over who was most intrinsic to the band.

But after all the build-up, people weren't expecting originality, they were waiting for a jukebox, the best of everybody in one glorious package. By the time the band's first British tour, opening for Ian Hunter and Mick Ronson, rolled into town in early 1975, and their debut album had been savaged by public and critics alike, and Gordon was denying that any member of Jet had ever even seen another band, let alone played in one. By then, however, it was too late.

Quite simply, Jet fell foul of the very hype that their record company (CBS) and management (RAM) had spent so much time and money on creating. With such diverse backgrounds to the various group members, everybody connected with the group had his own ideas of how their combined talents should sound. Any attempt on the band's part to introduce a hint of their own personalities into the proceedings would be quashed by a rousing chorus of "Come on boys, remember your heritage!"

And in the outside world, unaware of the callous machinations that ground away behind the sullen, leaden beast which was the bulk of Jet's eponymous first album, people grew tired of waiting for this new supergroup to deliver the goods. Instead, they just sat around looking for the joins, seizing upon every chord, every inflection, as the failed echo of something else.

When journalist Charles Shaar Murray described the band's second single, *Nothing To Do With Us*, as a disinherited second cousin to Sparks' *Something For The Girl With Everything*, he meant it as a compliment. Yet it was a comparison which would never even have been considered had CBS and RAM not so gleefully shoved such similes up the media's collective nose in the first place. And by the time Jet split, during the abortive sessions for an utterly eccentric second album late in 1976, they had already been forgotten — either that, or filed away alongside Jobriath as all-purpose cannon fodder and an object lesson in how not to promote an act, however gullible you consider their audience to be.

Jet would not go away, however. Their final recording session, in November 1976 (produced by Sparks' Trevor White), turned up four songs, *Antlers*, *Don't Cry Joe*, *Sail Away* and *Dirty Pictures*. A few weeks later, the latter pair were soaring up the independent charts under a whole new name — Radio Stars (with a whole new history — none to speak of) and a whole new audience. Punks didn't care for pedigrees.

Jet Discography:
UK Original Singles
  ○ *My River / Quandary* (CBS 3143, 1974)
  ○ *Nothing To Do With Us / Brian Damage* (CBS 3317, 1975)

UK Original Album
  ○ JET (CBS 86099, 1975)

☆ 38 ☆
Milk'N'Cookies

— *Little, Lost And Innocent* —

Their first Glam song, *Little, Lost And Innocent*, was released in February 1975.

A flash looking four piece with a predilection for white bow-ties and pink dungarees, and a very endearing line in what future generations would describe as "power pop", Milk'N'Cookies formed in early 1973, and landed their first big break when bassist Sal Maida, after a short (one album) time with Roxy Music, moved to New York to replace original Cookies' bassist Jay Weiss in July 1974. Island Records in London immediately started keeping tabs on the group, finally pouncing when Sparks' manager John Hewlett returned to London to rave about them.

"Ian North, the singer, had written to us saying that the band were great Sparks fans, and asked if we would come and see them next time we were in New York," remembered Joseph Fleury, then Sparks' fan club organizer.

"It was just around the time things were getting really difficult with Adrian Fisher (Sparks' lead guitarist.) He hated the band, he hated the music, he was simply in it for the money. So Ron and Russell were looking for someone to replace him, and for a while it looked as though Ian North might be suitable. In the end he proved otherwise, but in the meantime we brought Milk'N'Cookies back to England, and persuaded Island to sign them." Before the year was out, the band was in the studio with Muff Winwood (producer of Sparks' KIMONO MY HOUSE) cutting their first album.

Picking *Little, Lost And Innocent* as the song most likely to succeed, Island packed the band off on a nationwide promotional tour with instructions to look sweet, smile a lot and say lots of nice things. The band did as required, and with the single looking certain to justify Island's faith, they arrived in Scotland for a prime time interview on a local radio station. There, they smiled a lot, looked very sweet and said lots of nice things, right up until somebody mentioned the Bay City Rollers. Then they stopped looking sweet, stopped smiling, and said some positively horrid things about the lovable tartan tops. And that, to all intents and purposes, was the end of Milk'N'Cookies in the UK.

With the screams of several thousand indignant Roller girls still ringing in their ears, Milk'N'Cookies returned to London, there to be told that Island had decided against releasing the album, and that their contract had been curtailed. Joseph Fleury, to whom Hewlett and Island now entrusted the band, was not downhearted. Indeed, he succeeded in landing the band a new contract within days, this time with the Rollers' own record company, Bell. Ian North, however, had different ideas. According to Fleury, he made just one phone call, to Bell's managing director, and suddenly that deal, too, was off. The band returned to New York, re-established themselves on the local circuit, and by the end of 1976 were within a hair's breadth of signing to either Sire or Warner Brothers, at which point Island immediately changed its two-year-old tune.

Obviously forgetting the days when North would wander around their offices, happily insulting staff and roster alike, they offered the guitarist a solo deal, waving as bait the belated release of the Milk'N'Cookies album. North fell for it, and, having dissolved the band, returned to England. Whereupon Island decided they didn't want him after all (and that despite having finally released the album!) and Ian was left to ponder the ironies of life from a whole new perspective entirely, fronting punk era heroes Neo.

Milk'N'Cookies Discography:
UK Original Single
  ○ *Little Lost & Innocent* / *Good Friends* (Island WIP 6222, 1975)

UK Original Album
  ○ MILK'N'COOKIES (Island 9320, 1976)

☆ **39** ☆
Sailor

– *A Glass Of Champagne* –

Their first Glam hit, *A Glass Of Champagne*,
entered the UK chart on December 6, 1975.

Chart Hits		
	UK	US
Singles	3 (1975-77)	—
Albums	1 (1976)	—

Superficially, Sailor had very little going for them. They dressed, as the name suggests they would, as sailors, and their sound drew a straight line between Roxy Music and Sparks, and danced shamelessly all along it. Indeed, once the shock of their sheer musical mischieviousness had worn off, more column inches were expended on the true identity of the alleged Norwegian prince who sang their songs (Georg Kajanus) than on figuring out what made the band tick — and more time was spent drawing convoluted family trees which proved that far from simply piecing together a bunch of willing session droogs, which was most people's initial impression, Sailor actually packed some top line talent.

Phil Pickett arrived fresh from stints with the Albion Band, and a host of other English folkies. Drummer Grant Serpell played alongside Fancy's Mo Foster in Affinity, moving onto stints alongside Mike D'Abo and Ice. Guitarist Henry Marsh once played with the critically acclaimed Gringo. And the prince, Kajanus, had hitherto been known as Georg

Hultgreen, in which guise he worked with 60's folk heroes Eclection, and bedsitter bard Al Stewart.

Sailor itself formed from the 1973 pairing of Kajanus and Pickett, an eponymous duo whose 1973 album HI HO SILVER, undeservedly vanished without trace. Keeping faith in Kajanu's increasingly quirky songs, however, by late 1975, the band was riding high on the UK chart with the utterly insistent *A Glass Of Champagne*, tinkly keyboard and squeeze-box driven, and draped with Kajanus' strangely alluring, and so-slightly accented, vocals. When Record Mirror critics voted their tips for the top at the end of 1975, Sailor was right up there.

Sailor's world was one of high camp glamour, not at all dissimilar from the universe discernible on Sparks' recent INDISCREET album. Indeed, both *Girls Girls Girls*, Sailor's second hit, in March, and such early album cuts as *All I Need Is A Girl*, *Stiletto Heels* and *Sailor* itself, conjured up an inescapable aura of smokey wartime nightclubs, filled with carousing matelots and drunken floozies — the social corollary, perhaps, of the Berlin cabaret scene which more decadent minds were still leaning towards, but an effective affectation regardless.

Certainly it sustained Sailor over at least three albums, and was enough to grant them a third hit, too, close to a year after *Girls Girls Girls*. One Drink Too Many caught them still in the bar, on the pull, on their knees, and though the sailor suits were gone, the image prevailed.

Sailor Glam Years Discography:
UK Original Singles
- *Traffic Jam / Harbour* (Epic EPC 2562, 1974)
- *Blue Desert / Blame It On The Soft Spot* (Epic EPC 2929, 1975)
- *Sailor / Open Up The Door* (Epic EPC 3184, 1975)
- *A Glass Of Champagne / Panama* (Epic EPC 3770, 1975)
- *Girls, Girls, Girls / Jacaranda* (Epic EPC 3858, 1976)
- *Stiletto Heels / Out Of Money* (Epic EPC 4620, 1976)
- *One Drink Too Many / Melancholy* (Epic EPC 4804, 1977)
- *Down By The Docks / Put Your Mouth Where The Money Is* (Epic EPC 5566, 1977)

US Original Singles
- ○ *Traffic Jam* / *Josephine Baker* (Epic 50094, 1974)
- ○ *Glass Of Champagne* / *Panama* (Epic 50194, 1975)
- ○ *Girls, Girls, Girls* / *Jacaranda* (Epic 50229, 1976)
- ○ *Runaway* / *Put Your Mouth Where The Money Is* (Epic 50557, 1978)

UK Original Albums
- ○ SAILOR (Epic 80337, 1975)
- ○ TROUBLE (Epic 69192, 1975)
- ○ THIRD STOP (Epic 81637, 1976)
- ○ CHECK POINT (Epic 82256, 1977)

UK Important Archive Album
- ○ GREATEST HITS (Epic 82754, 1978)

US Original Album
- ○ SAILOR 197534039 Trouble (Epic 33248, 1975)

☆ 40 ☆
Slik

– *Forever And Ever* –

Their first Glam hit, *Forever And Ever*, entered the UK chart on January 17, 1976.

	Chart Hits	
	UK	**US**
Singles	2 (1976)	—
Albums	1 (1976)	—

Discovered by the Bay City Rollers' original — and Kenny's current — song writing team of Bill Martin and Phil Coulter, Slik was a Glaswegian Top 40 band, very similar to the undiscovered Mud in many ways, laboring under the singularly inappropriate name of Salvation. They became Slik, it was said, after seeing THAT'S ENTERTAINMENT and falling in love with the flickering image of old Hollywood.

Their first single was *The Boogiest Band In Town*, from the soundtrack of the movie NEVER TOO YOUNG TO ROCK, the tale of two talent scouts seeking out new artists for a television talent show. They ended up with The Glitter Band, the Rubettes, Mud and Slik, although it cannot be said that such an array of talent helped — the movie flopped almost as disastrously as the Slik single, and Martin-Coulter withdrew to rethink their strategy.

Buying back Slik's contract from Polydor, they resold the song to Bell in the hope that the company's experience of milking the teenage market might again come up trumps. And when it didn't, they called the band back into the office and outlined their next move. They were to don 1950's baseball kits, and record a song Martin-Coulter had already recorded (as an album track) with Kenny, *Forever And Ever*.

However, having seen one band, the Rollers, slip away from them bleating about artistic control, and Kenny already getting a little snotty on the same subject, this time around Bill and Phil intended playing everything by the book. With the Rollers they had had to start quite literally from scratch — Jonathan King aside, no-one had ever tried creating a teenybop phenomenon in Britain before, with the result that not everything in the Rollers campaign had gone according to plan. With Slik, the idea was to try and develop the members as musicians and showmen first, then allow the heart throb status to develop around that.

Having booked them into TOP OF THE POPS before *Forever And Ever* was even in the shops, and sewing up appearances on every other pop-oriented show in the country, the next step was to keep the band working the same live circuit they always had, the idea being that with the single rising up the chart, each of the band's performances would be given maximum attention, if only for the chaos at the box office. And then, with everybody clamoring to see them play venues which befitted their status, Slik was to play the Glasgow Apollo and London's New Victoria Theater.

The ploy worked. Within two weeks, readers of The Sun newspaper had voted Slik the best new band of the year. *Forever And Ever* was the nation's No. 1, and Phil Coulter was telling everybody who would listen that Slik were twice the band musically that the Rollers had been. "They have a solid musical background," he said. "They have the same potential as The Beatles." But Phil, the Beatles wrote their own songs!

In April 1976, Bell released the band's third single, the mournful *Requiem*. Disguised as monks, Slik filed around the TOP OF THE POPS stage chanting their requiem for a long lost love. Another hit seemed inevitable, but suddenly tragedy struck. On May 20, singer Midge Ure was injured in a car accident. The band's forthcoming tour was canceled, the loss of television exposure pulled *Requiem* up at a lowly No. 24, while the band's eponymous debut album, which might otherwise have been expected to clean up, could muster nothing more than one week at the lower end of the British Top 60. Plans for an American campaign were hastily shelved, and by the time Ure returned to fitness, the momentum was lost.

After one final gig, supporting Hello in Berlin, Slik returned to their hometown and, as PVC2, cut a solitary lost single for the local Zoom label. Then they broke up. Ure later turned up in Glen Matlock's Rich Kids and bored everybody rigid with tales of how he was almost recruited for the (pre-Rotten) Sex Pistols but turned the offer down when Slik started to break. He later established himself as leader of pomp-rockers Ultravox, playing alongside Chris Cross — brother of Hello's Jeff Allen, and then as a successful solo artist. His bandmates, meanwhile, became the Zones and recorded one album and two singles for Arista.

In the scheme of things, neither Slik nor their Martin-Coulter predecessors, Kenny, ever mattered more than their latest sales statistics. Whereas Chinnichap treated their charges as a canvas upon which to daub the outrageous visions that they felt the world of pop was most in need of, Martin and Coulter harked back more to the days of Tin Pan Alley, where the song alone was the key to success and the artist simply a vehicle through which it could be presented.

When The Sweet turned down *Dyna-Mite*, it was because they couldn't envision themselves being able to perform it as it should be performed. But Kenny and Slik were both to succeed, and succeed well, with their predecessors' warmed-up left-overs. In a way, they were the true children of the original bubblegum manufacturers, bands made to measure for a song, just as a suit is made to measure for a customer.

If Kenny hadn't wanted *The Bump*, Bill'n'Phil would simply have found somebody else who did, and wouldn't have given the banana boys another thought. Similarly, if Slik had turned down *Forever And Ever*, chances are they would still be playing the Glasgow club circuit today, fitting gigs in around their day jobs and wondering "What if . . ." until their dying day.

But if Slik and Kenny and the myriad other acts who were to be flung up around the cleavage of the decade were ultimately to prove as disposable as the songs around which they built their careers, there were plenty around them whose contributions were not to be written off quite so glibly.

Slik Discography:
UK Original Singles
- *The Boogiest Band In Town / Hatchet* (Polydor, 1975)
- *The Boogiest Band In Town / Hatchet* (Bell 1414, 1975)
- *Forever And Ever / Again My Love* (Bell 1464, 1976)
- *Requiem / Everyday Anyway* (Bell 1478, 1976)
- *The Kid's A Punk / ?* (Bell 1490, 1976)
- *Don't Take Your Love Away / ?* (Arista 83, 1976)

UK Original Album
- SLIK (Bell SYBEL 8004, 1976)

US Original Album
- SLIK (Arista 4115, 1976)

Afterwards

David Bowie and Ronnie Wood were together in a Los Angeles hotel room discussing David's role as the King of Glitter Rock.

"I'm very proud of that tag," the Thin White one said. "That's what the public made me, and that's what I am."

Ronnie Wood laughed. "Yeah, the reigning king." He handed David a slip of paper. "I don't like giving people tags, but here."

David looked at the piece of paper. It was a $15 price tag with "The King of Glitter Rock" scrawled on the back. He looked horrified. "Fifteen dollars?" Then he smiled. "Well, I guess Glitter Rock was always pretty cheap."

More
20th CENTURY
ROCK AND ROLL
— POP —

ISBN 1-896522-25-4
$13.95 USA
$17.95 Canada
£9.95 UK

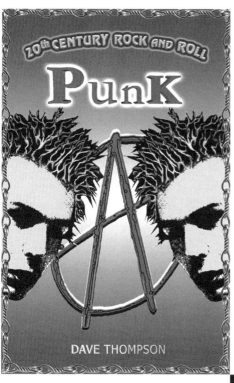

And more
20th CENTURY
ROCK AND ROLL
— PUNK —

ISBN 1-896522-27-0
$13.95 USA
$17.95 Canada
£9.95 UK

And even more
20th CENTURY
ROCK AND ROLL
— Women In Rock —

ISBN 1-896522-29-7
$13.95 USA
$17.95 Canada
£9.95 UK